Studio Practices, Tehniques and Tips

The *Ceramics Monthly* Handbook Series

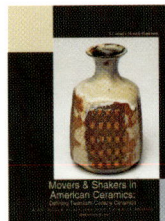

Movers & Shakers in American Ceramics: Defining Twentieth Century Ceramics
Elaine Levin
This remarkable collection of Ceramics Monthly articles, written by Elaine Levin over a period of 25 years, tells the stories of some of the most notable figures of the ceramic art movement in the United States during the 20th century. Levin relates the often long struggles and ultimate successes of 26 Movers and Shakers who dedicated their lives to a single vision—unselfishly pushing ceramic art into uncharted territory so others could enjoy and benefit from their efforts. From Binns, Baggs, Robineau and the Wildenhains, through Voulkos and Soldner, to Saxe, Rothman and Olsen, these personal stories are sure to educate and inspire ceramics artists well into the 21st century.
2003 • Paperback • 144 pages
ISBN: 1-57498-165-X • Order code: CA20
Price: $28.95

Exploring Electric Kiln Techniques
Edited by Sumi von Dassow
The electric kiln has made the experience of pottery accessible to people from all walks of life. For those who would like to better understand the art and science of pottery, this CM handbook focuses on the expertise of ceramics artists who have explored the possibilities and potential of electric kilns. These artists share their knowledge on a wide range of topics, including clay bodies, glazes, decorating, form and more.
2003 • Paperback • 144 pages
ISBN: 1-57498-160-9 • Order code: CA19
Price: $28.95

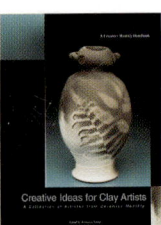

Creative Ideas for Clay Artists
Edited by Anderson Turner
Looking for new ideas? This CM Handbook features a collection of articles about creative artists, and ideas to challenge you and inspire your work. Pottery, sculpture and finishing techniques are covered. This is a must-read for anyone involved in clay. Whether looking for new designs, new inspiration or renewed creativity, you will find it here through these talented featured artists and their unique approaches to clay.
2001 • Paperback • 110 pages
ISBN: 1-57498-122-6 • Order code: CA16
Price: $28.95

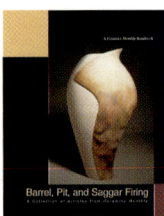

Barrel, Pit, and Saggar Firing
Edited by Sumi von Dassow
This CM Handbook reflects the growing interest in pit firing and related techniques. The articles included here were carefully selected to illustrate the wide range of approaches to barrel, pit and saggar firing. Works ranging from wheel-thrown and coil-built pots to complex sculpture are tied together by a similarity in the firing process. Standard versions of these firing techniques, as well as innovative variations, are discussed.
2001 • Paperback • 156 pages
ISBN: 1-57498-127-7 • Order code: CA17
Price: $28.95

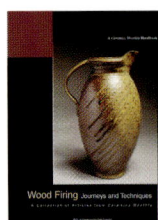

Wood Firing: Journeys and Techniques
Foreword by Dick Lehman
For some potters, wood is more than just a source of fuel for a kiln, it is a process. Wood firing can provide a link for ceramics artists to their surroundings and to pottery's beginnings thousands of years ago. Here are the experiences of potters who have sought to reconnect with a basic technology and who want to explore and master all the possible variables that this technique provides for the creative process. This book describes some of the technical, safety and physical challenges of wood firing through first-hand accounts and interviews with potters.
2001 • Paperback • 132 pages
ISBN: 1-57498-143-9 • Order code: CA18
Price: $28.95

Glazes: Materials, Recipes and Techniques
Edited by Anderson Turner
A collection of articles published in *Ceramics Monthly* dealing with glazes. Written by and about artists and experts, these articles cover a wide range of materials, recipes, and techniques used in the glazing of work by both studio potters and ceramic artists. This book is a great example of how the modern potter uses a combination of trial-and-error discoveries along with information from scientists and engineers in the field to achieve unique effects that are the signature of the current ceramics art movement.
2004 • Paperback • 144 pages
ISBN: 1-57498-174-9 • Order code: CA21
Price: $28.95

For information on ordering titles published by The American Ceramic Society, or request a ceramic art publications catalog, please contact Customer Service Department at 614-794-5890 (phone), 614-794-5892 (fax), info@ceramics.org (e-mail), or write to Customer Service Department, 735 Ceramic Place, Westerville, OH 43081, USA.

Subscribe to Clayart!
Clayart is the "electronic voice of potters worldwide," sponsored by The American Ceramic Society. Subscriber-initiated discussions range from questions/answers on materials and techniques to business advice and philosophical debate. Visit the website and subscribe at www.ceramics.org/clayart.

Visit our online bookstore at www.ceramics.org.

Studio Practices, Tehniques and Tips

A Collection of Articles from *Ceramics Monthly*

Edited by Anderson Turner

Published by

**The American Ceramic Society
735 Ceramic Place
Westerville, Ohio 43081 USA**

Founded in 1953, *Ceramics Monthly* is an internationally distributed magazine on ceramic art and craft. Each issue includes up-to-date information on exhibitions, available materials and trends, as well as profiles of individual artists, critical analyses, production processes, and clay and glaze recipes. While principally covering contemporary work, the magazine also looks back at influential artists and events from the past.

The American Ceramic Society
735 Ceramic Place
Westerville, Ohio 43081

©2004 by The American Ceramic Society.
All rights reserved.
Printed in the United States of America.

07 06 05 04 03   5 4 3 2 1

ISBN: 1-57498-200-1

Cover design by David Houghton, ACerS, and Melissa Bury, Columbus, Ohio
Cover image: "Wood-fired stoneware bottle" by Sheila and Tony Clennell.

No part of this book may be reproduced, stored in a retrieval system, or transmitted in any form or by any means, electronic, mechanical, photocopying, microfilming, recording, or otherwise, without the written permission from the publisher, except by a reviewer, who may quote brief passages in review.

Authorization to photocopy for internal or personal use beyond the limits of Sections 107 and 108 of the U.S. Copyright Law is granted by The American Ceramic Society, provided that the appropriate fee is paid directly to the Copyright Clearance Center, Inc., 222 Rosewood Drive, Danvers, MA 01923 USA, www.copyright.com. Prior to photocopying items for educational classroom use, please contact Copyright Clearance Center, Inc. This consent does not extend to copyright items for general distribution or for advertising or promotional purposes or to republishing items in whole or in part in any work in any format. Requests for special photocopying permission and reprint requests should be directed to Senior Director, Publications, The American Ceramic Society, 735 Ceramic Place, Westerville OH 43081 USA.

Statements of fact and opinion are the responsibility of the authors alone and do not imply an opinion on the part of the officers, staff, or members of The American Ceramic Society. The American Ceramic Society assumes no responsibility for the statements and opinions advanced by the contributors to its publications or by the speakers at its programs. Registered names and trademarks, etc., used in this publication, even without specific indication thereof, are not to be considered unprotected by the law.

For more information on ordering books published by The American Ceramic Society, subscribing to our publications—including *Ceramics Monthly*— or to request a publications catalog, please call 614-794-5890 or visit our online bookstore at www.ceramics.org.

CONTENTS

INTRODUCTION
by Anderson Turner 1

1 WORKSHOP PLANNING AND BUSINESS PRACTICES

A 21st Century Potter by Janet Buskirk 3
Finding Your Niche by Brad Sondahl 9
The Studio Sale by David Cuzick 11
Learning Through Apprenticeship by Alisa Carroll 16
Selling at Retail Shows by Sandi Pierantozzi and Neil Patterson 21
Studio and Showroom Organization by Dick Lehman 22
The Marketing Dance by Richard Selfridge 27
Attention to Detail by Tony and Sheila Clennell 32
Red Star Studios by Paula Sibrack Marian 35
Attaining Merchant Status by Mark E. Battersby 37
A Garden Exhibition by Alice Heystek 38
Questions to Ask a Gallery by Karen Shelly-Genther 41
Pack With Care by Debra Burke 42
Writing an Artist Statement by Ariane Goodwin 44
Is It Covered by Mark E. Battersby 46
Profiting Under the Right Label by Mark E. Battersby 48
Photographing Ceramics: Black-and-White Images
 by Glenn Rand and William Blanchard 50
Photographing Ceramics: Color Transparencies,
 Slides and Prints by Glenn Rand 54
Photographing Ceramics Revisited by Glenn Rand 57
Going for the Gold by Garth Clark 60

2 MATERIALS AND EQUIPMENT

Build a $75 Electric Wheel by Jolyon Hofsted 66
A Dry Clay Mixer by Brian VanNostrand 67

Modifying a Cement Mixer for Mixing Clay by Susan Nykiel and Ray Bub 68
The $1200 Studio by Lili Krakowski 70
The Versatile Extruder by William Shinn 74
An Environmentally Safe Spray Booth by Bill Campbell 79
A Utilitarian Booth Display by Carol and Jim Gross 80
Bamboo Tools by Mel Malinowski 82
Mining with the Potter in Mind by David Hendley 84
The Perfect Clay Body? by Jeff Zamek 86
Clay Body Absorption and Shrinkage by Jeff Zamek 91

3 KILNS

Salt and Refractory Coatings by Mel Jacobson 94
Insulating Existing Kilns by Regis Brodie 101
The Mysterious Hole by Marc Ward 104
A Castable Venturi Burner by W. Lowell Baker 108
The Oxygen Probe: A Potter's Tool by Nils Lou 110
Firing with Vegetable Oil by John Britt 112
George Wright: Oregon Potter's Friend and Inventor Extraordinaire by Janet Buskirk 115
Lessons from a City Kiln by Marc Leuthold with Sarah G. Wilkins 119
Kazegama by Steve Davis 121
A Fast-Firing Test Kiln by Rich Childs 124
Building a Modular Kiln by Bob McWilliams 128
Recycle That Old Kiln by David G. Wright 137

INTRODUCTION

The opportunity to edit this book came at an interesting time for me. My wife and I just recently purchased a farm in Garrettsville, Ohio, and have been slowly but surely updating it and planning my studio. My work area will be our roughly 1000 square foot pole-barn that was used as a garage. I've updated the electric and run all of the other necessary needs to the building and as I send this book back to The American Ceramic Society, I am waiting for the concrete guy to call me and tell me when he'll pour the new floor. So, I had a strong desire to find as much useful information as possible while researching this text.

Through my research, I discovered that there is a wealth of quality information inside the past twenty years of *Ceramics Monthly*. This should come as no surprise to any reader of the magazine, but at the same time collecting it all in a way that makes sense was a challenge. I chose to break it up into three sections 1) Workshop Planning and Business Practices 2) Materials and Equipment and 3) Kilns. It is my hope that these articles are presented in a way that answers important questions while providing inspiration.

Perhaps most importantly, the articles in this book are at their root about the desire to do and achieve more. From finding the motivation to write about their experiences to believing in their own abilities enough to try to make a life in clay, the authors of these articles all share a common energy and enterprising spirit. It is that spirit that is within all of us—the spirit to make, to learn, to teach—that drives our lives in clay forward. I hope you will be able to relate to and use some of the energy that is contained in each one of the articles in this book.—*Anderson Turner*

WORKSHOP PLANNING AND BUSINESS PRACTICES

"By allowing a man to pay for her meal, was Coyote promoting male-female wage inequity, or was she redistributing the wealth more equally?" and "Coyote did not know which he liked best: girls, cars or Spam on toast," each 9 inches (23 centimeters) in height, raku fired.

A 21st-Century Potter

by Janet Buskirk

Well, I never thought it would happen to me. I never thought I would be like that dweeby guy in the sport utility vehicle, out in the woods with his fax machine, computer and cell phone. But here I am, the 21st-century potter, sitting in front of a wood-burning kiln with my laptop computer. I stoke all five ports, then type for a few minutes, then stoke again.

A brief description of the players in this scenario: The kiln is an anagama owned by Brad Mildrexler. It is 2:30 A.M. on Friday. We lit the kiln Monday, fired slowly for a couple of days and started firing in earnest Wednesday morning. Three of us are taking slightly random shifts. Cone 14 is just bending in the front, and the only cone pack I can see through the back ports has two cones standing. I don't know what cones they are—we've never kept a log. Could they be 12 and 14? Anyone who might know is asleep.

The computer is an old IBM compatible that was given to me by a friend who had no need for antique technology. It is doing surprisingly well, considering that it has a virus and is currently covered with soot and sawdust.

As for me, I am a professional potter with a studio in Portland, Oregon. I typically fire lots of tableware in a gas kiln shared with my two studio partners, Jeanne Charles and Tony Hackenbruck. I do the occasional wood firing because I really like to burn things and to cut wood. And, oh yes, I like to make pots for wood firing.

There is one more player. A small brown mouse is scurrying around in front of the firebox, tidying up after all my spills. It is probably safer here than it has ever been while searching for food. No owl or coyote would hunt near the hot kiln.

How did I come to be here? What led me to a ceramics career and this type of firing? Growing up, I thought I would be a marine biologist. Being a potter never crossed my mind. But our lives often take odd little turns. Sometimes we are in the right place at the right time (some people might say that's the wrong place at the wrong time).

Teapot, 9 inches (23 centimeters) in height, thrown and altered white stoneware, fired to Cone 10 in reduction.

Janet Buskirk in her Portland, Oregon, studio.

Teaset, to 11 inches (28 centimeters) in height, slab-built porcelain, wood fired in an anagama.

When I finished college in the mid 1980s, I was not going to be a professional potter. No one in their right mind would consider that. Sure, I loved working with clay, but it wasn't practical. So I worked in a series of medical laboratories until my last boss quit taking his lithium, stopped sleeping, became delusional, made sexual advances to all the women in the lab, was institutionalized, blamed me, then fired me. The hospital offered me a severance package consisting of $950 and three months of medical insurance.

Oregon's beautiful summer was on its way and I didn't want to file a lawsuit, so I took the $950 (enough money to pay rent for almost 11 months then) and began making pots in earnest. Coincidentally, Portland happens to be a city where there are lots of potters who are willing to share information, equipment, kilns and expertise.

At that time, I knew nothing about marketing. I certainly had no business plan. I thought I was becoming a slacker, not starting a business. I went into the studio and, well, started goofing off. What came out were some slab-built, raku-fired coyotes. For each, I wrote a humorous story about the coyote's personal life. People loved those stories. The coyotes and their funny stories paid my mortgage for the next ten years.

My income was low, but so were expenses. For a young potter who was not concerned about such things as business insurance or a dependable pickup truck, life was cheap. How could I have known that I would someday have a web page, a reputation (those can be good or bad!) and literally thousands of dollars worth of professionally photographed slides?

Oh yes, there were also vast numbers of pots. In 1999 alone, I believe I sold well over 2000. That's a lot of pots. The lumbar region of my back will remember every one of them. Of course, so will my checking account. There was just enough money left over to put a new engine in my truck so that I could get to the next show.

The life of a potter is not what I had imagined it to be. I maintain a mailing list of over 2000 customers. I have a

Stoneware plate, 14 inches (36 centimeters) in diameter, with celadon glaze.

Casserole, 11 inches (28 centimeters) in diameter, wheel-thrown and altered stoneware, with scrap glaze.

merchant credit card account. I have business insurance. I spend a lot of time doing bookkeeping and accounting. I also use the knowledge I acquired in my college chemistry classes much more than I use knowledge from any other college courses.

My ceramics career began in 1986, and by the late '80s, most of my work was based on some type of social commentary. When I started to make the coyotes, their humorous stories often reflected some difficult aspect of my own life (more than one man I dated told me he would go to galleries and read my coyotes' stories to see if I was happy with my love life or not).

The coyotes established my career as a professional potter. They did not require a lot of technical skill to produce, but people bought them and they became my first "production" item. After five years of making up a different story for each coyote, I found I could no longer come up with so many new stories, so I began to repeat some. I still wrote new stories, but each of these was used for several coyotes.

During the time when the coyotes were my main production item, I also made high-fired dinnerware for fun. In those days, my dinnerware was really funky. I threw and altered pots, and made funky slab-built teapots. Most of this work seemed like it was precarious, like it could tip over if the wind blew too hard.

So much of my life as a potter has depended on being in the right place, at the right time, with the right people. In the late 1980s, I fell in with a wonderful group of potters who were all just setting up studios and looking for a place to fire their work. We all were friends with George Wright (see "George Wright: Oregon Potters' Friend and Inventor Extraordinaire" in the March 1998 CM), who rented us a studio for $15 per month. We also used his gas, wood and raku kilns, and learned a lot about different types of firings.

While I was working in this studio, we often fast fired a small wood-burning kiln. I had trouble understanding why some pots stuck permanently to the shelves, but one day I realized that the many stuck pots were worthwhile if just one came out with a subtle orange blush. That was when I fell in love with wood firing. Over the ensuing years, the focus of the work that I did for my soul changed from slab-built raku sculpture to wheel-thrown or slab-built work for the anagama. During that time my production work also changed. I slowly became a normal full-time potter, someone who makes a lot of bowls and plates.

Then, in 1991, I became very ill. Suffering from an undiagnosed intestinal illness, I was often too weak to work. My studio partner claims that the funky little porcelain cups I made that year were my best work ever. After I regained my health, I began to work more toward well-made functional pots. That year of illness had left me and my work much more serious. My work had somehow lost its innocence.

The 1990s were also a time of economic change in Oregon. Housing prices, which had been very low, doubled, then tripled, then kept on going up. Potters like me had to make our businesses pay more. So I began to learn about business. For a while, I tried to keep track of how long it actually took me to make each piece (I gave that up). I also began to examine which aspects of my business were most profitable. I had been wholesaling and consigning to galleries throughout the country. As I tightened up my business practices, I quit shipping work to wholesale accounts, and began doing more retail shows. I found that all of my wholesale accounts and distant consignment accounts took more time and made less money than the nearby consignment shops (which pay dependably).

I also learned the value of keeping a really good mailing list for studio sales. My studio partners and I have two studio sales each year, and we work hard to add names of potential customers to the mailing list. Anyone who expresses any interest in a new coffee cup is asked if they would like to receive a postcard for the next sale.

At last year's Christmas sale, we made over $9000. To put this in perspective, when we had our first studio sale in 1986, I was $25 short of being able to pay my rent. I made my rent goal at the next studio sale, but just barely. I regarded that as a success!

What are the secrets to becoming a successful professional potter? Of course, we must all learn about the technical aspects of clay, glazes and firing. We must also have some sense of design. But when this question was asked of a number of professional potters at an Oregon Potters Association meeting a few years ago, the overwhelming and immediate response was: "Keep your expenses down!" Everyone in the room could relate stories of potters who allowed their overhead to become too high, and were forced out of business. Our profit margin just cannot support large expenses.

The other thing every successful potter knows was best stated by Cynthia Bringle during a slide lecture a few years ago: "If you are going to make pots for a living, you have to really want to make a lot of pots."

Covered jar, 12 inches (30 centimeters) in height, stoneware, fired to Cone 10 in reduction.

7   WORKSHOP PLANNING AND BUSINESS PRACTICES

These days, I produce a lot of functional porcelain and stoneware. When I am not busy testing new glazes or repairing equipment, I sculpt my cat Chelsea (named after Chelsea Clinton). He probably does not deserve the fame. I also have been making wacky metal handrails and gates for my house, and, with the help of my studio partners, I have been slowly covering the foundation of my house with a ceramic and glass mosaic. ▲

Covered jar, 12 inches (30 centimeters) in height, wheel-thrown and altered porcelain, fired to Cone 10 in reduction, by Janet Buskirk, Portland, Oregon.

Coleman's Chun Flambé Glaze
(Cone 10, reduction)

Gerstley Borate	10.79%
Whiting	15.73
Custer Feldspar	15.57
Nepheline Syenite	20.43
Kaolin	1.48
Flint	36.00
	100.00%
Add: Tin Oxide	1.72%
Copper Carbonate	0.75%
Yellow Ocher	0.25%

I work with several Tom Coleman glazes, including a few from his booklet *Glazes I Use*.

Milky Blue Glaze
(Cone 10, reduction)

Barium Carbonate*	4.05%
Dolomite	9.52
Gerstley Borate	9.52
Whiting	2.73
Custer Feldspar	44.75
Edgar Plastic Kaolin (EPK)	1.53
Flint	27.90
	100.00%
Add: Tin Oxide	2.73%
Copper Carbonate	0.55%
Rutile	4.27%
Bentonite	1.75%

Janet's Clear Blue Celadon Glaze
(Cone 10, reduction)

Barium Carbonate*	1.53%
Bone Ash	0.81
Dolomite	6.10
Gerstley Borate	4.07
Talc	1.02
Whiting	8.14
Custer Feldspar	36.62
Edgar Plastic Kaolin (EPK)	3.05
Flint	38.66
	100.00%
Add: Tin Oxide	0.51%
Black Iron Oxide	0.41%
Yellow Ocher	0.81%

Purple Glaze
(Cone 10, reduction)

Barium Carbonate*	3.92%
Dolomite	9.79
Gerstley Borate	9.79
Whiting	2.78
Custer Feldspar	40.11
Edgar Plastic Kaolin (EPK)	1.65
Flint	31.96
	100.00%
Add: Black Iron Oxide	1.13%
Cobalt Carbonate	1.24%
Copper Carbonate	0.51%
Bentonite	1.86%

*All glazes containing barium carbonate should be tested for leaching.

Finding Your Niche

by Brad Sondahl

Two years ago, I moved my pottery studio to a county in the Idaho Panhandle; the population is so sparse, there are no stoplights in the whole county. It is next to a county as large as Vermont, which also lacks stoplights and, more significantly, the kind of population that usually accompanies stoplights. Not every potter ends up in such an underpopulated environment, but many potters move, and have to reassess their marketing strategies as a result.

I've always felt that because I'm self-employed, I could set up a workshop anywhere. In my many years as a potter, I've had seven studios and their locations have greatly affected my marketing success, but I've always been able to keep going. Other issues related to the pottery environment are: physical setup, name recognition, family considerations and local market conditions.

The first decision is whether to have a studio at home or in a separate location. Though a lot of successful potters have separate studios, the question for me was, "Where do I want to spend most of my time?" When I apprenticed, I spent enough time sitting kilns that I knew I would always have my workshop at home. But home studios can be controlled or prohibited by local codes; and noisy kilns make irate neighbors, so choose the location carefully.

The amount of space available and its suitability should also be considered carefully. An unfinished basement may provide plenty of room for a workshop, but hauling tons of clay and pots up and down stairs can be a bit of a nuisance. Generally, my studios have been too small. While this made them eco-

Brad Sondahl's summer studio with sales gazebo and outdoor kick wheel at Spirit Lake, Idaho.

nomical to heat and afford, there was insufficient storage space for materials and finished goods. Even a large space needs to be broken up into separate spaces to control kiln gases, excess heat and dust, dust, dust.

Okay, now you've set up a studio, and you're making pots, but no one has ever heard of you in Grangeville, Idaho. No matter what the quality of your pots, your name does not necessarily travel with you to new areas. If your pots are good, you can still sell them, but there will be no repeat customers until you've been there a while, so sales will be slower.

Art fairs are the great equalizers, allowing mass exposure to the target market. Unfortunately, getting into good fairs is another matter, subject to different systems of jurying, changing juries, tenure, etc. Galleries are dependable, and usually looking for new exhibitors, but each account requires a lot of pots to make a reasonable display, and returns are sometimes slow.

My best marketing strategy so far involved the purchase of a small place on the main street of a tiny resort town, the street being the only access to a 7-mile-long lake. Because customers didn't feel completely comfortable entering a private residence to look at pottery, I built a kiosk display in front. Then, because I didn't want to be tied down, I posted a sign asking people to pay by check under the door if I was gone. This strategy actually encouraged some customers to become loyal, because of the trust shown on my side.

At first, to develop a customer base, I took names and addresses off the local checks, and sent them handwritten invitations to special sales. After several years, the flow was self-perpetuating, with no advertising except a modest sign on site. To ensure repeat business, I added new items yearly, as well as new decorations and one-of-a-kind pieces for novelty. Sales of second-quality pots have sometimes brought about a kind of feeding frenzy with patrons.

Earlier, I mentioned that family considerations are important in locating your studio. It was my wife's occupation (as a pastor) that led to the move to this challenging new environment. I never would have chosen this particular location for sales, as it is too far off the beaten track. Fortunately, we still own our old location in the resort town by the lake and, as sales are mostly in the summer, we return there to sell what I've made throughout the winter. I throw pots at a kick wheel near the kiosk to keep busy and lure in more customers.

It's tough to find your niche in the world, but a potter's got to do what a potter's got to do. ▲

Sondahl in his winter studio in Nezperce, Idaho.

The Studio Sale

by David Cuzick

Vase, 8 inches in height, with wax-resisted Malcolm Davis Shino glaze and iron decoration, by Mary Cuzick.

As I prepare for my next studio sale, I think about why I'm a potter. I look over the latest series of covered jars, several teapots, some casseroles and a hundred cups waiting for handles to be attached. A dozen of these cups are all fat and round. The next few are like a cone with the foot flared out. About half of them are thrown off the hump. The perspective is different when the clay is up high; the cups that come from the hump are not the same as the ones from a single mound of clay.

I have been doing sales at my studio twice a year for 20 years. Preparing for each sale is hard work; it takes over my life for about ten weeks. So, why is it done, how is it done and is it something you should think about doing?

There are many reasons for having a studio sale. For one, I don't have to pack and unpack pots to sell at a fair. Nor do I have to pay for a booth space, though the costs of having a studio sale can be considerable too. I also don't have to contend with someone selling soup in the booth next to me, or someone else selling musical instruments and broadcasting loud music in the booth across from me—both are recent experiences. Finally, people come to my studio sale with the intention of buying, and I am able to develop a rapport with the ones who will be using the pots I have made. That's good for them and good for me as well.

The sale gives me a goal. It's my event, and I have to be ready with a good presentation. My livelihood depends on it. To start preparing for the sale, I pull out the calendar and mark off ten weeks. I will throw for seven weeks. The last three weeks will be used for glazing, firing and finally setting up the sale.

I bring out the list of all the things I make and start throwing them, day by day, marking each group of items off as I reach the quantity needed. I complete two or three items a day. For instance, today I will make 24 casseroles and 30 large bowls. I throw about $1000 worth of pots in a day, trimming the next day. Then I make more pots, trim and so on until the list is complete.

To keep creativity alive and to keep my pots from becoming too standard looking, I write notes to myself; these can range from a simple "make it differ-

Vase, 11 inches in height, wheel-thrown porcelain, sprayed with Hanna's Fake Ash Glaze, fired to Cone 10 in reduction, by David Cuzick.

ent" or "keep it loose" to "go have a beer before you throw." In order to keep creativity alive, it is necessary to make an effort to keep evolving.

One way of doing this is to read about pots, potters and cultures from the past. I seem to find a new interest before each sale and produce some pots reflecting my reading in that area. Last year, I made pots with leaf and floral additions influenced by the American art pottery movement; the year before, it was Jomon-style rope-paddled pots. Before that, I was interested in African, English, Korean, Japanese, Chinese, Greek and American Indian pottery.

They all, in one way or another, have influenced my work. I don't make copies, but I do allow the weight of history to inspire me. My point is to keep looking, to keep growing, to try to make better pots this year than last year.

Variety in shape and glazing is very important when conducting your own sale. If all of your pieces are glazed blue, but a potential buyer prefers green, then you've lost a sale. Vary the size, shape and surface quality of your pieces too. Think of all the possibilities for lids and handles. I try to vary the look without compromising my style.

After making pots for seven weeks, I begin glazing. It's daunting to look at all those bisqued pots stacked on racks or piled 3 feet high in the back of my glaze area. I often wonder how I will ever glaze so many. It's done one at a time, and I always seem to get through it.

The glazing weeks are both the hardest and the most exciting. I'm on my feet all day—glazing, loading and firing. Then comes the exciting part—opening the door after the firing. Each load is different, making it impossible not to peek into the still-too-hot kiln.

The cooled pots are pulled out with "oohs" and "ahhs," and a few "oh nos," then the bottoms are sanded and prices

Porcelain bowl, 12 inches in diameter, with Coleman's Red and Oxblood Red mixed 3:2 by volume, and Jensen Blue syringed around the rim, by David Cuzick.

Stoneware vase, 16 inches in height, with Turquoise Semimatt Glaze, and commercial artificial salt glaze sprayed over rim, fired to Cone 10 in reduction, by David Cuzick.

Cup, saucer and mug, to 4 inches in height, wheel-thrown and incised porcelain, with DC Blue and copper red glazes, fired to Cone 10 in reduction, by Mary Cuzick.

marked. (I will sometimes add up the retail price of all the pots in a single load; it's generally about $3000.)

Pricing can be difficult, especially for a beginning potter. The price should reflect the amount of time it would take a competent potter to make the piece, and how you feel about the way it came out of the kiln. The price should also have some relationship to what similar pieces are selling for in the area. Generally, pots are priced lower in Southern California than many other parts of the country. I have tried to raise my prices slowly but steadily over the years.

The glazing, firing and pricing continue. It takes three days to glaze a kilnload of pots. As the kiln fires, I glaze the next load. No matter what, it seems as though I always run out of time, and it is a struggle to complete that last load before the sale starts Saturday morning. I have even had sales when we opened the kiln midday Saturday. People love being the first to see pots still warm (hot!) from the kiln.

Setup for the sale takes two days. The best pots are displayed in the showroom. The others go on tables and racks placed around the backyard, loosely organized according to function—casseroles together here, platters there, cups on cup racks and so on. We also place pieces in boxes turned on end to create cubbyholes, and tuck pots in corners; some pieces are placed in the midst of a group of dissimilar pots to create a sense of finding something special. Other potters (including my wife Mary) participate in the sale as well, and we usually include a craftsperson from another medium to give variety to the show.

Of course, buyers don't just magically appear. We send out flyers to about 2000 customers from a mailing list that Mary keeps on computer and updates continually. I gather names at every fair I attend by putting out a guest book with a place for anyone interested to sign up for notification of the biannual sale. Guests can register on our website at www.cuzickpottery.com as well. I have also placed display ads in the daily newspaper; this is expensive, about $500 each time the ad appears, but worth it if you can afford it. On the day of the sale, signs and banners are put out to help newcomers find the studio and to create a festive environment.

There is a feeling of great relief and excitement when the morning of the sale finally arrives. At 9:00 A.M., people come streaming through the back gate to the show area. Often they rush in to be the first to see the new pots and make their selections. Many of them are friends now; they come to buy pots, to chat and to enjoy the party atmosphere. Mary makes 100 dozen cookies for the event, and we serve coffee and, in the spring, lemonade. Places for customers to sit while they consider purchases are all around.

We have three cashiers and four wrappers to help with the sales; it is very intense in the morning. Later on, when the crowd thins out, we have time to take a breath and consider how nice it is to do something we love to do and to receive so much appreciation for doing it. That's why I am a potter. ▲

Small teapot, 7 inches in height, stoneware with Shino #4 Glaze, fired to Cone 10 in reduction, by David Cuzick, Spring Valley, California.

Favorite Glaze Recipes

Turquoise Semimatt Glaze
(Cone 10, reduction)
Barium Carbonate	22.42%
Whiting	9.83
Custer Feldspar	56.82
Kentucky Ball Clay	10.93
	100.00%
Add: Zinc Oxide	6.01%
Copper Oxide	4.44%
Rutile	4.44%

A great glaze, but not food safe. Do not use on surfaces that could contain foods or beverages. Do not apply too thick. Very different on porcelain and stoneware. Good in salt. Also good using G-200 feldspar in place of Custer.

DC Blue Glaze
(Cone 10, reduction)
Colemanite	5.09%
Dolomite	13.40
Whiting	9.41
Custer Feldspar	25.45
Edgar Plastic Kaolin	19.50
Kentucky Ball Clay	1.70
Flint	25.45
	100.00%
Add: Red Iron Oxide	0.85%
Rutile	6.79%

Black Temmoku Glaze
(Cone 10, reduction)
Custer Feldspar	57.14%
Whiting	15.39
Kaolin	6.59
Flint	20.88
	100.00%
Add: Red Iron Oxide	9.89%

This glaze is from Clayart, the online discussion group; for further information, see www.ceramics.org/clayart.

Shino #4 Glaze
(Cone 10, reduction)
Soda Ash	4.55%
Spodumene	4.54
Nepheline Syenite	68.18
Edgar Plastic Kaolin	4.55
Kentucky Ball Clay	18.18
	100.00%

A very nice Shino. Needs lots of early body reduction.

Coleman's Red Glaze
(Cone 10, reduction)
Colemanite	10.80%
Whiting	15.73
Custer Feldspar	15.56
Nepheline Syenite	20.43
Edgar Plastic Kaolin	1.48
Flint	36.00
	100.00%
Add: Tin Oxide	1.72%
Copper Carbonate	0.43%

Oxblood Red Glaze
(Cone 10, reduction)
Colemanite	13.27%
Whiting	10.46
Feldspar	9.18
Nepheline Syenite	42.35
Edgar Plastic Kaolin	2.04
Flint	22.70
	100.00%
Add: Tin Oxide	1.70%
Copper Oxide	0.26%

This glaze needs good reduction to turn red. I often mix it with Coleman's Red to produce the best red of all.

Hanna's Fake Ash Glaze
(Cone 10, reduction)
Strontium Carbonate	10.0%
Whiting	30.0
Cedar Heights Redart	60.0
	100.0%
Add: Red Iron Oxide	3.5%
Yellow Ocher	4.0%

I always spray this glaze onto porcelain. It is very fluid at Cone 10.

V.C. 20 Glaze
(Cone 9–10, reduction)
Barium Carbonate	25%
Dolomite	10
Spodumene	25
Whiting	5
Custer Feldspar	35
	100%
Add: Tin Oxide	2%
Copper Carbonate	2%
Red Iron Oxide	2%

Note the very high amount of barium carbonate in this glaze. Do not use on surfaces meant to hold food or drink. This is a very fluid glaze over Cone 10.

Alisa Carroll and Peter Brondz; working as an apprentice provided postgraduate focus.

Learning through Apprenticeship

by Alisa Carroll

What do you do after you get a bachelor of arts degree in ceramics? Well, for me, it meant moving to a ski town in Colorado and being a ski bum, a waitress, a tutor, a massage therapist, a house-trim painter, a drywaller, a river-raft guide, a bartender, a babysitter, a ski-school video taker, a CPR instructor, a house cleaner and a bluegrass guitar picker—enough jobs to make me spin in circles. I needed focus. My friend, studio potter Peter Brondz, knew of my need, so he offered me an apprenticeship in Alaska.

Now, exactly what is an apprenticeship in this day and age, and how does it work? We often tried to figure this out to have a clear, articulate answer for the friends and customers who constantly inquired about, and sometimes misunderstood our relationship.

We had decided to begin with a commitment for three months. It lasted more

Wheel-thrown porcelain mugs, 4 inches in height, with dipped and trailed glaze, wood fired, by Alisa Carroll.

than three years, ending in December when I moved into my own studio. Naturally, our definition of apprenticeship changed over the years with my familiarity of his studio and systems, my financial situation and my ability to work with clay.

For me, apprenticing was an incredible opportunity to learn how to go about becoming a self-employed studio potter, not to mention how to humble myself, overcome frustration, set and achieve goals, be a good guest in someone else's creative space, and practice interpersonal communication in a business relationship.

Peter has a great sense of humor and is very flexible to work with. He is also a master at inventing efficient systems to accomplish daily tasks. This extends from the studio to the kiln sheds, sauna, kitchen, etc. I soon realized that being a pottery apprentice can, in a way, easily turn into being an apprentice to someone's life. Because I was eager to learn how to throw pots and survive my first winter in Alaska, I became a sponge, soaking up details.

Each year, we sat down for a meeting to set goals, solve problems and create awareness of each other's needs and desires. This resulted in a great list to refer back to throughout the year.

We also discovered a key component to facilitating communication is including a third party/mediator. This person's role was to clarify specific points, question each of us to elaborate on what we needed or expected, then help explain feelings or perspectives to us in an objective manner. The mediator was always an artist and mutual friend. Open communication and honesty were what made these conversations effective.

Last fall's meeting was held on a bluff next to the ocean. Prior to that, we had both spent time coming up with lists of the things that we provided for each other, how we both benefited and what we needed to work on.

The list of things I did for Peter went something like this: agree to be around and available to help approximately 40 hours a week; dust, stock and maintain bookkeeping for the gallery and craft shows; do the bank deposits; update the mailing list every month; help mix clay and glazes; help with loading, scraping

Bottle set, approximately 8 inches (20 centimeters) in height, salt-glazed stoneware, by Peter Brondz.

Stoneware pitchers, to 16 inches (41 centimeters) in height, with temmoku glaze, by Peter Brondz, Bird Creek, Alaska.

shelves, firing kilns; help with studio maintenance (e.g., oiling the timber beams, and repainting the floor and signs); conduct glaze tests; provide enthusiasm; and mop the floor (we took turns). Peter even had me help prepare his taxes for a while, until he realized how bad I was at it.

His list went something like this: provide a great space to work, a wheel, clay, glazes, kiln space, instruction, assignments, critiques, commission-free gallery space, enthusiasm, and all of the answers to my endless list of questions. Peter not only is an amazing artist, but he also happens to be one of the most generous men in the world. During the first year, he and his wife Lisa knew how poor I was, and fed me a burrito almost every day for lunch, as well as dinner when they could. By the third year, when I was actually making money in his gallery, he still insisted on taking no commission as his way to give back to the field of pottery. He said he had a good deal when he first started out, and he wanted to give me the same experience so I could save enough to start my own studio. It was an amazing gift, and I can only hope to honor the favor by doing the same for another young artist in the future.

What I learned as an apprentice to a studio potter is far more than I ever learned as a university ceramics student. When I told school friends that I was going to work in a potter's studio every day, most of them got this dreamy look on their face like, "Oh, if I could only have such a cush job." Only one of them said, "Get ready, girl; that's going to be a lot of work."

Being a first-year apprentice in someone else's space is nerve-wracking. There are a million chores and tools, and one specific way of doing everything down to how one wrings the water out of the mop. This was frustrating, but I would learn a better way to do something most of the time. Either way, I figured, when in Rome, do as the Romans do.

I wanted to be such a good apprentice and dreaded the time when I would screw up, which of course happened: Like the time I unloaded the kiln and dropped a perfect red teapot onto the cement slab. Like the time I forgot how many scoops of feldspar I had added to the glaze. Like the time I was on my way to the bank, but accidentally dropped a month-long gallery bank deposit into the United States mail with no address or stamp on it.

One revelation we were both sold on is the magic of assignments. We started out by keeping track of the hours that I worked. This became very nitpicky and felt like drudgery. Then Peter gave me an assignment on the board: Make 100 mugs. Now that was something I could be inspired about.

Assignments gave Peter an opportunity to consider what he believed I needed to work on and how to begin teaching me the skills. For example, he had me work on covered jars first, then move on to teapots. From my point of view, when I knew my assignment in advance, I could take a few days to research that shape, do some sketches of ones I wanted to try, and enjoy the challenge of completing a set goal.

Another thing that Peter contributed was the freedom to try to replicate his work. He figured that I needed to learn how to throw, for example, a pitcher, any pitcher, so it might as well be his. Then, after I acquired the technical ability, I could start to develop my own style of pitcher. What a relief! In college, I was under constant pressure to make something new, different, a unique form every time I sat down at the wheel. Teachers would say, "Your work should express you, be about you."

When beginning, it's overwhelming enough to try to throw a perfectly even 10-inch-high cylinder, then shape it into a pitcher, much less conceive of some artistic statement that resembles "me." I needed to simply have a space, some demos from Peter, then hours of practicing those techniques and steps.

Some potters are very protective of their glazes and forms, but not Peter. "Spread the wealth," he'd say. "Everything I do has been done before."

Peter has been making pots in Alaska for over 20 years. He has a Minnesota flat-top kiln, which I fired most of my work in. He also has a salt kiln and a wood-fired kiln in which many group firings take place. I had an opportunity to learn from the techniques and art of these other potters as well.

This community of potters also provided needed support and encouragement. When learning to fire a wood kiln, it's nice to have many resources to solve problems, as well as people who are willing to do things I would never dream of. Once, it had been pouring rain with 25-knot gusts for two days as we tried to bring the wood kiln to temperature, but it wouldn't budge past Cone 9. Some pyromaniacs in the crowd

Separate work spaces in the studio provided an environment conducive to individual development for the apprentice.

decided to hook up the propane burners to blast some extra heat into the firebox. Sounded fine to me, but I stayed well away from the combustion zone.

I also felt fortunate to have the resources of the University of Alaska, Anchorage, and its staff and students nearby. Peter is good friends with Martin Tagseth, a former instructor at the university. Having been a fly on the wall during their problem-solving sessions, one would think I would know enough to receive a diploma in kiln-building (if only I could remember everything they said).

With kilns, if it's not one thing going wrong, it's another. Peter and Martin would talk burners and bricks over many a cup of coffee, and I even had the opportunity to help build a kiln, but it will take many more before I'll feel that I have any real knowledge.

The university also brought many great artists in for workshops. Together, Peter and I took one with Linda Christianson; I was shocked and amazed that anyone could do things so incredibly different from what Peter does and make such cool pots. Peter just kept flashing me glances as if to say, "Yep. She's breaking all my rules."

There was also the time when he sent me down to Homer, Alaska, to be the guest apprentice of his friend Paul Dungan. Paul broke all the rules too. It was great—loosened me up. As an apprentice, you have to remember to be your own person, your own little wild artist; to ask ridiculous questions; challenge ways of doing things; experiment; endure it when the master looks in at what you're doing and either holds his breath or rolls his eyes; shock 'em!

My best learning experience came the summer before last when Peter and Lisa went to Africa on their honeymoon. I was on my own! I had signed up to do a Fourth of July craft fair, and had to make pots to fill the kiln and fire it. Yahoo! It was a trying experience, up at 3 A.M., napping on the dog and trying to figure out how much reduction was actually occurring. The firing was a smashing success, as was the fair.

We had a long-standing joke concerning all the little tidbits of knowledge that Peter passed along. He knew how broke I was and always told me I could get $10 if I would send his latest tip to *Ceramics Monthly* for publication in the Suggestions column. I even made a list, thinking one day I might cash it in.

Then the day came when we were in the studio together while he was glazing, and I was decorating my already-glazed pots. Usually, we gave each other alone time to decorate, but I didn't mind him being around until I felt him staring at me from behind.

"What now?" I asked, ready to be called on something I was forgetting.

"You just turned that bowl upside down to get that thin brushstroke around the foot," he said in shock.

"Well, yeah," I said. "How on earth do you do it?"

"I just squish my brush in there. It never occurred to me to turn the bowl upside down."

I said, "You have got to be kidding me. In 20 years of decorating pots, it never occurred to you to turn the pot upside down?"

"No," he said. "That's a great technique. You should send that one in to *Ceramics Monthly*." ▲

"Tamari Pourers," to 5 inches in height, porcelain with Shino glaze and black slip, wood fired to Cone 10, by Alisa Carroll, Bird Creek, Alaska.

Selling at Retail Shows

by Sandi Pierantozzi and Neil Patterson

When we were first seduced by clay, we didn't make things to be sold but rather because we loved it. As our work evolved, so did the realization that we might actually be able to make an income from doing something that we enjoy.

We've both done numerous gallery shows and some wholesale business, but there are distinct advantages to retail shows. Any large, well-attended craft show provides massive exposure for the artist. Even though many of our customers came to the "Philadelphia Museum of Art Craft Show" because they received one of our announcements (we mailed over 800 cards to former students, friends, collectors and customers), there were still quite a few who had never seen our work before.

Another advantage to a good retail show is developing customer relations. We enjoy having the opportunity to meet the people who embrace our work and want to have it in their lives. There is a whole range of feedback from customers, some of which is very insightful. At times, a customer can help you see your work with fresh eyes.

A real plus at a retail show is having control over the display of your work, although this can feel like an overwhelming task; it is a challenge to arrange every detail of your display. It is refreshing to see our pots set up in environments that we've created specifically for the work.

One of the best things about doing a craft show is meeting other craftspeople. Not only can you develop lasting friendships, other artists are an important source of information. We have found most to be very generous in giving valuable advice about other shows, galleries, etc.

Of course, there are aspects of doing craft shows that we do not enjoy. All of the schlepping is probably the biggest hassle. Doing a craft show can also mean a week or more out of the studio, especially if travel is involved. Then there is the expense (booth fees, electric, mailings, display, travel, hotel, etc.). We have found that most craftspeople start to enjoy a show after they've made enough sales to cover expenses. This is all just part of the bigger picture of being able to make and sell our work.

Perhaps the hardest thing about doing retail shows is being juried into them. Since the judges for most shows change from year to year, there is no way to be assured of acceptance, even for a well-established craftsperson. This can be a big factor in determining yearly income.

Acceptance into a major show is always exciting and comes with a certain feeling of validation for our work in the professional realm. On the other hand, it is important to treat the possibility of rejection realistically, and if we're not chosen, to understand that our work is still valid and that we may have better luck next time.

It is also important to know our limits and try to pace ourselves when preparing for a show. A retail show offers the advantage of making whatever we would like to make, whether it be old favorites or new forms, versus just working to fill orders. We have found that having a range of prices, as well as a selection of large and small pieces, attracts a wider audience.

We feel fortunate to have such venues as the Philadelphia show, which enable us to show and sell our work to a wide and appreciative audience. The contact with the people who are buying our pots adds a feeling of completeness to the cycle of making our work. ▲

Studio and Showroom Organization

by Dick Lehman

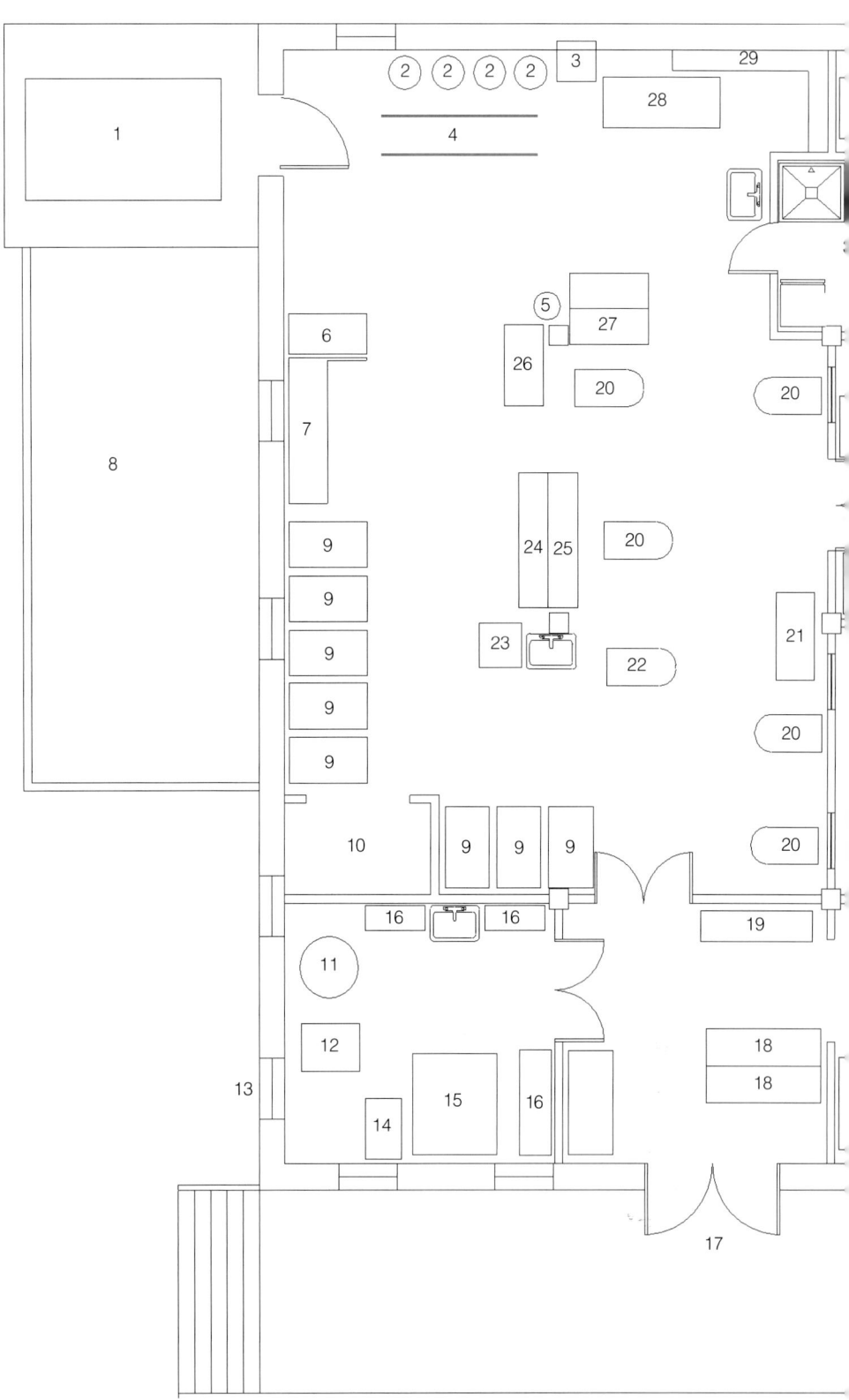

As a production potter, I had long wished that I would someday have the opportunity and the means to build a new studio to my specifications. For years, I had lived within the design constraints of "existing space." I wanted the chance to start from scratch, to design the space *my* way; however, the cost of construction remained formidable, and the opportunity to build elusive. The devastating news that my studio building had been condemned (in an eminent domain take-over by the county) actually gave me that opportunity—although not on the terms that I had originally envisioned.

Given just 60 days to vacate my studio, I had no time to build. Instead, I hastily moved into a vintage (1890s), brick, three-story factory building (of "slow-burning-mill" construction). The space was completely wide open, so I was able to design the entire studio as I eventually wanted to have it, but had the luxury of implementing the design as I could afford it—incrementally over a period of years.

What has finally emerged is very much like the original vision; however, having the experience of actually working in the developing space over a period of years gave me the opportunity to fine tune many details. In the end, this made the space far more useful and efficient than it would have been had I needed to make all the decisions in the turmoil and disruption of those first weeks or months following the forced move. Let me describe the space, highlighting various aspects that, over the years, have been most useful in maximizing both production and retail sales.

Originally, I shared this mammoth 60,000-square-foot building with only one other business—a hardwood furniture manufacturer. Over the intervening years, other shops have joined us, creating a "collection of producing artists and craftspeople." Today, there are 19 shops housed in what has come to be called the Old Bag Factory.

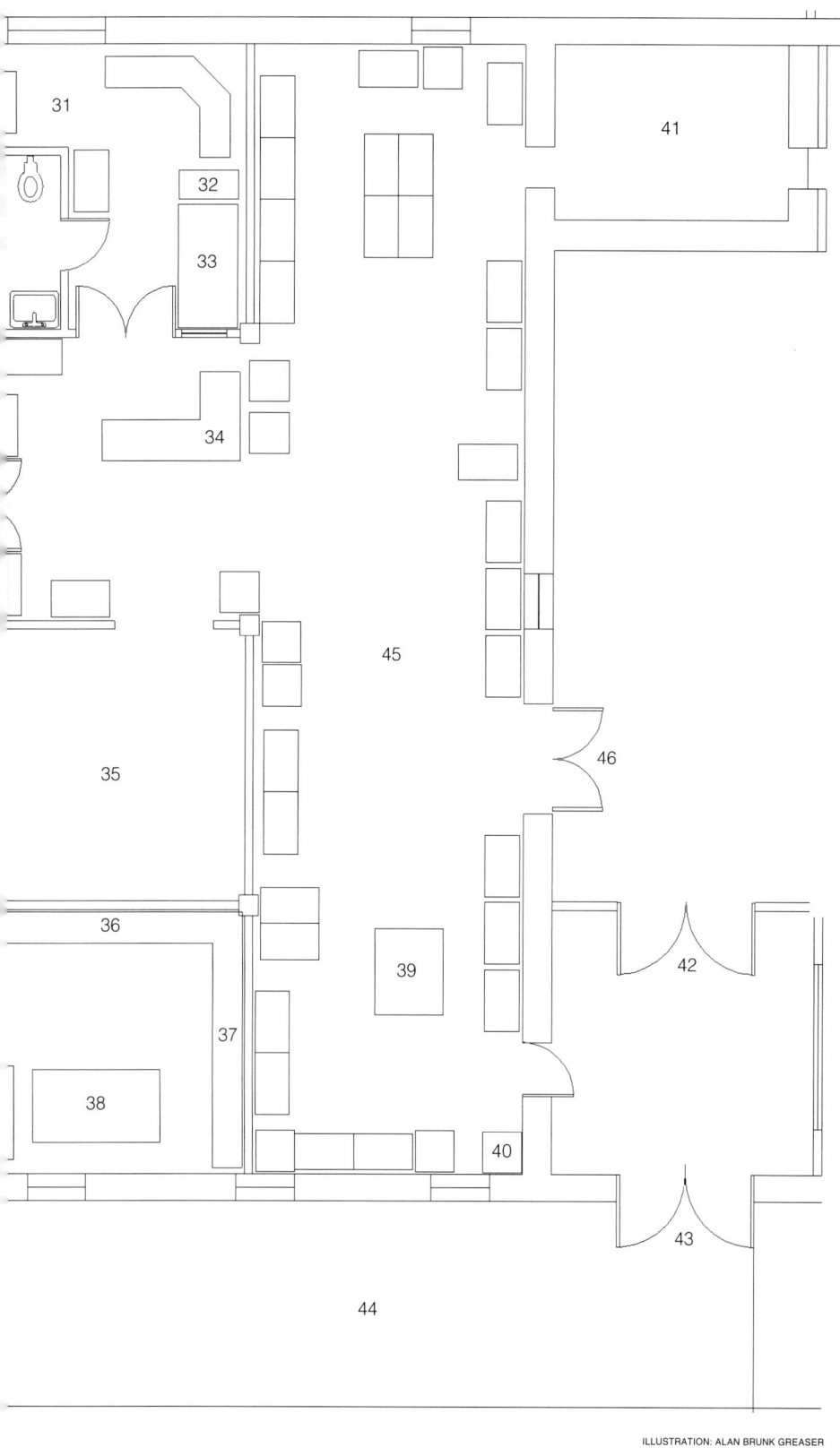

1) Car Kiln
2) Large-quantity Glaze Buckets on Wheels
3) Spray Booth
4) Kiln Track
5) Extruder
6) Storage
7) Tool Bench
8) Fenced Raku Area
9) Rolling Ware Carts
10) Photo Booth
11) Electric Kiln
12) Mixer
13) Exhaust
14) Hammer Mill
15) Wet Clay Storage
16) Glaze Chemicals
17) Loading Entrance
18) Supplies and Accessories Storage
19) Wet Clay
20) Wheel
21) Slab Roller
22) Trim Wheel
23) Porcelain Wedging Table
24) Stoneware Pug Mill
25) Porcelain Pug Mill
26) Stoneware Wedging Table
27) Bats
28) Glazing Table
29) Glaze Storage
30) Restroom with Shower
31) Office
32) File
33) Desk
34) Check-Out Counter
35) Gallery with Pedestal Display
36) Dry Clay Storage
37) Wet Porcelain Storage
38) Packing Area
39) Dinnerware Table Display
40) Storage
41) Old Vault Showroom
42) Airlock Entry Way
43) Secondary Entrance to Complex
44) To Ramp
45) Showroom with Display Units 30 and 80 Inches in Height
46) Main Entrance to Pottery

ILLUSTRATION: ALAN BRUNK GREASER

As customers enter and pass through the entryway, a look to the left would reveal the 5000-square-foot showroom of the custom hardwood furniture manufacturer. Looking toward the far end of the furniture showroom, they would be able to see directly into my pottery studio. The line of sight takes a customer's eyes directly into the showroom space and back into the well-lighted gallery space.

Because the 1300-square-foot showroom and gallery space is rectangular, I have located the display units toward the outside walls to maintain a feeling of openness. Part of the showroom utilizes an "old records vault" complete with heavy steel doors and combination locks—just part of the charm of an old building such as this.

The display units, which hold approximately 2500 finished pieces, are made of cherry. I designed half of them with built-in lighting and glass shelving. The rest are lighted by a halogen track system in the ceiling.

The half walls and low 30-inch-tall display units that ring the gallery space allow customers to see into the studio space where we potters are working (and, in turn, allow us to see the customers). For the few areas in the showroom that are out of our direct line of sight, I installed rounded mirrors. These are effective not so much as a security measure or to deter shoplifting, but rather to make it possible for us to be aware of where people are in the showroom and to determine whether sales assistance might be in order.

As an interesting aside, I should mention the flooring, which is made up of three rather squeaky 1-inch-thick layers of pecan wood. Aside from their charm, the squeaks generate a bit of marketing information as well. As we have listened to people walking in the showroom over the years, we have learned to distinguish the separate and distinct "gaits" of first-time visitors, repeat customers, shoppers on a mission to buy a gift, and time-killers. While not infallible, these audible clues actually assist us in antici-

Trimming tools are organzied in PVC pipes glued to a castered table.

pating just how much and what kind of customer assistance is needed.

I should note that all the sales in the showroom are made by those of us who make the ware. I currently employ three other potters. Usually the sales responsibilities are shared equally, although whose turn it is to assist may be determined by something as simple as who has the driest hands. Over the course of the year, the Old Bag Factory has nearly 140,000 visitors. Of that total amount, nearly 10,000 visit the pottery.

This commitment to making and selling has had a huge impact on how the showroom and studio were arranged. All the throwing wheels are situated so that each potter can see, by looking through windows and doorways, and can be seen immediately by customers entering the showroom. A smile or nod from 35 feet away may be our first contact with visitors; however, if a customer stays in the pottery for more than a few minutes, one of us will make formal contact.

Similarly, the office is laid out in such a way that I can be working at my desk and still, through windows, see the entire showroom and gallery area. Miniblinds in those windows allow for privacy if I am working on something I would rather the customers not see (making a bank deposit, for example).

Often we sit in the back of the studio for lunch, somewhat out of the view of customers, but with enough visibility for us to see customers who need assistance. In this way, the studio can remain open over the lunch hour when it is most convenient for many of our local customers to quickly stop by to make a purchase.

The gallery itself is reasonably well lighted all the time. However, the halogen track-lighting system is activated by a motion sensor. When a customer walks into or near the gallery, the sensors activate lights. I can see at least two benefits to this arrangement: the first is the energy savings achieved by not lighting the gallery when no one is in it. Secondly, there is that sort of "taaa-daaah" feeling experienced by the customer as the lights come on. And if for some reason I am out of direct sight of the gallery at that moment, the lights alert me to the customer's presence.

The check-out counter is located very near to both the office and the studio workspace. If I am in the office, it is just a few steps out to help a customer with a sale. And, of course, by having the sales area very near the workspace, it gives increased security to the cash register, and eliminates needless extra steps to make sales.

Not shown in the floor plan are the 24×48-inch wheeled carts that each potter uses. These are useful in moving clay from storage to pug mill (we always pug what we are going to use just before we throw with it), and from pug mill to throwing area.

There are at least two other tools, which are absolutely indispensable, that do not show up explicitly on the floor plan: The first is a cut-off tool I made to fit the end of the pug mills. As the pug exits the mill, it moves forward on stainless-steel rollers (found at the local scrap-metal yard for a small price). Hinged above the rollers is a variably spaced series of cut-off wires. These may be arranged to cut at any interval, and are simply tightened in place with wing nuts. When the pug reaches the desired length, the wires are pulled down to cut 4–6 pieces at one time.

For smaller amounts, the 4-inch-diameter pug size is a little inconvenient (the slices are so narrow as to be difficult to use). To cut smaller weights, I clamp a wire to the end of the pug barrel, using a kind of "vise-grip" tool. This allows me to split the pug into two halves before cutting to length. (For even smaller weights, I clamp on a cutter, which splits the pug into four pieces before it is cut to length.)

The second indispensable tool is a small rolling cart, which holds all of our trimming tools and trimming accessories. At a liquidation sale, I purchased a slide-projector cart (simply a four-castered stand with a small table top on it). I added a piece of plywood to enlarge the table top and to this glued, in upright positions, a series of PVC pipe of varying diameters to hold the trimming tools that we use. I say this tool cart is indispensable because it takes what is normally a messy, cluttered box full of tools, and organizes them in a fashion that (while it still may be a bit messy) allows us to see all the individual tools at a glance.

Another benefit to this way of organizing tools is that it also allows us to see when something is missing. More than once we have noticed a trimming tool or metal rib missing, and found it among the trimmings—before it was dumped into the barrel of scraps destined for the hammer mill. (Only one trimming tool has actually gotten into the hammer mill and, based on that one experience, I have ruefully concluded that it is much better to find tools beforehand than to fish out all the "parts" afterward.)

I have tried to put casters on everything in the studio that can reasonably be moved. As a result, all the throwing carts, the ware carts, a glazing table, the trimming tool cart, and all the large glaze buckets are on casters.

I learned about the blessing of glaze buckets on casters from my potter friend Phil Yordy, who works in Saint Jacobs, Ontario, Canada. His studio is on the ground floor of six connected grain silos. There are no straight walls in his entire space (a problem for display units, etc.); however, when glazing, he simply wheels ware on carts into one silo where all the glaze buckets are within easy reach in a circle around him—much better than a line of buckets. The arrangement saves many steps.

Since I have no silo, I decided to put my buckets on casters and encircle myself for glazing. And it is easy to wheel the buckets back to a storage area when they are not in use.

The car kiln is located near the glazing area to minimize movement of pots between glazing and loading. For the same reason, the glaze spray booth is located adjacent to the kiln.

The photo booth is normally used as a storage room, filled with wheeled ware carts when it is not in service. It is an easy task to remove the ware carts, relocate the castered strobe, softbox and boom, and lower the pulley-controlled photo backdrop. In less than 10 minutes, the photo booth is operational, and at the end of the photo session, it may be fully restored to storage space in another 10 minutes.

Having easy access to a photo booth has been a real blessing. It is not a particularly high-tech or expensive arrangement; most of the equipment I have made or have picked up as used equipment at camera swap meets. But the arrangement affords me the setting in which to make publication-quality images at any time.

I also find that I am more apt to keep better photographic records of my work since it is so easy to do. And the economy is astounding. With a consistent set-up, the results are always of predictable high quality. Rather than paying $75–$100 per pot, we can easily set up and shoot 20–30 pieces in an evening for only the cost of the film and processing. (If we are in a rush for slides to enter a show or competition, an evening of photography followed by dropping the film off at an overnight processor can have the finished slides in our hands by 4:00 the next afternoon.)

Materials storage, and clay and glaze mixing areas are located in separate rooms on the south side of the studio. A ramp allows clay supplies to be forklifted right to the loading entrance, then quickly wheeled into storage areas. Package services can use the same entrance for the delivery of supplies.

The clay mixer, hammer mill, electric kiln and glaze materials/station are lo-

I have tried to put casters on everything in the studio that can reasonably be moved. As a result, all the throwing carts, the ware carts, a glazing table, the trimming tool cart, and all the large glaze buckets are on casters.

Pug cut-off tool: As the extruded pug moves forward on stainless-steel rollers, a wire clamped onto the end of the pug mill slices it in half vertically; then infinitely adjustable cut-off wires (tightened in place with wing nuts on a hinged lid) are pulled down to slice the halved pug into specified throwing weights.

cated in the southwestern-most room. This may appear to be an odd combination of items. However, the decision was driven by the need for these processes to have access to the good-quality exhaust system located in this room.

Wet-clay storage occupies parts of three of the auxiliary storage rooms on the south end of the studio. We attempt to keep at least a four-month supply of clay mixed and aging.

Finally, I have located the packing area as far from the production areas as possible. This decision keeps the inevitable mess, which always seems to accompany the use of packing materials, from contaminating work in progress and glaze materials.

We do quite a bit of shipping, sometimes for people who come into the studio to purchase gifts for others, but more often to people who telephone in orders. As a service to customers, I have a toll-free number. The volume of sales that this generates more than pays for the fee. And it is, I trust, an appreciated part of customer service.

I do not publish a catalog picturing our pots so nearly all phone orders come from previous customers who know what we offer. The northern part of Indiana is one of the fastest growing areas in the state for tourism. Consequently, while 70% of sales are from regional customers, a growing amount comes from tourists. The toll-free telephone number and reasonably priced shipping are real conveniences for them, and a boon to our business as well.

Your convictions and preferences about sales, marketing, production, space needs and work style are likely to be different than mine. Your personal temperament and budget are likely to imply different organizational decisions. But I hope that what I have shared here will be useful in helping you make the most of what you have to work with. ▲

The Marketing Dance
by Richard Selfridge

"Dog Day Afternoon Teacup," 8 inches high, slab-built terra cotta with majolica decoration, fired to Cone 04, by Richard and Carol Selfridge, Edmonton, Alberta, Canada.

Twenty-five years ago, we would go just about anywhere to try to sell our work. Yes, you could say we were hippies; we would sell our functional pots off a tie-dyed bedspread in a Friday flea market at the university or a folk festival, even in the middle of a shopping mall. We really liked the direct contact with the end users and the "attaboys" that we got when passing over our latest, fresh-from-the-kiln experiments to an appreciative public.

In those golden granola days, you could live on $300 a month (who needed a dental plan or children's college fund?), and anything with a matt glaze and a splash of decoration would usually sell. If we only had to wrap up half the stock at day's end, we were laughing all the way to the grocery store.

We thought we could identify our customers. They looked like us (head bands and bell bottoms); they liked the same things (music and handmade art); and they considered our inexpensive work a "consumer durable" (like an old car or stereo system). Of course, our most expensive item was about $40. But things changed—us, our work, our audience and our marketing approach.

Our first "reality check" came in the mid 1970s at a Calgary ceramics seminar, where Randy Johnston recalled how he had tried to sell his subtle wood-fired pots at a music festival. He thought this was his target audience because "they liked the same music." In retrospect, he wished he had sold the food that day.

Selling good work requires the right context. Just because it looks earthy doesn't mean it will sell well on a blanket on the ground. It's hard to dance like Ginger Rogers if you're partnered with Bozo the Clown. The real nadir of my mistaking our audience came on a snowy winter weekend (I only lasted one day) at an antique and gun show, where I sold nothing and was frightened by the "gun nuts" in the bargain.

Why did I do it? My friend, who sold leather goods, was going; besides,

The front porch of the Selfridge's home/studio serves as a showroom for functional stoneware and porcelain.

we both liked antiques and thought that at least half the crowd would be "our people."

I also remember the remark of a panhandling wino with a proper British accent. He assured me at a farmer's market on Mother's Day that "things may be slow now" (people were only buying flowers, house plants, chickens and vegetables), but "when our crowd gets here, sales will be much better."

What follows is a description of some of our principles for selling work in this post-Thatcher/Reagan global economy.

First, a brief note on what our work is: Carol and I work collaboratively, making stoneware and porcelain (gas reduction fired or wood fired to Cone 10–11) and illusionistic majolica-glazed terra cotta (fired in an electric kiln to Cone 04). Most of the stoneware and porcelain is sold from our studio showroom (the front porch and yard of our Victorian house) and at two open-house events (900 mailed invitations). The illusionistic majolica is sold in about 15 galleries across North America. Wholesale represents at most 35% of our income. We have lived solely from our work for the last 25 years; although we are not rich, we own a home and travel a little and help our three kids with university expenses.

With the hard economic realities of cutbacks and governmental off-loading of public services, especially for those on the economic bottom in North

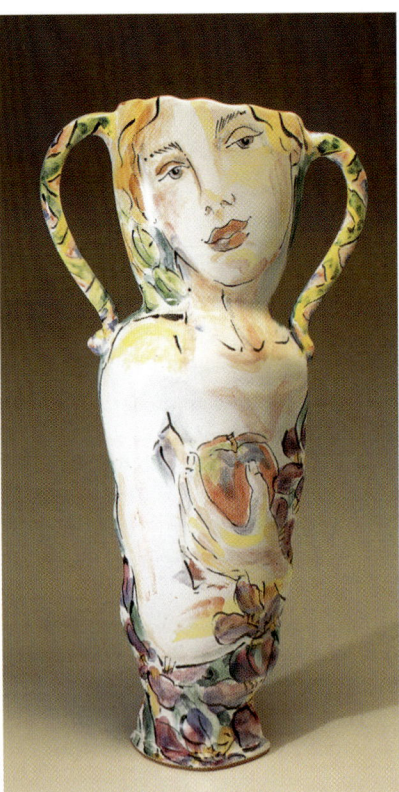

"Eve's Red Apple Amphora," 30 inches in height, slab-built terra cotta with brushed majolica pigments.

America, fund-raising has become an activity for citizens at all levels of society. Whether it's a bake sale to send preschoolers on a field trip or to support a new cancer facility, we don't want for worthy causes.

As artists, we are inundated with requests for donated work. Often those who do the asking, especially for upmarket celebrity events, are our patrons and buyers. These past customers and their fellow benefit attendees are a significant part of our target audience in our city of 850,000.

An instructive example of our community involvement occurred when Carol and I participated in a fund-raising dinner at the request of two of our regular customers. This was for the Minerva Foundation, which funds ABC Headstart, Hope Foundation, Kids Kottage, Kids with Cancer and many other worthwhile endeavors.

Usually, people ask us for a donation of our work for a benefit auction (more about that later), but this time the Minerva request was different. They were having a fancy dinner with an inspirational speaker talking about overcoming adversity. The speaker was Silken Laumann, Canada's two-time Olympic rowing medalist, who persevered despite a career-threatening leg injury in-

Studio Practices, Techniques and Tips

"Japanese Geisha Teapot," 21 inches high, terra cotta with majolica decoration.

"Cubist Mixed Floral Vase," 20 inches in height, majolica-decorated terra cotta, fired to Cone 04.

curred in a boat crash just before the Barcelona Olympics.

Two hundred thirty people paid $350 per couple to dine in the Empire room of the Macdonald Hotel in Edmonton. The hotel is a palatial chateau-style landmark—the place for visiting royalty; e.g., the Queen of England and the Rolling Stones. Instead of the traditional flowers for centerpieces, they wanted to borrow, for the evening, one piece or an ensemble of our majolica pots for each of the 27 tables.

The reasons why we accepted illustrate some of the important marketing principles we've learned since those days of "the gypsy pottery caravan hits the road" of 25 years ago:

1) As an artist, you want to control your life as much as possible; other people's ASAP deadlines and artificially enforced themes are a quick way to kill creativity. The organizers asked us to participate ten months before the banquet, so we had plenty of time to set aside work. We merely postponed by a week or two some of our regular gallery shipments. And the event itself took only about a day of our time.

2) You want to present your work in the best possible appropriate context. This venue was elegant and up-market (as good as any local gallery), with the added twist that, even though they were not used to serve the meal, many of the pieces suggested the possibility. The work was presented in such a way that it was the center of attention, something that the diners discussed, especially after the master of ceremonies acknowledged our presence as the makers. Yes, we attended as guests, mingled and dined. It was not seen as a selling situation, but as an opportunity to view our work, more like the way we see things in a museum or in someone's home. Although we were mentioned in the program, there were no prices or

promotional materials present, reinforcing the idea that this was our contribution to the event.

3) Controlling the costs of public relations, or knowing when to say yes and when to say not this year is crucial. We are asked about twice a week for contributions of our work, and like everyone else, we frequently are solicited by telephone for funds. Money is something we don't have a lot of, so we have decided to only give goods to causes we support. This also lets us deal with the problem of worthy charities that use professional fund-raisers who often keep more than 80% of the funds they raise.

The delightful thing about the Minerva event was that we only lent our work. These pieces actually took the place of about $1800 worth of flowers, which might have been contributed by some benevolent florist. Our costs were in lost time for planning and transportation. Fortunately, the hotel is only ten minutes from our home/studio, and the work was transported without much packing in two minivans and set up with the help of one of the volunteer/customers who asked us to participate. When you compare this with the enormous amounts paid by corporations to publicists to present their companies as good corporate citizens, this event was very cost effective.

4) If you can, it is usually a good idea to show solo rather than with a lot of competing goods. It seems counterproductive to us to advertise and draw a crowd so that others can make the sales. Fairly early on, we decided that it was better for us to stage an event, bring out our loyal clientele, and sell to them in an environment that we could control to some degree, rather than to be in the "scrum" of a sort of juried crafts fair. It may be that, as a buyer, it is nice to find a "bargain" hidden among the dross of a craft fair, overrun with beginner work that was "juried in" because of the organizer's greed for fees and admission receipts. But as a seller, it can be discouraging, even without the gratuitous insults of people who think it's easy. ("My aunt took pottery once." She better not have taken any of mine.)

I am sure there are some excellent juried craft shows, both retail and wholesale. However, the idea of sending out invitations to your former clients to meet you in a large hall where they will be confronted with the work of 200 others selling goods never made much sense to me. Our philosophy has been that, unless you run some kind of factory (Warhol comes to mind), the amount that anyone (or two with no assistants in our case) can make in a lifetime is really very little. Ideally, you should have a path from a sale of your work back to you, either directly or through a continuing relationship with a store or gallery. If you concentrate on quality, your past work should sell your present. Unlike the guy selling "Rolex" wristwatches on the street corner, you want your customers to be able to find you again.

The people who come to our studio showroom see it as a destination. They come to buy "homecraft" in a historic residential neighborhood, not a commercial shopping area. Although they don't usually throw their wallets in from the street, very few are tire kickers or only looking for entertainment.

We might not have done the Minerva event if we were among 30 other artists asked to loan work. The impact of our pieces being the visual stars of the evening, and not playing merely a supporting role, was important. Sometimes a secondary role at a fund-raising auction can be valuable, particularly if the other items are more up-market than yours. But it all depends on the audience, their affluence, and their familiarity with your work.

"Persephone's Fruit Platter," 28 inches in length, thrown and altered terra cotta, with majolica pigments brushed onto white base glaze, fired to Cone 04, by Carol and Richard Selfridge.

5) Sometimes it is important to show your work again to your target audience. Our experience has been that the way for your customer base to grow is by letting past customers "sell" your work for you. Even if you donate a piece to be sold as a fund-raiser, the person who buys it at the event will usually display it prominently or give it as a gift. The high bidders become your new customers, and they bring new blood to your mailing list. On our open-house invitations, we always tell our clients to bring a friend, and these new friends are then our new regulars. The Minerva event had a liberal sprinkling of our regulars, almost one or two at each table. They were reminded about us and enthused about our work to their dinner companions.

6) Projecting the image that your work is valued, changing for the better and in demand by a growing audience is necessary for continued success as an artist. Unfortunately, the only constant in contemporary society is change and a demand for novelty. People always want to know what is new and unique, and what important "success" you have had lately.

It is also a truism that you are seldom valued in your own hometown until some consensual validation comes from outside. Although they may seem like a lottery where the tickets are good slides, we enter juried exhibitions (only a few are open to Canadians) and we have had some success. We let our regular customers know about these minor triumphs by making postcards of these pieces with the info about the show, then send them out with invitations for our open-house events. They also provide validation of the gift giver's "good taste" when they accompany the gifts we sell from the studio.

Along with these cards, our invitations also include a "brag sheet" about our recent new work, our exhibition successes and distant gallery representation, and some of our donations to worthy causes. The Minerva dinner and the photo of me pouring tea for Carol and Silken Laumann provided an interesting visual for our winter open-house letter, extending the scope of our contribution to our larger audience. The cachet of having your work collected by a celebrity or given as a gift to a visiting

Carol and Richard Selfridge outside their home/studio gallery.

dignitary will certainly enhance your work's value to your normal clientele. You do, however, have to let them know about it.

7) If you are careful, sometimes what you give away comes back double. When you let people know you donate your work for worthy causes, you have to expect that more will ask you. How you answer is a public-relations dance where you have to be fast on your feet.

First, be sure to reserve the "yes" for an event that will be attended by your target audience. It can be a benefit for the indigent women's shelter, provided at least some of those attending are not indigent women and they know of your work and appreciate it. Don't expect the bidding to go through the roof at a picnic or rummage sale. Black tie usually means they bring their wallets.

Even more important is the way the work gets there. Don't drop it off yourself or send it by courier. When previous or potential customers ask you for a donation, you should arrange for them to pick it up at your studio/showroom. Usually, they bring a friend and often they decide to buy something for themselves or remember that they need a gift for someone else.

Provided that you only give away work you are proud of, not seconds or inferior pieces, this can be an opportunity to clear the decks of older inventory. Sometimes the best pieces are the last to sell, especially if they have been in the dark at a distant gallery. Often these older pieces are perfect for representing you to the grateful fund-raising community.

Saying "no" can be difficult because you may be disappointing valued customers. Sometimes it is easier to just give them a couple of mugs and some postcards, especially if you think the event will be "thin" on your target audience. If the request is to back a sensitive or partisan organization or a controversial issue that divides your clientele, or from an art association that you know would never show the kind of work you do, then it is not too hard to say "not this year." It is particularly galling when other visual artists ask us to help them raise money for their installation or performance when they only want to associate with lowly craft media on the one day of the year when they have a fund-raiser. Unfortunately, too many artists went to art school where they had a pottery sale of beginner works (candidates for the recycle bin), sold so that they could bring in a "real artist," seldom a lowly potter. All of us want our work to be taken seriously, certainly not to feel used or gratuitously insulted. We do, however, support theater and dance groups, and in return, often receive complimentary tickets to events we would pay to attend anyway. In the end, these are really decisions about how we will distribute our goods as a form of advertisement.

We try to dance with the folks who brought us, to pay back the community that has bought, collected, praised and valued our work. We are now getting a lot of wedding-present business from the children of our aging hippie customers of 20 years ago. These kids grew up using our pots and see them as the kind of things they want to give and use. We are part of their community.

At the Minerva banquet, Carol sat next to the heart surgeon who replaced her mitral valve 12 years ago. (When he says he wishes he were talented like us, we laugh and say we think he's pretty good with his hands.) His wife has brought scores of people to our studio. They, like many of our customers, have become our friends. It is a pleasure to support their fund-raising endeavors, to nurture that voice in them that says individual people can still make a difference in this complicated world. ▲

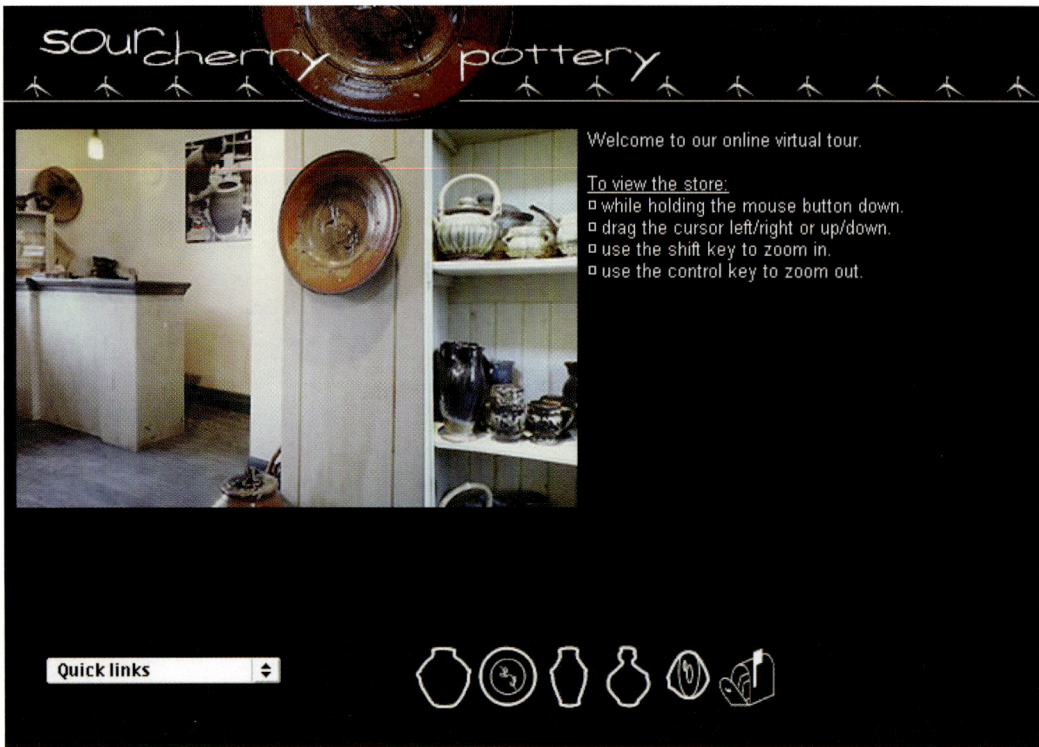

A virtual tour page allows 360° navigation of the studio showroom at www.sourcherrypottery.com.

Attention to Detail
The Making of a Pottery's Website
by Tony and Sheila Clennell

We had decided to move our home and business. In addition to establishing a new customer base, we needed to build new kilns and a studio. We were very lucky indeed to have our son Sean in the building business.

It was during the construction of our workshop and showroom that we became aware of Sean's attention to detail. No shortcuts could be taken. The final product would be his signature of fine craftsmanship.

As it happened, the studio was to be his last building construction job. Longing for a new challenge, Sean packed up his tools and headed back to college where he successfully completed a webmaster program. His goal was to establish a design house with a focus on artistic website solutions. Since we had been uprooted and were looking to attract new customers, we decided to hire him to develop our website www.sourcherrypottery.com.

As visual artists, we wanted a site that would be visually interesting and connected to who we are as studio potters. We wanted our site to be our "electronic business card." We wanted it to help establish a new customer base, contact galleries with a portfolio of our latest work and also sell pots. Our purpose was not to use the site for catalog-style shopping, but for more personalized service. Prospective buyers can e-mail us directly for a detailed description of work currently available.

When asked what makes a good website, Sean, in typical computer-guy speak, answered in a short four-word formula: purpose, functionality, aesthetics and navigation.

Welcome to the world of computers. Web surfers can travel the world in seconds, so they are not the most patient people on the planet. Once you've got their attention, you have to keep them looking.

How many times have you visited a website only to stare at a blank screen for what seems like a lifetime? You go off to make a sandwich and a pot of tea, then come back to see that only 21% of the data has downloaded. Many visitors would hit the quit button and be off down the cyber highway. A general rule is to keep your download times to about 12 to 16 seconds.

One difficulty with artists' sites is the amount of time it takes to download

Stoneware teapot, 8 inches in height, fired in the throat arch of the wood kiln; sliding firebox doors open to reveal a thumbnail image on the website's wood-fired pottery page.

photographic images of the work. Our solution was to use thumbnail images with the option to enlarge the thumbnail in a separate window without affecting the browser window. We also use "progressive" images; in layman's terms, coarse images that appear instantly (capturing the viewer's attention), then become progressively sharper as the image downloads.

As in pottery, it is the attention to detail that distinguishes the amateur website from the professional, the ordinary from the excellent, the memorable from the forgettable. The details of a pot can be in the form of decoration, attachment of handles, all the things done to make it individual.

Keeping in mind that the website should not overpower the individuality of the work, Sean used the details that we incorporate into our pots to create positive and negative silhouettes, background "wallpaper" and "push buttons." These include a close-up of a carbon-trap glaze, hacksaw decoration, the door of our wood kiln and the tip of a flame.

Eye-catching, bright, neon colors would suit many potters' works, but ours is best suited to colors that are quiet and subdued. When deciding on a color palette for the website, choose one to provide continuity with your artistic identity.

This is where the webmaster matches the work to the wallpaper or carpet sample. We've all had that happen to us at a craft show or in our studios. We may roll our eyes, but know a color match means a sale in the end.

There are thousands of different fonts or type faces. Your choices can be a statement of who you are or to whom you are targeting your work. Sean picked a font he thought would complement our style of pottery. Although our work is traditional in nature, it does have some contemporary edges. Your font choice could be more formal or informal. How about New Wave Ink Blot Baby? We'll leave this one for you to ponder over with your webmaster.

Motion pictures—what a concept. It is true that the more senses you can appeal to, the more successful your product will be. The computer age hasn't yet mastered the touchy feely or the smell thing, but there are some senses that can be stimulated. We squealed like little kids when we opened our site for the first time and saw the rusty door of our wood kiln's firebox opening and closing as it introduced images of our wood-fired pots. We were delighted to see the high-fire pots engulfed in flames as they were presented. Sean even added a virtual tour of our showroom with zoom-in capabilities.

Finally, our website was to be a marketing tool, so we needed to do something to maximize the number of visitors. Sean's advice was quite simple: offer something free and they will come. We decided on a drawing to win a wood-fired teapot. When we have a new body of work, we will have a new contest and a new prize. We value our customers, we are proud of our work, and we want everyone to see it. It's as simple as that.

A friend of ours was once asked by an aging Bernard Leach: "What makes a good pot?" After she had named form, function, decoration and so on, he stopped her and answered in one word—integrity. With Sean's permission, we would like to add that word to his list of website requirements. ▲

Wood-fired stoneware bottle featured on website, 14 inches in height, by Sheila and Tony Clennell, Beamsville, Ontario, Canada.

Red Star Studios

by Paula Sibrack Marian

Kansas City, Missouri, is nearly smack in the center of the country. And Red Star Studios is nearly at the "crossroads" (the intersection of I-70 and I-35) of Kansas City. The neighborhood, affectionately known as the "Upper West Side," is situated between downtown and Union Station.

The 80-year-old building was originally a Red Star Yeast factory. The process of renovation had already begun in the neighborhood when potter Steven Hill and fiber artist Susan Hill first toured the vacant, boarded-up factory. The facade reminded Steven of the Alamo (an icon from his birthplace and imaginary childhood games). Both thought the space would be perfect for a gallery, classes and workshops, plus shared and private studios.

Owning a ceramics center had long been the couple's dream. A sought-after workshop presenter, Steven has had the opportunity to teach at over 100 schools and ceramics facilities throughout the United States and Canada. By the mid 1990s, he had started to look for a way to give workshops locally. His hope was to expand his studio, to offer classes, to begin an artist-in-residence program for aspiring potters and to provide workspace for other ceramics artists. Establishing Red Star Studios has made this possible.

The project was a collaborative effort. Susan envisioned how the studio would look; since her background is in interior design with a strong interest in architecture, the structure of the studios was clear in her mind. Steven determined how the studio would work, although he admits that he had no experience "being the boss of anything. You need to have a vision when you're doing a big project like this, or the little obstacles along the way can make you crazy. Neither Susan nor I have any problem with vision."

Red Star Studios' grand opening was on November 20, 1998. Like its namesake, the studio has been something

The Red Star Studios building, formerly a Red Star Yeast factory, houses gallery space, a community studio and ten private studios.

of a leavening agent, in that it has inspired other artists, as well as creative restaurateurs and entrepreneurs, to relocate to the neighborhood. Many of the residents in the area are new as of the last ten years, says Steven. And both new and old have an incredibly strong sense of community; they all watch out for each other.

Steven now splits his claywork between Red Star and his home studio. "I make pots at home, where I have some solitude. I decorate, dry them out and transport them (a 20-minute drive) to Red Star to glaze and fire them."

Steven doesn't have a kiln at home anymore, as he tore down his 22-year-old downdraft kiln to use the bricks to build a soda kiln at Red Star. The studio is also equipped with a 70-cubic-foot car kiln. Fortunately, transporting the bone-dry pots to Red Star hasn't been a problem. "I don't pack them very well—that would be too much work—but I drive very carefully," Steven admitted.

Steven credits involvement with Red Star Studios with several positive changes in his work. Prior to Red Star, his work had moved ahead slower, he confessed. The studio gave him a reason to do more new things, partly to set an example for his students and also due to the artistic stimulation of the community. "The whole process of creating became more public and I was setting an example for people to experiment and do new work."

Not only did Steven's clay forms change when he moved to Red Star, but he also seriously re-evaluated his glazing, opting to discontinue the use of manganese. In a flurry of glaze experimentation, he came up with an entirely new glaze palette. Having others watch him go through that process encouraged glaze experimentation throughout the entire studio.

Prior to Red Star, potters would often ask Steven if they could work for or apprentice with him, but his home studio

Evening and weekend classes are offered in the community studio space.
The gallery showcases works by potters from across the country.

Since dismantling his kiln at home, Steven glazes and fires his work at Red Star, which allows students to learn by observing the process and experimentation of an accomplished potter.

was too small to accommodate more than one person. The larger studio space has allowed an artist-in-residence program for aspiring potters. Red Star Studios' first resident artist, Conner Burns, has moved on and is currently setting up his own ceramics studio in Natchez, Mississippi. Current artist-in-residence Donna Ropp will remain at the studio through May.

Ongoing classes at Red Star Studios are varied. Beginning throwing, intermediate/advanced throwing and handbuilding are all taught in the evenings or on Saturdays.

There are also four to six workshops per year, accommodating up to 70 people for a demonstration and 18 for a participation workshop. The Red Star formula for a well-attended workshop includes a festive opening on Friday evening, workshop Saturday and Sunday, public slide lecture Saturday evening, and a show featuring the workshop artist in the gallery.

Workshop artists have included Robert Briscoe, Pete Pinnell, Sylvie Granatelli, Malcolm Davis, Nick Joerling, Jeff Oestreich, Ellen Shankin and Matt Long. "Many of our workshop leaders are long-term friends, but some I invite just because they make great pots," Steven explained.

Twice each summer for seven days, Steven takes center stage for his "Functional Stoneware Single Fire Pottery" workshops. He has found that teaching helps clarify his own work. "I have to dig deep to identify the important issues to share." Generally the theme of a workshop is about *why* as opposed to just *how*. "A good workshop can unlock someone else's why."

Red Star also has ten private studios (occupied by the artist-in-residence, the studio manager, the gallery director and seven other potters, ranging from serious hobbyists to professionals), and 20+ people working in a shared studio. All members, students and their guests are invited to a monthly open studio on Friday evening. Entitled "Down and Dirty," the event fosters communication; it has featured critiques, panel discussions on marketing, using the extruder and demonstrations by outside artists.

The Red Star Studios gallery carries the work of about 20 potters from across the United States. Many of these potters are the Hills' friends; all represent Steven and Susan's vision of the best of functional pottery. Of course, the gallery also features Steven's pottery and Susan's fiber work.

The private studios have cases for members to display and sell their own work. Twice a year, in early December and June, there is a show and sale in which all members are invited to participate.

Two shows, "Stoneware: For Daily Ritual" and "Porcelain: Another Touch," will be on view in March when NCECA (National Council on Education for the Ceramic Arts) comes to Kansas City. (See the conference preview in next month's CM for information about hours and shuttle bus service.)

Located near the intersection of I-70 and I-35, at 821 West 17th Street in downtown Kansas City, Missouri, Red Star Studios is typically open Thursday through Saturday, 10–4, or by appointment (up-to-date information can be found on the website www.redstarstudios.org). According to Steven, "Our goal is to make Red Star a destination for potters traveling across the U.S." ▲

Attaining Merchant Status

by Mark E. Battersby

Today, nearly all commercial firms accept credit cards. Not only can customers buy whenever the impulse strikes them, credit-card sales mean almost instant money in the business' bank account. In fact, any business that does not accept credit cards cannot compete in today's marketplace. Not providing customers with the ease of using credit cards means that sales will be lost. Unfortunately, the ripple effect of new federal guidelines issued for the so-called subprime credit-card businesses that cater to customers with poor credit or low income is already trickling down to studio ceramics businesses. The impending passage of the first reform of our bankruptcy laws in over 25 years will also make that coveted "merchant" status more difficult to obtain and more expensive to maintain.

The government's new guidelines have already pushed some credit-card companies specializing in the subprime market—estimated to be as much as 37% of all credit-card loans—to move toward changing their accounting methods and to tighten their lending practices. The crackdown's impact on those who process the credit-card sales of small businesses is also causing the industry to be more selective about who will be permitted to accept credit cards and at what price.

Credit-Card Basics

It is important to understand the basics of credit-card transactions—and the charges that accompany merchant status. That understanding means more than merely deciding which cards to accept—Visa, MasterCard, Discover, American Express, etc. The charge paid to these card companies will vary, depending on your sales volume and the size of the average transaction. The average fee usually runs between 2.5% and 5.5% percent of sales, although American Express is usually a bit higher. As with everything else, shopping for the best and most affordable rates makes a great deal of sense. Never assume that the rates charged by banks and credit-card companies are the same, or that they are the same for every ceramics business.

Among the terms encountered will be the discount rate, which is the percentage that is deducted from the total transaction amount and paid to the credit-card company and the issuing bank (2.5% to 5.5%). It is comprised of the transaction charges, the interchange rate and the transmission costs.

The transaction charge is essentially the profit that the processing network makes. It is usually included in the discount rate, but it may be charged separately. The transaction charge is often the only element of the discount rate that can be negotiated. If one bank has a transaction fee higher than another bank, ask the bank why that is so. And don't forget to ask whether additional services are available for that higher fee.

The interchange rate is the cost of processing the charge through the particular credit card's network. For example, the current interchange rate for "swiped transactions" is 1.3% for MasterCard and 1.35% for Visa. Federal regulations require an additional charge of about 0.3% each for the "nonswiped" transactions. Thus, the total interchange rate for nonswiped transactions is 1.6% for MasterCard and 1.65% for Visa.

The transmission cost is the fee charged for running the sales information through the processing network. It is expressed as a cost per ticket and runs about 18¢ to 23¢ per transaction.

Applying for a Merchant Account

With credit-card fraud topping $200 million each year, banks and other lenders were skittish about commercial credit-card accounts even before the crackdown and the threat of new bankruptcy laws. Any merchant going to a lender to open a credit-card account has long been required to make a full financial disclosure, just as though asking for a loan.

For every potter whose bank has denied him or her a merchant account, there is a so-called independent service organization (ISO) just waiting to serve. The ISO contracts with the bank, in effect, bearing the risk of doing business with the potter. Naturally, the ISO will charge for its services. A word of warning: although there are over 1400 ISOs in the United States, they are not regulated. Investigate the extra charges before entering into any agreement.

Accepting Plastic

While computer terminals have helped combat fraud, the technology has also increased costs for merchants, as the scanners are more expensive than the manual imprinters of the past. On the bright side, the electronic processing of credit charges often means the money is available much sooner. An imprinter can still be obtained for about $25; however, a scanner, under a four-year lease, will usually run $75 to $100 per month. Of course, scanning equipment can be purchased, but be sure to find out what the bank will charge to connect that equipment to its system. The extra costs may make renting less expensive than buying.

Another, less expensive, option is also available: software for your own computer. Just make certain beforehand that it is compatible with the bank's system.

Staying the Course

At the time of a sale, your bank will authorize any charges and notify the credit-card company (or an agent acting on its behalf) of the charge. The credit-card company will collect the money from the bank that issued the card, send it to your bank and bill the customer. Once your bank has the money, it will deposit it (minus the discount rate) into your account.

It is an unfortunate reality that any business that has too many "chargebacks" may be in danger of losing its merchant card account. It is a good idea to know what the chargeback rate is, as well as the limit set by the credit-card company (usually about 1% of credit sales). If your business is getting close to that limit on a particular credit card, perhaps customers could be asked to pay using one of the credit cards that isn't in danger.

So-called "procedural chargebacks" occur because the business didn't follow the rules set by the bank. The frequency of these chargebacks can be reduced by developing a routine that is always followed. For example, always check the expiration date before running the card through the scanner.

Customer-initiated chargebacks occur when customers attempt to cancel the transaction for some reason, usually because the goods were damaged or because they claim the charge was excessive. A chargeback differs from a simple return of your merchandise because the credit-card company is involved. In other words, the customer has complained not to you, but to the credit-card company. If the customer complains directly, you can repay the customer without affecting your chargeback status.

With a little investigation, every studio artist should find that attaining merchant status is not only possible, but affordable. All that is required is better understanding of the entire credit-card process and a little shopping for the best deal.

Works displayed in a garden setting.

A Garden Exhibition

by Alice Heystek

Potters are fortunate in having a large and very diversified audience. This took me a long time to figure out but finally led to the idea of exhibiting my pots in the garden of my home. It's exciting to meet the people who come to my show. I love it when they say nice things about my work. (How would they dare not when they are standing on my turf?) And I am gratified to find that the people who buy pottery like to meet the individual who made it. So I have fun and they have fun.

For many years, I lived in South Africa, and became fairly well known for my work. While there, I once loaned my garden to a group of craftspeople as an exhibition space. It worked very well for them, so just before my husband and I returned to the United States, I tried a garden show too. Since retiring to central Florida, I've done several more. I thought I was pursuing this marketing strategy because my reputation as an artist hadn't traveled with me from South Africa. Whatever the reason, it has now become my preferred way of exhibiting.

What is the proof of the pudding? Well, I can count on healthy sales, as much as 90% of the total in the past. I don't have to pack and transport my pots all over the place and back, and none are collecting dust on consignment anywhere. Best of all, I have a chance to make sure the people who come to my show understand about the care and time that go into each piece.

You may want to try this too, so I offer you my personal checklist. Notice how many things can be done ahead of time. Notice also how many things, once accomplished, will never need doing twice. Anyone with an artist's imagination can stage a garden exhibition:

1. Compile a list of exhibitions in which you have participated in chronological order, both private and group. If it is a long list, stick to the most important; it will be more impressive. Also list all the magazines and books in which your work has appeared. If you can keep both lists on one page, it will encourage more people to read them.

2. Prepare a brief biography. This should be made as interesting as possible (you can juice it up a bit). Include any honors you may have received. Write in third person. You will be happy you did after you see how many times you use the first person singular in your artist's statement.

3. Write a new artist's statement every time you have an exhibition. Busy editors and art reporters are pleased to use this statement for quotes, or to find an idea for a headline. Let them know what is important to you about your work, making sure it sounds genuine and personal. Sending along the first three items on this checklist will help ensure that the people writing about you have their facts straight.

4. Put together a mailing list. Whether it is a computer database or a 3×5 card file, make sure it is easy to revise and that there is room to add comments about the customer or what he/she bought. People appreciate being remembered.

I started out with lists of people whom other people knew. Friends and neighbors can make an astonishing contribution, and their friends may become your mutual friends. Even if they don't buy your work, at least they were interested enough to come to the show. They then have a story to tell other people, and your reputation will grow. The names of people who don't come to my shows two times in a row are deleted from my mailing list to save postage. A very good source of new names is your guest register.

5. Always keep a photographic record of your work. These images will come in handy for publicity.

6. You can never have too much publicity. For your reputation to grow, you need to reach an ever-widening circle of people who are familiar with what you do. Start well in advance, researching listing opportunities in your local newspapers, craft magazines and TV channels. Look for what's free to everyone, such as a calendar of upcoming events. Ask for the names of the editors in charge of exhibition coverage and human-interest stories. A direct call to the editor is sometimes all that's necessary.

Local newspaper and television editors will sometimes send out a reporter to interview you and maybe even a photographer, but it is up to you to see that they have the correct facts, issued by you in writing. I once opened the weekend section of my newspaper and discovered a huge color photo of me and my work illustrating an article describing my forthcoming show as if it were to start that very day—a whole month too soon!

7. Acquire display furniture, and plan the layout. I use new, unpaneled doors, painted white, with a long grass mat on top. A kind neighbor made bracket-type supports in two different heights, so as to vary the display; they pack flat when not in use. To vary the heights still further, the same neighbor made a couple of pedestals, each 15×15×30 inches in height. I can rearrange the groupings from year to year.

8. Develop a logo. Over the years, my signature in stylized letters has become my logo.

9. Prepare an information card to accompany each purchase. It should contain a bit about the quality of the work and something personal about your design philosophy.

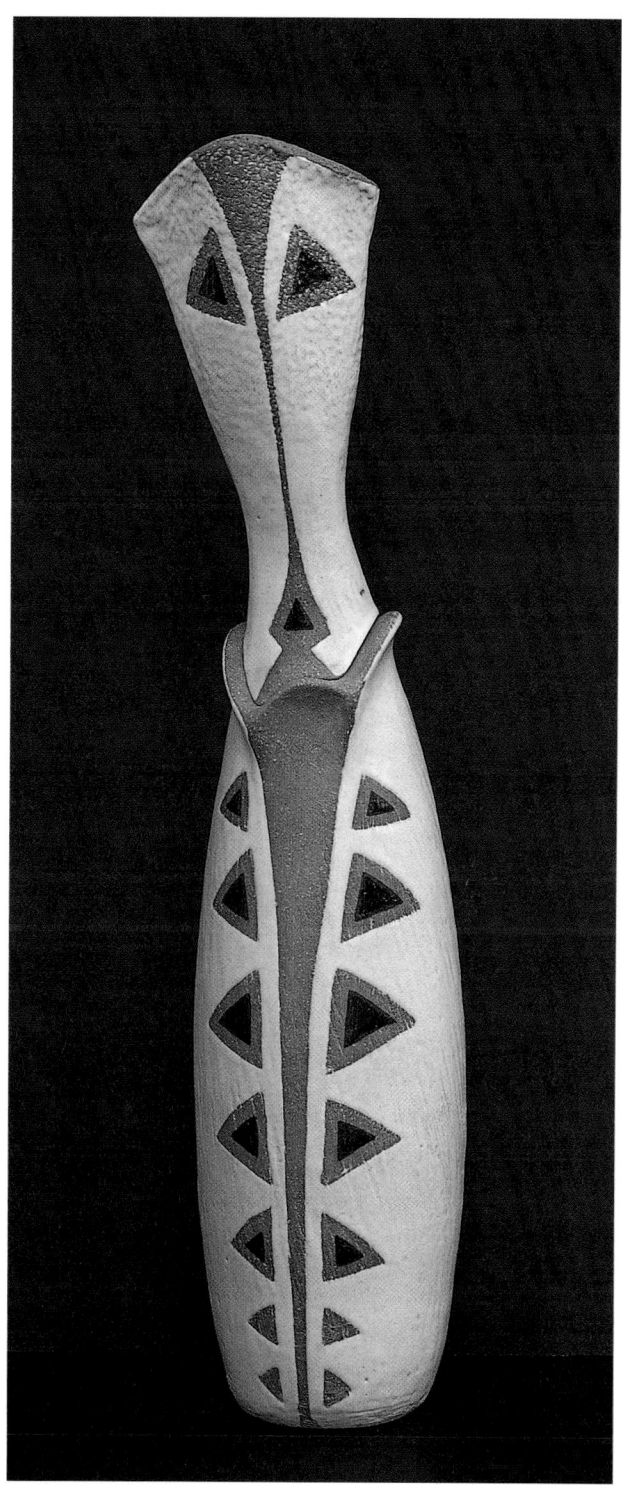

"African Totem," 23 inches (58 centimeters) in height, handbuilt.

10. Place signs at turnoffs from the main road or roads—with arrows pointing in the direction of the turn. Be sure you have enough. You will also need signs at your house—with arrows pointing customers to your garden so that they won't ring your front doorbell.

11. I don't feel the need for business cards, but a brochure is a good idea. Send it to editors, gallery owners and other people who may be interested in your work. Have plenty so that people at your show can take one home.

12. Keep any invitations you receive that seem especially well done and striking. They will help you decide on the design of your own invitation. It is worth taking the time to design a good invitation if you want people to take you seriously. I buy 8×11-inch invitation stock, which is fairly stiff but can be folded, making four pages. On the cover page is a picture of one or two pots, plus my logo. Page two has short descriptions of the pots on the cover and their sizes. All the exhibition information (who, what, where, date, time, duration and telephone number) goes on page three. Finally, my house is hard to find, so a map, including significant landmarks, is printed on page four.

13. I send a postcard (with a very photogenic pot on the front) to people who have been to my shows in the past, asking them if they know anyone who might be interested in receiving an invitation. People relocate frequently these days, and there are always cards returned. This actually helps me keep my invitation file up to date. And several people will call with new names for my list. I am happy to chat with those who take this kind of trouble for me.

14. A price list can be computer printed at the last minute. About 12 copies are enough. If they are glassine covered, people won't carry them away.

15. Purchase several folders with pockets to hold promotional materials; see numbers 1, 2, 3, 9, 11, 13, etc. A signed folder makes a nice souvenir for the patron who purchases a pot.

16. Among the extras to have on hand are red circle labels for sold works of art, small white labels for numbers corresponding to the price list, a sales record book and a guest register.

As mentioned previously, the latter is an excellent source of new names for your mailing list. Generally, I sit at this table myself, greet the people, and make sure I can read everyone's writing. I tell them this is important if they want to receive notice of my future activities; if they don't want to, I thank them anyway for taking the time to come to my show. Sometimes I ask where they heard about the show. It's good to know which publicity was the most effective.

17. Refreshments are optional and not always desirable. After all, the focus should be on the work. Besides, drink glasses, napkins and half-eaten remains create a mess, which constantly needs cleaning up and doesn't improve the looks of your garden.

18. My enthusiasm is equal to one weekend. I really think this is enough. It's like popping popcorn. When you hear the noise die down, the corn is popped. I open the exhibition on a Friday afternoon, from 2:00 until 4:30; on Saturday and Sunday, the exhibition is open from 11:00 to 4:30. This is an exhibition, not just a sale, so the pots should be left in place until the end of the show. Purchases can be collected on Sunday after 3:00. I don't mind delivering if returning is too inconvenient for the buyer, but most people like to see how many are sold, and don't mind coming back.

Sometimes people come early before the show is really open to be sure they have first choice. In the interest of fairness, it's best to ask them to line up and wait a bit.

By now, it must have occurred to everyone that rain could be a problem. An alternative exhibition date can be stated on the invitation and in the newspaper in case of inclement weather. You may also want to consider renting a marquee when the forecast is gloomy. Finally, since almost every marketing technique mentioned here may be utilized to exhibit your work in a rented space, you might prefer not to take a chance on the great outdoors.

Mounting a garden exhibition takes a lot of work, but I have learned to think of it as though I am giving a big party. Introduce people to one another. If you help them enjoy the show, they will stay awhile and really look at your work. They will remember it, tell their friends about it and look forward to the next show. Believe me, the person having the most fun will be you. ▲

"Tall Gourd with Striped Black Clay Decoration," approximately 16 inches (41 centimeters) in height, by Alice Heystek, Leesburg, Florida.

Checklist

1. List of exhibitions and publications
2. Biography
3. Artist's statement
4. Mailing list
5. Photography
6. Publicity
7. Display furniture and layout
8. Logo
9. Information card
10. Signs
11. Brochure
12. Invitations
13. Postcards
14. Price list
15. Folders with pockets
16. Extras to buy
17. Refreshments
18. Duration

Questions to Ask a Gallery

by Karen Shelly-Genther

What is the biggest nightmare an artist has when shipping work to a gallery show? Breakage? No, it should be insured. If it breaks, it's paid for. How about the work not getting there or, worse yet, going to the wrong address?

Let's say two partners split up; one continues to run the gallery. For the first month, everything is amicable between the two old partners-then unpaid bills become a problem. Words are exchanged and the former partners stop communicating. Meanwhile, some unsuspecting artist ships work out according to instructions in an acceptance letter. Unfortunately, the work arrives at the wrong partner's address and delivery is refused. But the show is scheduled to open in two days and the artist lives across the country. Stranger things have happened.

How do you know what kind of gallery you are dealing with, where it really is located (in relation to or within a major city), who comes to the opening, what kind of client base it has, what sort of advertising will be done for the show you are participating in, and what the working climate is like? These are all valid and important questions-ones you shouldn't hesitate to ask.

While you are at it, ask about the gallery director or owners. Are they artists themselves? What's their background? Ask for references from other artists who have shown there. What is the sales rate? That should say a lot about who is coming to the shows.

This doesn't mean your work isn't going to end up in Podunkville, but Podunkville may prove to be just right for you. You never know who will see your work and tell someone else, and so on. But is exposure the only thing you are looking for out of this venture?

Also ask questions about the jury. Is it a group of three or more? Or is it one person's opinion? Do they accept repeat artists? Or can you do only one show per year there? What are the criteria that determine which pieces are accepted? Are they looking for originality, quality, or simply lining their pockets with your jury fee and accepting everything that is entered? What is the turn-down rate?

Unfortunately, there is no gallery checking guide in existence. Anyone can advertise a show, take jury fees and shipping fees, then set up in a basement.

Think about the costs involved. First send a self-addressed, stamped envelope (SASE) for the prospectus, then send in your slides along with a check to cover the $10-25 jury fee. When (if) you hear your work is accepted, the delivery date might be only two days away, but it normally takes five days to ship from your studio to there, which means extra money for overnight delivery.

The work makes it to the show on time but there is no guarantee that the right person will come in a purchase it. It could be packed back up and returned to you C.O.D. when the show closes. The total expenditure can include shipping both ways, the jury fee and a few stamps. Don't forget to add in a few long-distance phone calls as well.

Remember, the gallery is working for you. You are not working for it. You should expect to be treated fairly and with respect. If you are careful about who you deal with, you will probably fare well. But if you are too anxious to have your work in a show, any show, then you are subjecting yourself to the worst that can happen.

Ask questions. If the gallery personnel balk at answering anything, that should immediately turn on a warning light. After all, your sales are paying the bills. Try to enter shows you may actually be able to attend. If you do plan to attend, notify the gallery ahead of time so that the local press can be alerted. Attending the opening could result in local newspaper, radio and/or television publicity. Meanwhile, you have the opportunity to scope out the gallery, see your work displayed outside your studio, find out how the gallery advertises and handles an opening (food, entertainment, etc.), and evaluate the crowd of potential buyers.

There are certainly legitimate galleries out there where work sells practically before it is unpacked. Your job is to find them with the least amount of personal pain possible. ▲

Pack With Care
by Debra Berke

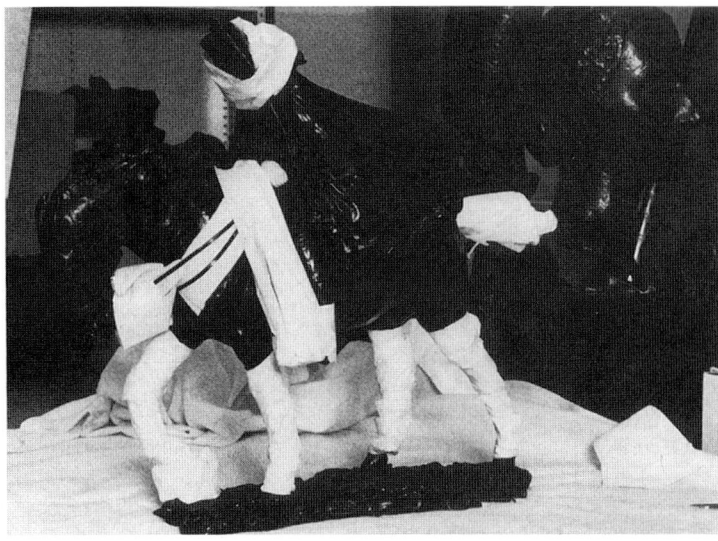

Appendages should be wrapped, then rounded off with tissue paper so that the resulting tissue ball encases protrusions as part of a smooth whole.

Gallery and museum personnel tell horror stories about poorly packed ceramics. For example: "We couldn't believe it, a raku wall piece was sent to us laying on crumpled newspaper without any padding between the top of the box and the piece. Of course, the box was tipped during shipment. And, it arrived broken!"

When museums transport irreplaceable ceramics like Inca stirrup jugs, George Washington's china, or a Robert Arneson sculpture, breakage is intolerable, so specialized packing techniques and materials have been developed. Potters and clay sculptors, too, can prevent the embarrassment and expense of customers receiving broken objects or the chance of being taken out of an exhibition because the artwork arrived in pieces.

Shock, vibration, rapid temperature change, and contact with water or humidity are the primary causes of breakage. The goal of good packing is to protect against the worst hazards to which an object may be subjected during transport. The container and not the object should absorb shock and vibration.

Before packing, photograph your artwork to document its preshipment condition so you'll have records should the object be lost, stolen or damaged during transit. Never tape labels directly onto the object, as this may damage its surface and/or leave adhesive residue. A label identifying the object and its component parts with your name and address should be affixed to the package exterior.

To obtain reasonably priced shipping containers and cushioning supplies, contact a local museum for a list of packaging suppliers, or look in the telephone directory under Boxes, Packaging Containers and Packaging Materials. Art packing supplies are often the same as materials used in transporting high-tech electronics, so most areas should have a distributor. Other ceramists have been creative in finding inexpensive sources for packing materials: a Vermont potter obtains surplus insulation from a nearby factory.

The shipping container must be strong, puncture proof and able to withstand rough handling. Double-strength cardboard boxes are adequate for most ceramic objects. Select boxes 3-4 inches larger than the object to be shipped to allow room for cushioning materials. Transport large or heavy items in a crate. Reusable molded polyethylene crates can often be purchased. Instructions for building wooden crates are given in *Safeguarding Your Collection in Travel* by Caroline Keck, published by the American Association of State and Local History, Nashville; and *Way to Go: Crating Artwork for Travel* by Stephen Horne, published by the Gallery Association of New York State, Hamilton. Obtain these reference materials through your local library or its inter-library loan program.

An initial wrap with tissue or muslin protects against the more abrasive materials used in cushioning. Either of these wraps also serve as a moisture buffer. When using tape, make sure it cannot come in contact with the object.

All projecting parts of any object should be rounded off with tissue so that the end result is a ball of tissue with the protruding pieces an integral part of the whole. For example: When packing a teapot, stuff loosely crumpled tissue inside the vessel, around the handle, and around the entire form. Then cover the teapot with another sheet of tissue to keep the crumpled tissue in place.

Put the part of the object that can handle the most shock at the bottom. Component parts of an object, like teapot and lid, should be packed separately. Make supports and mounts for heavy portions of the object and to secure the object in position.

Cushioning materials float the object inside the container and absorb shock and vibration. A general rule is to provide 3-4 inches between the objects in the same container and the container walls. Polyurethane and polyethylene foams care the best cushioning materials, but less expensive sponges and papers can provide sufficient cushioning if used correctly. Pack very carefully when using the expanded and exploded plastics (peanuts) because they can settle and leave the object exposed.

One cushioning technique is to wrap the rounded-off object in layers of bubble sheeting, then pad the extra space inside the container. Another technique for fragile objects is to pack them in successive layers of foam. To do this, measure the shape, mark the contour on the foam with pencil, and cut the foam with a bread or electric knife. This technique is excellent for objects that must be repacked in the same box for return.

Double boxing (packing an object in two sequential boxes) is an excellent cushioning procedure, and the one most commonly used by potters. The immobilized object is cushioned inside one box, then the first box is nested inside a second box that is at least 2 inches larger on all sides. The space between the two boxes is completely filled with newspaper or foam.

If the packing configuration is complicated and if unpacking in an incorrect order can cause damage, then include written unpacking instructions or a sequence of Polaroid shots. Also include an itemized packing list to protect against small items being accidentally tossed out with the packing materials.

Neatly wrap and label the container. Shoddy looking boxes invite rough treatment, whereas a neatly wrapped box may command more care by handlers. Put arrows on the sides to signify which end is up, and letter neatly on the top face "open this side." Do label the package "Fragile", but it is best not to write "works of art" because this may invite theft.

Contact local museum staff for referrals for qualified shipping companies. They are knowledgeable and usually willing to help. Transportation may be via the U.S. Postal Service, United Parcel Service (U.P.S.) or other commercial deliverers. Cost depends on size, weight, distance and deadline for arrival. U.S. mail and U.P.S. can ship up to 70 pounds and 108 inches in length and girth combined. When using the U.S. mail, send by return receipt. U.P.S. is particularly useful for fragile objects and has next-day delivery available. Air freight is the fastest method, but it is expensive and packages are subjected to much handling. Van and truck lines have fragile product shipping services in specially equipped vans with air-ride shock absorption and climate control.

An artwork is truly completed when it reaches the intended destination, be it in a home or an exhibit case. Therefore, potters and clay artists should be as creative and analytical when packing and shipping their ware as they are in producing it. ▲

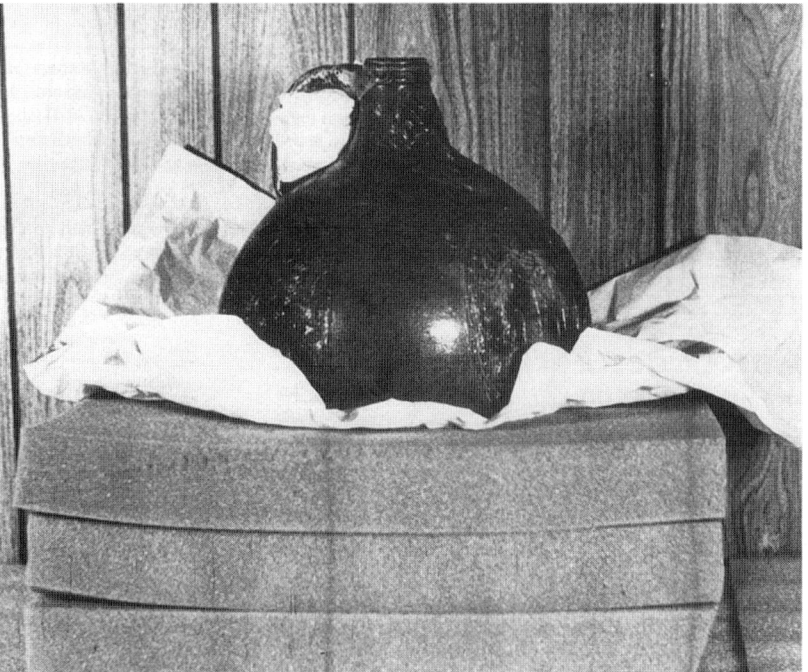
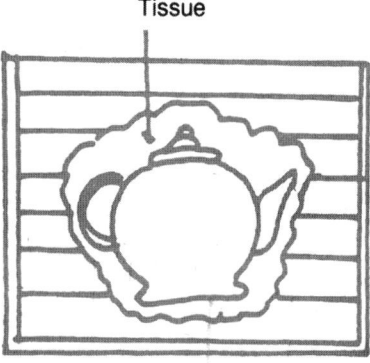

Even a very fragile object can be successfully packed and shipped. Such work should be delivered and returned in the same crate or box (3 to 4 inches larger than the ceramic object). Pack the work with tissue paper until smoothed over and thereafter in foam layers, each custom cut to conform to the shape of the tissue wad. A rare 16th-century Bellarmine jug and an illustration of a teapot show the progressive assembly of a protective package.

Writing an Artist Statement

by Ariane Goodwin, Ed. D.

Working on an artist statement can be deeply trying, so much so that even the most responsible, professional artist never even begins the process. The statement lingers, in an unformed lump, on an invisible shelf of "marketing shoulds."

There are several reasons for this, the most daunting of which is the writing itself. Sure, you know an artist's statement is a good marketing tool. You know that people who love your work want to know more about you. You know that offering your audience more ways to connect with you increases their delight in what you do, and the perceived value of your work. But, you protest, there are all those *words*.

Right you are. An artist statement is all about words, which are a completely different language than wedging and shaping, glazing and firing. Clay is in the world of our senses; while words are the landmarks of our mind, once removed from sight and touch.

Sometimes, when the world of words captures our world of senses, we feel a delight in the connection. After all, we have lived longer with words than we have with clay in our hands. Think about it: what is more organic to humans than language? Our first intentional sounds proclaim us as individuals even before our first baby steps. So why is it that as adults, who have found a place in the world with what pleases us most (clay), one of the fundamental connections to that deep pleasure (our words) eludes us as soon as the idea of writing an artist statement pops up?

I imagine that a combination of art critics and formal education has something to do with this. One promotes language, in service to noble judgments (the emotional emphasis here is on "judgments"), and the other unwittingly teaches us to mistrust words. In school, someone else told us *when, where,* and *how* we could, or could not, use *which* words to communicate in writing. This mistrust smolders, mostly unnoticed, until our words are thrust into a context where they can be judged (criticized) by others, as in an artist statement.

Often, when we sit down to write a statement, every thought we ever had about our work vanishes. We are convinced that we have nothing to say about our own work, or certainly nothing of value. Sometimes, we toss our unformed thoughts into a mental scrap bucket, turn out the light, and head out of the studio. Or we fake it, ending up with insubstantial or overblown words masquerading as us.

There is an alternative response. Begin with the thought that you have a lot to say that is neither self-important nor trivial, but relevant, revealing and wonderful. Because, the good news is: *you can use your own words*. There is an unselfconscious language that you use all the time when thinking or talking about your work. The trick is to learn how to catch yourself doing it, then faithfully write it down.

Why bother? An artist statement builds a compelling bridge between you and your audience. For the buying public, the artist statement provides a better understanding of the work and more reasons to take your pots home. For you, the statement gives you one more way to validate what you do.

Working with clay and writing an artist statement are kindred activities. In both cases, you need raw materials, a commitment to set aside sufficient time, patience with yourself and a willingness to practice. You did not learn to throw or handbuild in one sitting; nor will you learn to write an artist statement in one sitting. But when that first statement sits gleaming in your hand, the satisfaction will be the same.

Getting Started

To begin, gather the necessary raw materials: 1. A spiral notebook (if you like lined paper), or a folder (if you like unlined typing paper), or a beautifully bound leather journal encrusted with jewels; they all work equally well. 2. A favorite writing implement (pen, pencil, magic marker or keyboard), one that lets your hand, and thus words, flow across the page. 3. A timer (for two- and three-minute writing exercises). 4. Uninterrupted time (two hours is good).

Warming Up

Timed writing exercises are wonderful for warming up. Writing fast eliminates cautious thought (a creativity killer), reduces internal censorship and trims away excess, pushing us to center on what is essential. Treat it like a game, where you are trying to beat the clock. The great thing about writing is that, like claywork, you can scrap (crumple up the paper or hit the delete key) awkward first efforts and start again. Nothing is lost, and your writing "muscle" grows stronger with each mistake.

• Set your timer for three minutes.
• Then, without thinking about spelling, grammar, punctuation or your Aunt Martha, tell a friend about your work. Work as quickly as is comfortable.
• When the timer goes off, stop. You probably will not be able to resist reading what you wrote, but absolutely do not erase, edit, or do anything else to change it.
• Put it in the back of your writing folder; or if you are using a journal, turn the page and fasten it with a paper clip; or if using a word processor, save the file. What is important here is that you wrote, not what you wrote.

Silencing the Inner Critic

Before you begin writing in earnest, there is one critical detail to attend to. Just as you want clay to be free of imperfections, you want the process of writing your artist statement to be free of your inner critic, who is as potentially damaging to your work as any trapped air.

• Close your eyes and imagine your internal critic. Who appears on the scene when you have to write? For me, it is my eighth-grade English teacher, with her rigid back and her rigid relationship to language. Sentence diagrams lorded over her narrow kingdom. Words that flowed

like liquid silk over my tongue, expired daily on her blackboard.
- Still with eyes closed, bring this internal critic of yours into full view. Firmly, authoritatively, but respectfully, give your internal critic its marching orders. Carefully explain—ignore sputtering and interruptions—that you are going to work on writing and that, as much as you will need your critic's help later on for revisions, right now the critic must find something else to do.
- Escort your critic outside the room; leave her/him in the hall with crayons or clay, or climbing a tree, whatever (but be specific). Come back into the room and open your eyes.

Enjoy the peace and calm, but be watchful. Your job is to remain alert and catch your critic sneaking back to whisper that you are not good enough, or smart enough, or honorable enough to do this good work. Periodically, you may have to escort your critic back outside. This is a new relationship, and no self-respecting critic easily gives up ruling the throne of judgments.

This exercise is good for any time you set about writing anything. It only takes a minute or two to establish these internal boundaries and effectively rein in the judgmental part of yourself. It is also fun to see how this benefits other areas of our lives.

Reservations/Motivations

The next two exercises continue clearing away the obstacles to hearing our own language:
- Set the timer for two minutes.
- Write down every reason why you cannot, should not or will not write a statement. Mince no words; forget about complete sentences. Just fume and fuss! Here's where you get to meet the Doubt Dragons face to face; when exposed on paper, their potency dissipates.
- After two minutes, stop.

Now that you have all your reservations listed, move on to motivations:
- Set the timer for two minutes.
- Quickly, write down every reason you can, should and will write an artist's statement. Be as fanciful and playful as you wish. Here, you have the opportunity to engage large visions, and affirm why you are doing this, sending a powerful message of intent to your best ally, your sub/super-consciousness.

- After two minutes, stop.

Again, put these exercises away. You have done what you needed to do. In the beginning, process is everything and the product (the artist statement) is still just a glimmer in your mind's eye.

The Product

Your ability to write an artist statement will improve with practice. Just as your work grows and changes, so will your artist statement.

An artist statement is not a résumé, a historical summary of your work, a critique or a list of accomplishments. An artist's statement *is* a celebration of your work, a reflection on your work, a personal revelation about your work, a psychological bridge between you and your audience, and an effective marketing tool.

To write an artist statement, you will need to tap into the natural language of your mind, for you and only you can tell *what* and *how* and *why* you do the work you do.

One way to capture these words about your work is to overcome any self-consciousness that pops up when you try to write about yourself. Timed writing exercises are perfect for this. At the same time, they should give you an abundance of fresh words from which to choose for your statement.

The following exercises are designed to engage the imagination, putting the focus on playfulness and your creative spirit. Do them one at a time, over a few days, or all at once. By casting a large net, you could come up with a record catch, but be grateful for any keepers.

Statement Writing Exercise 1

- With eyes closed, imagine you are in your studio and suddenly one of your pieces starts to talk to you.
- Set the timer for three minutes.
- Write down everything the piece says, no matter how absurd; just keep your hand moving across the page. Allow yourself to be awkward. It's the beginner's way. Tell yourself that you are free to write absolute junk!

Statement Writing Exercise 2

- Close your eyes and imagine that someone from your childhood, whom you have not seen for a long time, comes into your studio while you are working.
- Set the timer for three minutes.

- What do you want to tell this person about your work? Write like one possessed. So much to tell; so little time.

Statement Writing Exercise 3

- With eyes closed, imagine a piece of your work has come to life in the studio. What does it do?
- Set the timer for two minutes.
- Write for the child in you, the one who loves adventures and magic.

Catching the Abundance

An artist statement is a lifelong process, evolving alongside your work. It will grow and change, becoming a significant contribution to the totality of your artistic story. The important thing is to keep casting your net. Let your wild child create your own zany, timed, writing exercises on a weekly basis.

Tote around a small, spiral notebook in which you can jot down any phrase that comes to you in a conversation, a dream or daydream, in the car, in the studio, in the shower, anywhere inspiration strikes.

Include personal comments in your technical notebook. What were you thinking as you applied that last glaze, or centered that large platter, or unloaded the kiln at dawn?

Enlist a friend to talk with you about what you do and why; take notes or record the conversation. Often we say the perfect thing to someone else. Be ready to catch your words before they vanish downstream.

Pluck out quotes, of your own, that appear in any articles written about your work. The following quotes came from *Ceramics Monthly* (May 1998). If I was either of these artists, I would send out every one of my pieces accompanied by these compelling words. See if you agree:

I know that truly good pots owe more to the generosity and spirit with which they are made. Imparting this spirit in pots is infinitely more difficult than simply making well-crafted pots. It requires focus tempered with an affection for what I am making.—Cary Hulin

Clay takes you back to the source.—Dennis Smith

Nothing should block us from writing about our work, being clear about what makes it unique. With a little exercise and occasional note taking, an artist statement should easily take shape. ▲

Is It Covered?

by Mark E. Battersby

Unfortunately, far too many potters and ceramics artists do not understand the importance of securing adequate insurance for their business. Or, if they do understand its value, many believe they cannot afford full insurance coverage. However, when armed with the knowledge of just what the business actually requires, every professional artist and craftsperson should find

It pays to learn what types of coverage the business needs, how to shop for the best value, what the policies cover and, most importantly, what they don't.

that there is a lot of available insurance coverage between the extremes of insuring for every contingency and having no insurance at all.

It pays to learn what types of coverage the business needs, how to shop for the best value, what the policies cover and, most importantly, what they don't. It also pays to evaluate just what risks the business actually faces and to make an attempt to find ways of reducing that risk of loss. This strategy alone can substantially lower any operation's insurance premiums. This is called risk management.

Just what types of insurance coverage are available? A number of potters and ceramics artists have discovered standardized business-insurance packages that include many types of coverages tailored for the average small business. According to the experts, a basic business-insurance package should consist of four fundamental coverages—general liability, workers' compensation, auto and property/casualty—plus an added layer of protection over those, often called an umbrella policy.

Workers' Compensation

Although nothing about insurance is really easy, of the four types of coverage, workers' compensation comes closest to being a "no brainer." Why? Quite simply, workers' compensation is required by law in all 50 states. In fact, the rates, in many instances, are set by the states.

Of course, those preset rates don't necessarily mean that a potter or ceramics artist must—or should—automatically accept that rate. First, the ceramics professional must ensure that the business is properly categorized so that it is charged the appropriate rates. After all, no artist wants to have his or her business categorized as an explosives manufacturer when the closest they come to blowups is an occasional irate customer.

General Liability

The general liability insurance that is typically packaged in a business policy, along with property and casualty insurance, covers the legal expenses if someone sues for injuries sustained on the operation's property or from its works—products the business manufactures, distributes, sells or promotes.

Remember the case of the woman who sued because she spilled hot coffee from a container held in her lap while in a car? When it comes to product liability, the focus has shifted away from the respective obligations of maker and user, to the operation of the product itself. Now, the operating premise is that a person who has been injured by a "defective" product is entitled to be compensated for his or her injuries. It is no longer a prerequisite to recovery that the product manufacturer acted negligently. Also, liability is not restricted to the product's manufacturer; anyone in the chain of distribution, including the retailer, is vulnerable.

What is a defective product? Generally, there are three ways that any product will be considered "defective." First, it can be defectively manufactured. This means that the usual design specifications were not met and that the product is not what it is supposed to be.

The second type of "defect" is in the design of the product itself. In other words, the product does meet its intended design standards, but the design itself is unsafe.

Finally, the third type of "defect" is a marketing one. Every potter and ceramics artist has an obligation, or duty, to warn the user of any potential hazards or dangers from its use. The focus here is upon how the product behaves when used as intended or in a reasonably foreseeable way. In other words, the courts feel that almost any injury should be avoidable with proper notice.

The old rule was to buy general liability insurance equal to the business' net worth. Unfortunately, that doesn't work when people sue for the amount of the insurance policy, as well as the artist's net worth.

When it comes to any liability insurance, the real trick is determining how much coverage is really needed. The old rule was to buy general liability insurance equal to the business' net worth. Unfortunately, that doesn't

STUDIO PRACTICES, TECHNIQUES AND TIPS

work when people sue for the amount of the insurance policy, as well as the artist's net worth.

Today, the soundest approach often is to figure out what amount the ceramics operation could be sued for. Fortunately, the big numbers feared by most studio potters and ceramics artists may, in reality, not be that big. Despite many well-publicized court cases, it is rare to see an award in excess of $1 million.

Property/Casualty Insurance

Property/casualty insurance covers damage to an artist's property from fire, storm, theft and other perils. Most policies these days are written on an "all risk" basis so that the policy will usually cover any damage that isn't specifically excluded.

It's important to be aware of policy limits. Despite that all-risk designation, for instance, damage from an earthquake or flood is often excluded in most standard policies. Fortunately, potters and ceramics artists who do not live/work in California or along the Mississippi River can buy that extra coverage for nominal amounts—if they are aware that such risks are not covered.

How much the policy actually pays, of course, depends on whether the artist has paid for "replacement cost" coverage, which reimburses for the value of the damaged property at today's prices if it is decided to replace it. If the policy owner has opted for "actual value," on the other hand, the business will receive only as much as that 25-year-old kiln would cost to replace minus the cost of depreciation, which may be quite a bit less.

Auto Insurance

As with workers' compensation, auto insurance is fairly straightforward. It does, however, offer more of an opportunity for a potter or ceramics artist to save money.

Auto insurance for a business works the same as it does for individuals; that is, there is comprehensive coverage for damages to the vehicle, collision coverage for damage to someone else's vehicle and liability coverage for injuries. It should be noted that when an employee or subcontractor uses a vehicle on the artist's behalf, the business can be held liable. This is true even though the operation may not actually own the vehicle.

Umbrella Policy

In addition to these four basic groups, many insurance specialists recommend an umbrella policy, which protects the operation for payments in excess of all other existing coverage or for liabilities not covered by other policies. Because the studio potter or ceramics artist won't need this umbrella for everyday claims, several million dollars of extra coverage should be relatively inexpensive.

Does a homeowner's insurance policy cover a home-based business? Surprisingly, the answer is yes, although in a very limited way. Loss of business property in the home is usually reimbursed up to $2500, and up to $250 for business property damaged or lost away from those premises. Even if the business is a sideline, these limits may be too low to cover all the equipment and materials that have been accumulated.

It is also important to know that no business liability coverage is included in a standard homeowner's policy. Fortunately, it is possible to add coverage to the homeowner's policy or to a separate commercial policy.

Shopping for Insurance

It should go without saying that an excellent first step for reducing insurance costs is to shop around. In today's marketplace, insurance brokers are very eager to bid—and many independent brokers will shop their own bids among several of the companies that they represent.

Actually verifying the level of claims service that each agency provides is another good rule when looking for someone to handle all of the business insurance needs. After all, when a claim arises, no one wants an agent telling him or her to call an 800 number. An agency that is willing to become involved in the claims process and work with the claims adjuster can have a positive impact on the settlement of any insurance claim.

Another extremely important area is loss-control services (which include everything from fire-safety programs to reducing employees' exposure to injuries). After all, the best way to reduce insurance premiums over the long haul is to minimize claims. The best way to do that is through loss-control services.

Obtaining the proper levels of insurance coverage at competitive prices, increasing the amounts that will be self-insured (using higher deductibles) and, above all, understanding what insurance is needed and included under the various types of coverages offered to the average ceramics business, will produce lower, perhaps even affordable insurance. The alternative of no insurance can, of course, prove to be quite a bit more expensive. ▲

It is also important to know that no business liability coverage is included in a standard homeowner's policy. Fortunately, it is possible to add coverage to the homeowner's policy or to a separate commercial policy.

Profiting Under the Right Label

by Mark E. Battersby

Is there a right way to conduct a studio business in the United States, one that might save you from endless paperwork and high tax bills? The easy answer is as a sole owner (sole proprietor), because it requires the least amount of paperwork. Unfortunately, with a sole proprietorship, you must go it alone, unable to bring anyone into the business.

Similarly, operating a business partnership, as with a sole proprietorship, leaves you and your partners liable (obligated according to law for any debts incurred). Liability, in its many forms, is a strong argument for doing business as a corporation.

With a corporation, however, there is a great deal of paperwork and, in some cases, double taxation of profits paid by the incorporated business in the form of dividends. An S corporation eliminates the problem of double taxation by treating the corporation much in the same manner as a partnership, passing along profits and loss to the shareholders.

How does one decide the best method of operation? Let's take a closer look at the options available:

Sole Proprietorship

A sole proprietorship is nothing more than a business operated by a single individual. Often, the only formality involves notifying the state government that you, the potter or ceramics artist, will be using a fictitious name for the ceramics business.

A sole proprietor (owner) has unlimited liability. Schedule C of Internal Revenue Form 1040 is used to report income and expenses of a sole proprietorship. Should the sole proprietor die, the business ceases to exist.

Partnerships

A partnership is an organization of two or more persons who pool some or all of their money, abilities and skill in a business and divide profit or loss in predetermined proportions. Partnership shares can be based on capital contributions, time devoted to the business or some other mutually agreeable formula.

Partners are individually responsible for debts of the partnership—which is why S corporations are often favored. An S corporation, as you will see, is a corporation that is treated, at least for tax purposes, as a partnership.

In other words, a partnership does not pay federal income taxes, rather income or loss "flows through" to the partners, who are taxed on their individual shares of partnership taxable income. Of course, the partnership is a tax-reporting entity that must file an annual partnership return.

Corporations

The courts have historically upheld the principle that a corporation is separate from its shareholders, officers and directors. Shareholders risk their capital investment, but their personal assets are generally considered beyond the reach of business-related creditors and lawsuits, provided the incorporated operation is sufficiently capitalized and treated as a separate entity.

Corporate ownership offers a number of advantages, including limited financial risk for the owners, increased availability of capital and easy transferability of ownership. Dissolution of the business is among the strongest arguments for incorporating.

The owner's ability to more readily value and sell his or her share in the incorporated business at any time is invaluable. It is one means of assuring that a business will go on, even if one or more of the principals leave.

Incorporating your ceramics business usually will protect your individual assets from lawsuits should you run into financial problems; however, even when the business is incorporated, pockets of personal liability are still present. Whether as an employee, officer or director of an incorporated operation, when you sign a loan individually or guarantee anything personally, you are putting your personal assets at risk.

Taxes can be both an advantage and a disadvantage for an incorporated business. Depending on a number of factors, the use of a corporation can increase or decrease the actual income tax paid; however, corporations are able to offer a much greater variety of fringe benefit programs to employees and officers than any other type of business entity.

The Downside of Corporations

Some disadvantages of an incorporated pottery or ceramics arts operation are also inherent in corporate ownership. Corporations are the most difficult and costly business ownership form to establish, they are usually at a tax disadvantage, and they often face a multitude of legal restrictions.

Each state has different incorporation laws, some of which are quite technical and complex. Establishing a corporation usually requires the services of an attorney—despite the many advertisements for do-it-yourself any-state incorporation guides.

States also charge incorporation fees that add to the cost of setting up this type of business. This fee varies from state to state. Delaware, for example, has traditionally attracted corporations because it has relatively low costs and easy requirements for incorporating.

As separate legal entities, corporations are subject to federal and state income taxes. Corporate earnings and any dividends (payments to shareholders from earnings) are taxed on an individual basis. From the viewpoint of stockholders who receive dividends, this is effectively double-taxation of corporate earnings—once at the corporate level, then again at the shareholder level when those already-taxed earnings are distributed as dividends.

S Corporations

Many states provide tax relief to corporations meeting certain size and stock ownership requirements by recognizing them as Subchapter S corporations. This allows them to choose to be taxed as partnerships while maintaining the advantages of incorporation.

The S corporation shareholders are treated similarly to partners in a partnership. The income, losses and deductions generated by an S corporation are "passed through" the corporate entity to the individual shareholders. Thus, there is no "double" taxation. In addition, shareholders of S corporations can personally deduct any corporate losses.

Limited Liability Companies

The Limited Liability Company (LLC) is a relatively new form of business organization that is used in some states (and accepted by some professional licensing organizations). Although the business entity is usually treated as a partnership for federal income tax purposes, the LLC entity provides that all-important limited liability protection for the owners at the state level.

Similar to an S corporation, a properly structured LLC is taxed as a partnership for federal income tax purposes. That is, the entity itself pays no income taxes, instead passing along all income or losses to the individual members or owners. They, in turn, report—and are taxed on—those amounts on their individual, partnership or business income tax returns. At the same time, LLC members (shareholders or partners), like corporate shareholders, cannot be held personally liable for the debt or liabilities of the business.

Under federal tax rules, an LLC is taxable as a partnership only if it lacks two or more of the following corporate characteristics: (1) limited liability, (2) continuity of life, (3) free transferability of interests, and (4) centralized management. The majority of LLCs that qualify for classification as partnerships usually lack the corporate characteristics of continuity of life and free transferability of interests. In other words, an LLC rarely survives the withdrawal or death of one of its principals (continuity of life), and as it would lose its LLC status when it issues stock, there would be little or no transferability of interests.

Why should any potter or ceramics artist consider the unproven or untested LLC as an entity for his or her professional activities? Common among many is a desire for limited liability and the flexibility offered by this hybrid partnership. The LLC allows both the limited liability normally associated with the corporate form of organization and the flow-through, single level of taxation ordinarily associated with the partnership form of business organization. Even better, the LLC also imposes few of the constraints normally associated with S corporation elections.

The Decision

Determining which entity is right for your business is a major consideration, before and during operation. Sole proprietorship or partnership may simply be a question of how many people are involved as owners. Whether or not to incorporate can often hinge on whether adequate insurance is available.

If insurance coverage is available, you may decide not to incorporate. In those situations where insurance protection is not available or affordable, incorporation and the limited liability it provides might be advisable.

Obviously, the decision depends on many factors, not simply taxes. Liability, the number of people involved, the availability of insurance and, of course, the most beneficial types of financing that will help the business grow—all play a role in determining how to profitably operate your business. ▲

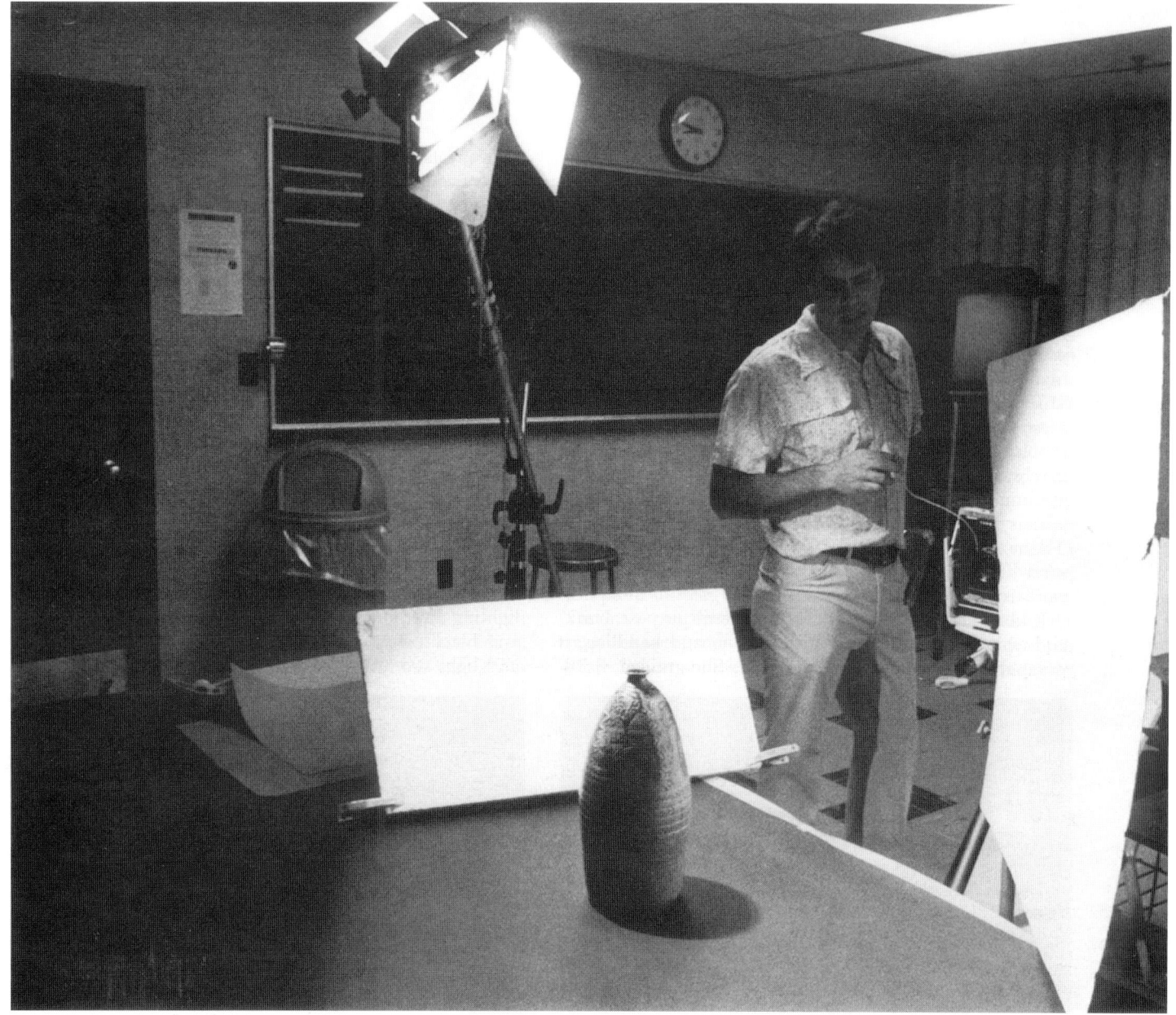

Glenn Rand photographing one of his works using light reflected from one source. The results are shown on page 53.

Photographing Ceramics
Black-and-White Images
By Glenn Rand and William Blanchard

Ceramists need photographs of their works for a number of reasons from entering juried shows to keeping personal records. In many situations the quality of the photography may favorably influence introductions of your ware to shops and galleries, and the better the photographs, the greater the likelihood of their use in any publication. Most print media request 8x10 inch, black-and-white photographs. The Author's Guide for *Ceramics Monthly* goes even further: "Good quality photographs are very important in determining manuscript acceptance. Those submitted for article consideration should be glossy, black-and-white, in focus, and with a full range of contrast."

In some instances it may be best to hire a professional photographer, since you may not have the proper equipment, time or experience to meet your requirements. Should this be the case, select a photographer carefully- check with other artists who have hired similar services, compare prices and ask to see examples of previous work. But if you wish to take your own photographs, the following suggestions for basic equipment and procedures will help assure that your photos achieve consistent quality.

When it comes to cameras, the market is full of choices. For personal records, you might use point-and-shoot type cameras; but the prints will not be suitable for publication.

A 35mm single lens reflex (SLR) camera is only acceptable for producing 8×10-inch prints, but is best for slides. If you will be making primarily prints and transparencies, you might look into a 2¼-inch format camera, available in twin-lens reflex, range finder and SLR models. The SLR systems are more expensive, but they eliminate grossly inaccurate framing in the viewfinder (parallax problems) caused by shooting at close range. Large format cameras (producing 4×5-inch or larger negatives) are unnecessary unless you have an interest in doing posters or a great deal of work on a professional level. The normal lens is good for most jobs, but you may want a set of close-up accessory lenses (macro lenses), if your work is small.

Kodak Tmax 100 (TMX) is a satisfactory general purpose black-and-white film. With careful processing and handling, it is capable of producing good quality, fine-grained, 8×10-inch prints.

Perhaps the most underrated and most useful piece of equipment is the tripod. Keeping the camera stationary allows you to compose the picture and position lights to give the best view. Otherwise you must coordinate holding the camera level, focusing precisely and pressing the shutter button – all factors that can lead to slight blurring of the image. The tripod also allows longer exposures that in turn permits the use of smaller lens openings which promote sharper pictures.

For lighting, the simplest and least expensive source is the sun. You can achieve excellent results by shooting outdoors or near windows. But changing weather or the setting sun may frustrate your efforts. Two or three available flood lights would be handy; these should be directional (with reflector) and perhaps "barn doors" (light blocking devices) on at least one. Other advantageous lighting equipment would include a small mirror, white and black pieces of board, aluminum foil, utility clamps and light stands.

You will also need a visually uninteresting background. Various seamless materials can be used for backdrops, such as rolls of colored paper (purchased from a photographic or art supply store), butcher paper, brown wrapping paper or fabric. For backdrop colors, select a white to medium gray or brown. White pots on black background or black pots on white may look good to the eye, but not usually on film. Tack the

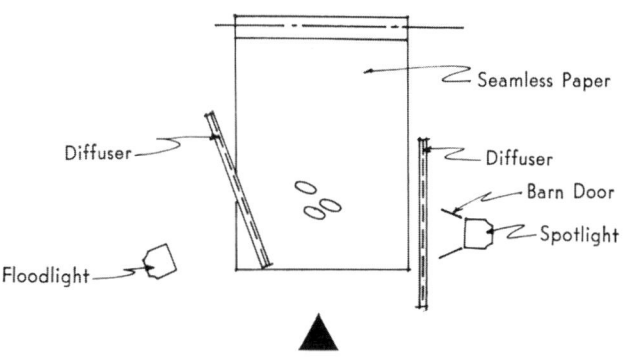

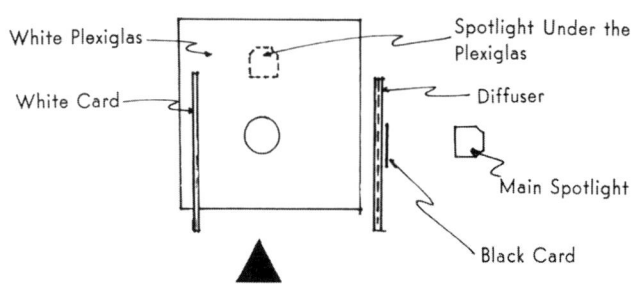

Above *A spotlight under Plexiglas created a circle of light when aimed at the plate. Light from the main spotlight was softened with a diffuser, and a black card taped where the light's intensity was concentrated eliminated specular highlights.*

Left *"Barn doors" (light blocking devices) gave direction to light from the main source on the right; the flood on the left lightens shadows from the main source. The photograph originally had a wider margin but was cropped tightly during publication.*

backdrop to a wall and run it onto a table, forming a smooth curve. Make the backdrop large enough so that you can frame well in from the edges. Camera viewfinders are seldom perfect; even when a picture looks safe, it may include the backdrop edge.

Though there are no hard and fast rules governing a good photograph, you will want pleasing composition and lighting, accurate exposure and the very sharpest detail. Take time to compose what will be seen. All too often the artist looks through the camera and sees only the central object, not noticing an extension cord, light stand or shadow, until the pictures are developed. Look through the viewfinder for distracting materials around the edges. At the same time be sure the camera is close enough to avoid leaving too much empty space around the pot. A good rule of thumb is that an 8x10-inch photo for publication should have from ¾ - to 1 inch background all around it.

Begin with one light. Typically, photographers place it 45° high and 4-5 feet back. But you may like the effect of 90° side light, back light or direct overhead light. Each pot may suggest different lighting moods. To reduce dark shadows, shine a second light into the shadow, or position reflectors to bounce in fill light. For balance, place the second light about twice as far away as the main light. To avoid shadows on the backdrop, keep the pot toward the front of the table and the lights high. You may wish to use a separate light to illuminate the backdrop evenly. For very soft light, try aiming one or two lights toward a white ceiling or side wall, creating indirect light; or shine light through a translucent shower curtain or other diffuser. However, the more diffuse the light, the less subject texture shows. For increased texture, you need a direct light (spotlight) relatively perpendicular to the axis of the camera and the subject. Use as few lights as possible-more lights create more heat, shadows and speculars (bright spot reflections). Glassy surfaces show what is reflected in them, not what is illuminating them. Thus if the only viewfinder indication of the light source is a specular highlight, some extraneous or distracting object might be shown in the reflection.

In bright sun, the shadows will probably be too harsh and dark. Reflector cards (illustration board or crumpled aluminum foil stretched on cardboard) can be positioned to bounce

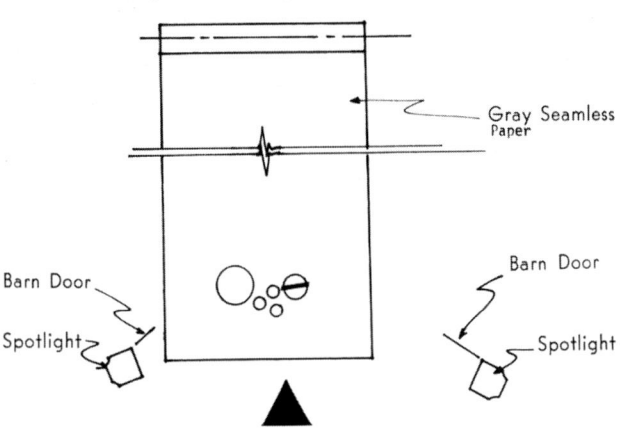

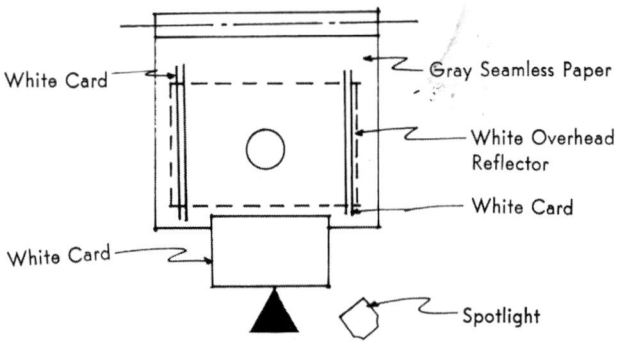

Above *Matt or semimatt surfaces can be directly lit for increased texture without specular highlights. Barn doors on the spotlights keep the background in shadow.*

Right *For this softly lit photograph the spotlight was aimed at a white overhead reflector; the white card in front was angled toward the work.*

STUDIO PRACTICES, TECHNIQUES AND TIPS

light into the shadows. You may also make a tent with a translucent shower curtain to diffuse direct sunlight.

Simple cameras often have automatic exposure control. Most 35mm and 2¼-inch cameras permit you to set f-stops and shutter speed manually. Since you will probably use f-16 for maximum depth of field (distance of clear focus), you have only to determine the correct shutter speed. Even without a meter, outdoors you may use the "Sunny 16 Rule"–in bright sunlight use f-16 and set the shutter speed at the time closest to the film's ISO rating. For example, with ISO 64 film, shoot at f-16 and 1/60 second.

To coordinate light and camera action indoors, you will need a light meter. There are many types, some built into cameras, others handheld. An incident meter will tend to give better and more consistent results. If you do not have an incident meter, take the light reading from an 18% gray card placed beside the subject. Such cards are available (with instructions for their use) from your local photo store. You may wish to "bracket" exposures for the best selection: If the meter recommends 1/15 second at f-16, shoot three pictures using 1/8, 1/15 and 1/30 second as shutter speeds.

Taking good photographs can be a time-consuming effort. To adequately photograph a ceramic object, you might find that setting the lighting and constantly checking the image through the viewfinder may take two hours, while the processing and printing may take another hour. (If you are not set up to make your own prints, consider taking your film to the more expensive, but more reliable, custom processors, rather than snapshot photo-finishers.) Considering every step carefully is well worth the time invested to ensure good photographs of your work. ▲

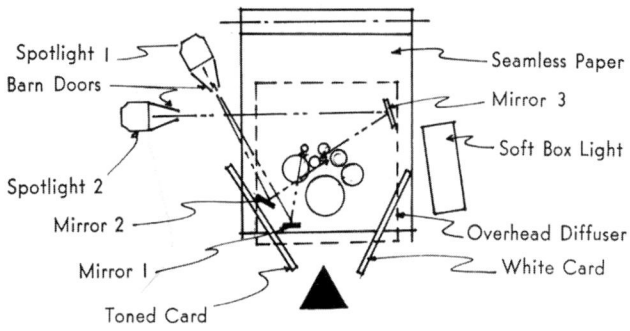

Above *Complicated lighting can be worth the effort; a diffused box light (fluorescent) from above is augmented by reflected light from one white card on the right and a mid-gray card on the left. Directing a small spotlight off mirror 2 added illumination to part of the tumbler; the dominance of the rose was diminished through lightening with the same spotlight and another mirror. Spotlight 2 and mirror 3 added back lighting to the shakers.*

Right *The photograph and diagram of the setup on page 50.*

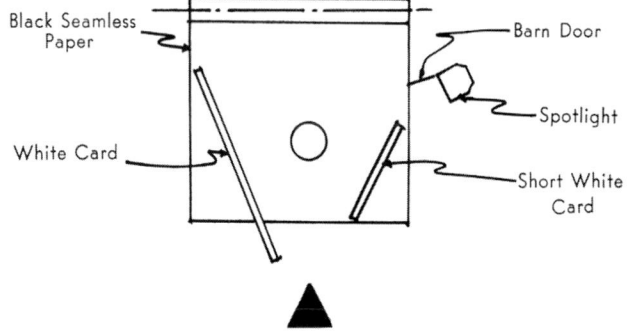

Photographing Ceramics
Color Transparencies, Slides and Prints
By Glenn Rand

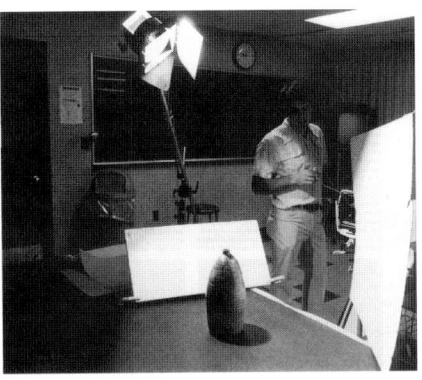

For serious color photography, you will need a tripod, cable release, background to shoot against, and lighting equipment for the shot, including large sheets of colored paper or board: much of the same equipment as used in making black-and-white photos. Photograph with a camera size which gives the end product you wish. If you want slides, then a 35mm SLR camera is more convenient and provides better quality than reduced copies from a 4x5, or vice versa.

Color photography of ceramic objects usually involves 35mm slides: for records, lectures, entering fairs, exhibitions, and marketing. Slides are convenient and relatively inexpensive, but on occasion larger transparencies may be required for color publication in publicity materials, books and magazines; or a color print might be more apropos for gallery presentations.

In color photography, consider that most of the concepts for color use which are employed in your ceramics apply in the photographic reproduction of that work.

When shooting color, the film type and light source have great bearing on meeting your requirements. The "tungsten" indication on film designates its photo emulsion is manufactured for 3200-degree quartz lights and for tungsten bulbs which also produce light at 3200K (degrees Kelvin). The designation "photoflood" refers to film which is produced for 3400K bulbs and 3400K quartz lights. These Kelvin "color temperature" designations refer to the actual color of light overall. Daylight (5500K) is relatively blue, while tungsten light is more yellow in comparison. Our brains correct slight shifts in the color of light overall, but the films used in color photography make no such correction, holding constant their engineered color balance. When the wrong film/light combination is used, the result is an image with an obvious (and usually unfavorable) color shift. Thus, film designed for one light source should usually not be exposed in another without a camera filter which compensates for the change.

In addition to various light sensitivities, films are made for specific purposes. For a print, you should use a negative film. Kodak Portra will give the best results for most situations: Kodak Portra 160 in daylight; Kodak Portra 100T with tungsten lights. For 35mm slides Ektachrome 100 (EPN). For reproduction purposed it is essentially grainless and less likely to fade with time than Ektachrome films. Ektachrome 64T (EPY) is good for use with tungsten light, favor blue-oriented ceramic colors and have the advantage of fast processing. For larger transparencies Ektachrome 100 (EPN) will give the best results in daylight; in tungsten light the best film is Ektachrome 64T (EPY), the standard in the commercial field for studio work.

As in black-and-white photography, compose the picture and check lighting possibilities through the camera's viewfinder. Consider effects possible with colored reflectors, but remember colored backdrops may both enhance and compete with the subject. A black background is particularly useful in color transparencies for publication because it masks minor shifts in color caused by the lighting, film, or publication production processes.

Sharpness is the key to good representational photographs. Focus carefully; if you cannot focus on both the closest and farthest parts (as is often the case), set the focus about one-third of the way into the object. Then close the f-stop down to the smallest lens opening, usually f-16 for maximum depth of field.

Though it is better to shoot good negatives for print applications, you can get good results directly from slides.

Regardless of the finishing process, color images are not as rugged as black-and-white; the surfaces of prints and transparencies tend to scratch easily. Protective sheets designed for use with color photography are available for prints, transparencies and slides. For storage of all photographic materials, avoid hot, humid or dusty environments. ▲

Salt-glazed stoneware, 26 inches in height, by Bill Bracker, Lawrence, Kansas. To add subtle hues to a monochromatic work, a blue card reflected light from the single spotlight on the left. Orange and yellow cards flat on the left reflected a complementary color on the opposite side.

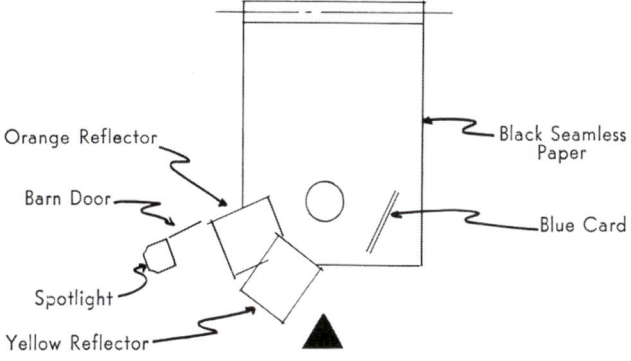

Reduction-fired stoneware platter, 12 inches in diameter, thrown, with combing and incising, by James Reinert, Owosso, Michigan. The brightness of the glaze on this work made the lighting choice difficult: the low angle of light emphasized the texture at the center of the plate, but also created specular highlights on the rim (in this case a desirable sacrifice). White and yellow cards filled in light from the left. Ceramics reflect the color of objects around them during use, on exhibition, in every circumstance. The photographer may control these surrounding colors in the same manner as the direction of light and the color of the background on which a work is seen. A black background is particularly useful in color transparencies for publication because it masks minor but unwanted shifts in color caused by the lighting, film characteristics, or publication production processes. Images like this one which can be cropped both horizontally and vertically are more likely to be published because they offer the book or magazine designer more options in layout.

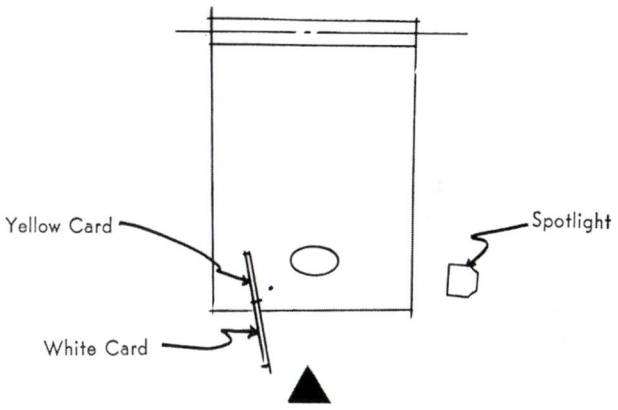

Salt-glazed stoneware, 5 to 8 inches in height, by Bill Bracker. Setting work on Plexiglas can add dramatic reflections. The filtered yellow floodlight on a rear wall adds back lighting, silhouetting the ceramic forms and softening the transition from the black Plexigals to the wall. Placing the main spotlight low minimized specular highlights; the blue reflector neutralized some yellow light and slightly accented the work. A white card filled in light from the right.

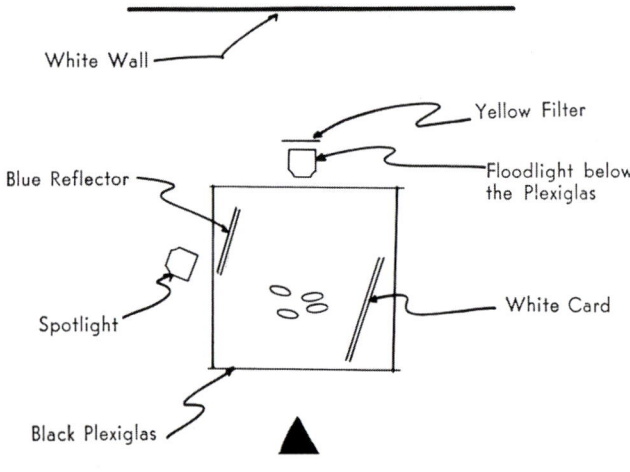

Wood-fired stoneware, 5 inches in height, by the author. This technique is known as camera masking. The pot was lit from the side, with a yellow card filling the shadow on the left. One film exposure was then made. (The black wall in the background received little light for minimum exposure in that area.) Next—without advancing the film or moving the camera—white illustration board was placed on the back wall and a slide projected onto it (a projection screen may shine back at the camera, causing lens flare.) With the spotlight turned off, a light reading was taken from the projected image, and a second exposure made. Images such as this may add interest to slides for jurying and have potential for book usage.

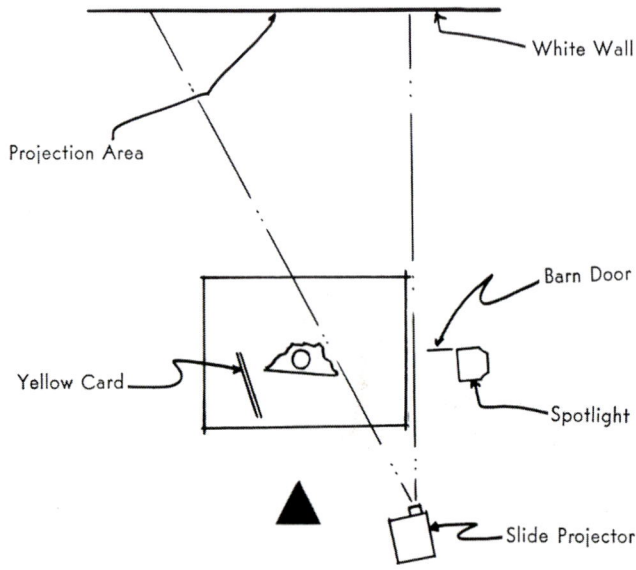

Photographing Ceramics Revisited

by Glenn Rand

During the past decade, the importance of good photographs for marketing and documentation has grown steadily. Now, galleries and magazines prefer large-format "transparencies" over slides; a ceramic artist can't feel comfortable just popping film into an Instamatic, pointing it at the piece and submitting the results for publication or as a show entry.

Today, there is a need to produce photographs on a more "professional" level. This doesn't necessarily mean the photographs must be shot by professional photographers, but that the same care in photographic technique is taken. Part of this technique involves how a photograph creates a successful illusion of three-dimensional form from a two-dimensional image. The photographer controls how an object will be seen by selecting an appropriate vantage point and the lighting under which the object will be photographed.

If you are competing (for a gallery slot, acceptance to a show, a teaching job, etc.), and your photos do not look as good as those of other hopefuls, then you obviously have a problem. Ceramists are forced by the fragility, size and weight of their work to rely on photographic reproductions to make their efforts readily accessible to a large audience. And, for better or worse, the person whose work is best translated to photographic form will tend to win in photo image-based competitions, regardless of the three-dimensional realities.

Perhaps the best way to provide this "professional" look is by creating visual excitement. That is what a photograph needs to overcome its two dimensionality. But what is really required?

First determine the purpose of the proposed photographs. If you need insurance photos, then very likely that point-and-shoot camera will work fine. If your hope is to have the work reproduced in color on the cover of a magazine, you may need some help. Unless you are willing to go to the expense of purchasing or renting a view camera, lighting equipment and a studio, it will probably be better to hire a professional.

If that is your choice, first ask to see samples of work similar to what you expect. Let's face it, you may make silver-lustered constructions unlike anything else on the market, but your work photographs very much like polished chrome. If the professional has not shot ceramics before, it doesn't mean that he/she has not photographed something similar. But don't assume that because a photographer takes good portraits or has work in the "Museum of Esoteric Art" that he/she can produce the types of photographs you expect. If you have an idea of what you want, be sure to tell the photographer. (You can always show pages from magazines you want to be seen in.)

Expect to pay for photographic services. Remember, the work you are having shot probably took some time and effort to make it good. It will most likely take a similar effort to make the photograph represent what you have created. And you expect to be paid for your efforts, don't you?

If you decide to take the photographs yourself, you should first give some thought to equipment and materials. Most of you probably use a 35mm, single lens reflex (SLR) camera to produce slides and negatives for prints in either black-and-white or color. But the results in all reproduction techniques are improved by using the largest size film possible. The 2¼-inch (also called a medium-format) camera may be used to make slightly larger and more controlled images than the 35mm, but the 4×5-inch view (also called large-format) camera is the workhorse of commercial "tabletop" photography, It gives the photographer the most control.

You will need a tripod regardless of the type of camera you use. Just be sure it will give steady support. Unless you are photographing at speeds less than 1/125 of a second, there is little chance of holding still for maximum sharpness.

Lighting equipment is also important, even if you are utilizing the sun as the main light source. If you choose to work in a studio, which I recommend, you will want two or more lights.

The type of film will also make a great difference. Just keep two things in mind: lighting (color shifts will occur if the light and film are not matched) and use (negative film for prints and transparency film for slides or reproduction in all print media). The three example photos suggest suitable techniques for different lighting circumstances. ▲

This pot was photographed at the studio of Kioshi Morioka in Kyoto, Japan, using the sun as the main light source. The problems created by sunlight are twofold. First is the brightness. To expose for the highlight detail and still hold detail in the shadow areas, you need to use fill cards to bounce light into the shadows. Second, the sun gradually changes position relative to the work (as the world rotates), so you must be prepared to make adjustments in fills. Naturally, filling the shadows of a spherical form is not as much of a problem as it would be if the object were geometric in shape.

The jar was photographed on a white, seamless background because the white naturally reflects light into shadows. To lessen the impact of the white, I allowed the shadow of a nearby tree to fall on the background. A fill card was also used to open up the shadow on the side away from the sun.

Above Right In doing photographs of work by Madeline Ricks, I ran into two problems. The first was she wanted the work shot on 35mm film because she uses the images mainly for exhibition entries. But, due to her use of bright glazes and lusters, it would have been easier to photograph with a view camera. For a shiny surface to show color, the color must be reflected in the surface from the lighting. (With view camera movements, this is easier to handle.) So, gold foil added to a white fill card placed in front allows the gold luster to read properly in a color image.

The first part of the photographic process was to support the piece so that it could be shot against the background. This was accomplished by hanging it with black button thread. Thread was used because it reflects little light and the black color blended into the background. Many people think that monofilament fishing line would be better because it looks transparent, but the material reflects light rather than letting it pass through. Threads were also used to keep the work from rotating.

A medium gray background was used to produce tones from light to dark. This gradation is created by holding back direct light from the background material, and allowing the long sweep of seamless paper to drop off in illumination.

Primary lighting was electronic flash. The work was also illuminated by a Hazylight (softbox) above, with a small Boxlight (small rectangular light) passing through a diffuser panel as fill. Because the majority of the sculpture's surface was brightly glazed, the broad diffuse lights gave reflected shape to the piece.

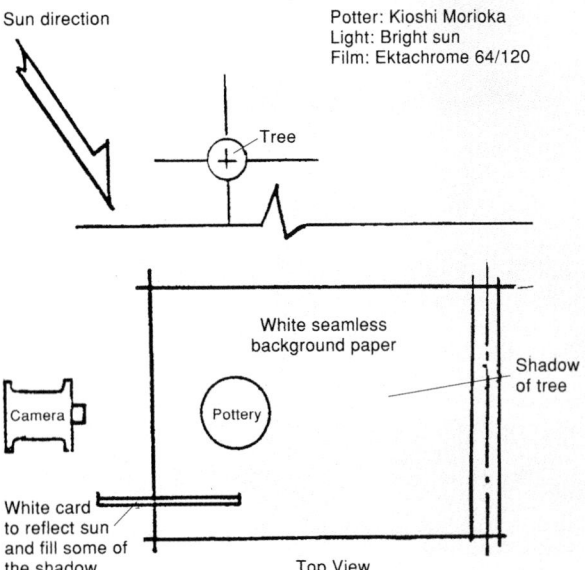

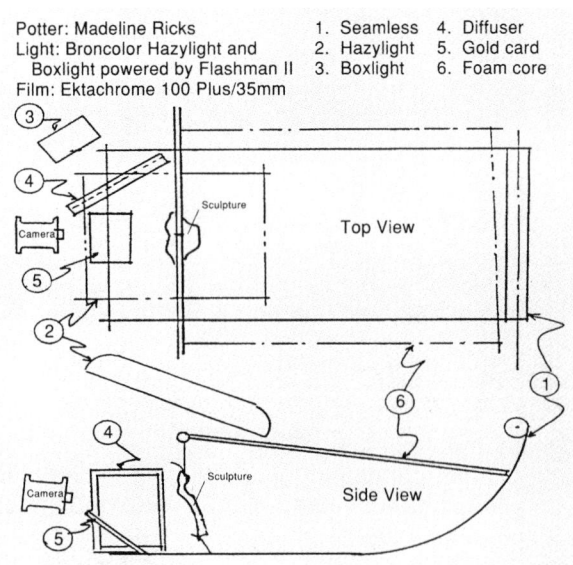

STUDIO PRACTICES, TECHNIQUES AND TIPS

The concept behind photographing this salt-glazed porcelain bottle by Anne Bracker of Lawrence, Kansas, was to make an image that would enhance the work's color and pattern. This was accomplished by building a set with black pebbles on a tray and a painted sunset backdrop. The painting covered about one-third of a white posterboard, which also served as a light diffuser/reflector. The lighting of the image was by a floodlight aimed at the board, with "barn doors" (adjustable light-blocking panels) controlling the illumination so that no direct light struck the bottle. This was important, as the glaze would have caused a "hot spot" on the pot in direct light. A large white fill card was positioned in front of the bottle. The camera was positioned over the fill card, shooting down into a field of black pebbles. Water was added to just below the level of the base of the bottle to reflect the colors of the abstract painted sunset.

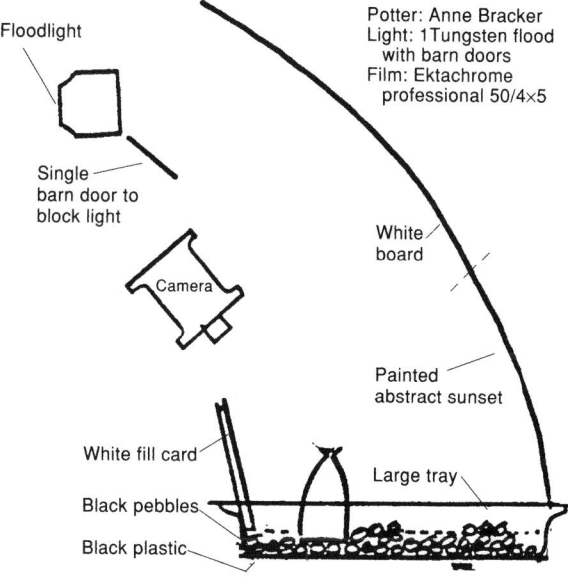

Photographic Recommendations

Purpose	Special Medium (Camera)	Lighting
Insurance	any color print (35mm)	no
Documentation	slide (35mm)	no
Lecture Support	slide (35mm)	yes*
Show Entry	slide (35mm**)	yes
Magazine (small-size, black & white editorial)	5x7 glossy print (35mm)	yes*
Magazine (med.-large, black & white editorial)	8x10 glossy print (2_)	yes*
Magazine (color editorial)	transparency (2_ or 4x5)	yes*
Magazine (b & w illustration)	8x10 glossy print (35mm)	yes*
Magazine (color illustration)	transparency (4x5)	yes*
Poster	transparency (4x5)	yes*

*In some cases available light will have to suffice. But this may restrict usage in publications. They generally require better quality than is typically achieved with this technique. The range of tones in printed photographs is less than in the film form, and this normally requires lighting control to gain proper photo tones for printing purposes.

**Many shows require entries to be in 35mm slide form. This does not mean that the original photographs must be that form, but if you do plan to duplicate from larger images, use duplicating film.

Equipment

Type	Use	Effect
Floodlight	broad light	large amount of light for the cost; shadows are somewhat soft, but still distinct
Fresnel Light	collimated light	focused, and directional light; shadows are sharp and distinct
Soft Box	diffuse light	very broad and soft light, shadows are nondistinct
Fill Card	add soft light	shows detail/color in shadow areas; flattens contrast range
Diffuser	diffuse light	can be used with any kind of light
Seamless	background	allows for controlled, uncluttered look
Barn Doors	blocks light	attached to the lights to control the size and shape of light on the subject

Suggested Films

Type	Light	Film
Black & White Print	any	T-Max 100
Color Prints	D/S	Ektachrome 100 (EPN)
Slides	D/S	Ektachrome 100 (EPN)
Slides	T	Ektachrome 64T (EPY)
Slides	D/S	Ektachrome 100 Plus (EPP)*
Transparencies	D/S	Ektachrome 100 Plus (EPP)
Transparencies	T	Ektachrome 64T

D/S = Daylight or Strobe   T = Tungsten lights

*Ektachrome 100 Plus (EPP) is designed to improve color saturation, while maintaining good neutrals.

GOING FOR THE GOLD
The Marketplace for Ceramic Art
by Garth Clark

"Perforated Vessel," 9 inches (23 centimeters) in diameter, ceramic and steel, by Tony Marsh, Lakewood, California; at Garth Clark Gallery in New York City.

September marked the 20th anniversary of the Garth Clark Gallery. A major promoter of contemporary studio ceramics, the gallery opened with an exhibition of works by Beatrice Wood in Los Angeles in 1981. Two years later, owners Garth Clark and Mark Del Vecchio established a second venue in New York City. Through the mid 1990s, active exhibition schedules were maintained at both sites; however, the partners closed the Los Angeles gallery in 1994 to concentrate on the New York site. Altogether, the gallery has featured solo shows by approximately 140 ceramists from around the world during the past two decades.—Ed.

Even though the marketplace is crucial to any professional ceramist's life, and always has been, I have never attended a single conference where selling has been the subject of a serious paper or discussion. It is as though talking about this subject will pollute the purity of the creative spirit, yet the issues of sales are the constant unspoken subtext of anxiety and desire whenever artists gather.

This ambivalence is a modern attitude, what writer Maya Angelou terms a "learned affectation." The ancients were untroubled by selling, and saw it as an integral part of the overall process. No lesser figure than the Greek poet Homer wrote of the importance of marketability in a poem entitled "Kiln" from around 100 B.C.:

*If you will pay me for my song, O potters
then come Athena, and hold thy hand above the kiln!
May the kotyloi and kanastra turn a good black,
may they be well fired and fetch the price asked
many being sold in the marketplace and many on the road,
and bring in much money, and may my song be pleasing.*

But then he also warns against a loss of integrity:

*But if you turn shameless and deceitful
then I summon the ravagers of the kiln
May they hit these pots hard, may the kiln collapse
And may the potters wail as they see mischief
But I shall rejoice at the sight of their luckless craft
And if anyone bends over to look into the spy hole
may his whole face be scorched
so that all may learn to deal justly.*

With that warning ringing in our ears, we can proceed to look at how ceramics, art and money fared at the end of the second millennium, and specifically at the arrival and mechanics of a fine arts market for ceramic art. The gold standard for visual arts is painting. Canvases by modern masters, such as Pablo Picasso, fetch $49 million and "wet art" by living artists sells for up to $18 million. This is an intimidating standard. Yet, before we castigate ourselves for not having reached the same lofty fiscal heights, let's place this in perspective. The painting market is about 600 years old, and has been developed shrewdly and uninterruptedly throughout these centuries, beginning in the Renaissance when painters considered themselves, first and foremost, businessmen. This market is bolstered by thousands of academics, dealers, consultants and museum specialists—all directly or indirectly working at maintaining the status quo.

The ceramics market, by comparison, is minuscule, underdeveloped and still in its infancy. As a field for individual artists, it is little more than 100 years old. The so-called fine arts market for ceramics is less than 50 years old—in real terms, maybe only 25. But the market for ceramics is nonetheless remarkably resilient. With the barest of resources, practically no academic support and the slightest of museum interest, it has, since the late 19th century, survived all kinds of vicissitudes, periods of indifference and a vulnerable, underfunded eco-structure to emerge in the last decade of the 20th century with surprising strength and promise.

Ceramics started to make serious inroads into the world of dealers and collectors who had previously shunned the field in the 1980s, as the entire art world entered the greatest bull market of the century. It was a British artist who had the most impact on New York's art market, one that was traditionally resistant if not outright hostile to ceramics. Andrew Lord's first exhibition in 1981 at Blum Helman, one of New York's most influential galleries, was a sellout success. Jasper Johns, Robert Rauschenberg and other artists were among those who acquired the work. The critics tripped over each other in the race to lavish praise on the work and, with their total ignorance of ceramic history, credited Lord with every innovation made in the last 300 years. But the work was powerful and held its own against the toughest competition from the fine arts.

With this, another benchmark was achieved. Lord has often been the subject of great resentment for his stance that ceramics must be priced and treated exactly the same as any other artwork, and for having the determination to make the concept stick. He opened a door. Those who feared to follow have only themselves to blame.

However glamorous the Blum Helman exhibition might have been, much of the ensuing progress was made by a small group of dedicated ceramics dealers in the U.S., Britain, Germany, Holland and Japan, who opened galleries that were unquestionably galleries of art in their design of space, presentation and professionalism. Slowly but surely, ceramics advanced its position and its profile.

In 1990, with the collapse of an overheated art market, one would have expected ceramics to be pushed back into obscurity. This has not happened. The fact that ceramics held its own and that prices did not collapse, nor did the collectors disappear the way they did for some years in the painting market, earned some respect and some material interest on the part of fine arts. Ceramics was more solid than the arts community expected.

Now, I do not want to create too much of a Pollyanna scenario, because even the top end of ceramics is still marginalized, but it is now marginalized within the fine arts rather than without. While this may sound like a shift in degree rather than kind, it is in fact the beginning of a whole new paradigm. It has many ramifications, including the fact that New York's critics are taking time to bone up on the history of the field before rushing to print. The review of the Picasso show at the Metropolitan Museum of Art by Roberta

Smith actually quoted the opinions of major ceramists, including Robert Arneson and the ubiquitous Bernard Leach, regarding Picasso's claywork.

This opening up of the ceramics market is not all good news. When ceramists so eagerly sought entrance to the fine art galleries, they did not realize the extreme selectivity of the art market mechanisms. Many thought that one day ceramics would become accepted as art, and that there would be a blanket change of designation for all ceramists. They did not realize that the art market would only allow a small group of ceramists to cross over from crafts to art, leaving most of the field still excluded, and much more frustrated and embittered than before. As Truman Capote warned, beware of answered prayers; they are the cause of the greatest pain.

To show how this market has broadened and increased, I have compiled a scrapbook of images (slides, announcements and advertisements) for ceramics exhibitions that took place in New York in only one season, from September 1998 to June 1999. The purpose was to evaluate the texture, the diversity and the heft of this relatively new market, keeping in mind the understanding that as late as 1985 New York was considered a hostile environment for ceramics. Unlike now, ceramic shows were then reviewed by the *New York Times* in the Home section next to recipes of coconut cream pies. So the change has been real and dramatic.

Looking at some recent price tags shows just how much the fine arts market for ceramics has grown. For instance, the price of a handmade pot by a good if not wildly famous potter—and I hope that Jeff Oestreich won't mind his pitcher serving as the example—has increased in value from a high of around $200 in the 1960s to about $1500. That is an impressive jump of 750%. But if we look at those artists who function in the fine arts market, the figures are very different. Over the same period of time, the prices for Peter Voulkos works have risen from $1000 to $200,000, an increase of 20,000%. A Betty Woodman "pillow" pitcher sold for $250 in 1975; they are now $18,000, an increase of 7200%. A major work by Adrian Saxe has jumped from $600 in 1980 to $30,000 in 1999—an increase of 5000%. And Beatrice Wood's work went from $1000 in 1980 to as much as $45,000 in 1999—an increase of 4500%.

Then there is Robert Arneson. One of his sculptures has fetched $250,000, the highest price for 20th-century ceramics. This represents a whopping increase of 166,000% from the 1960s when $1500 was a high price, and Arneson's market values are continuing to increase strongly as work disappears into public collections. In certain areas of his work, notably the portraits of the 1970s, only a handful are left in public hands, so the competition when one comes up for sale is fierce.

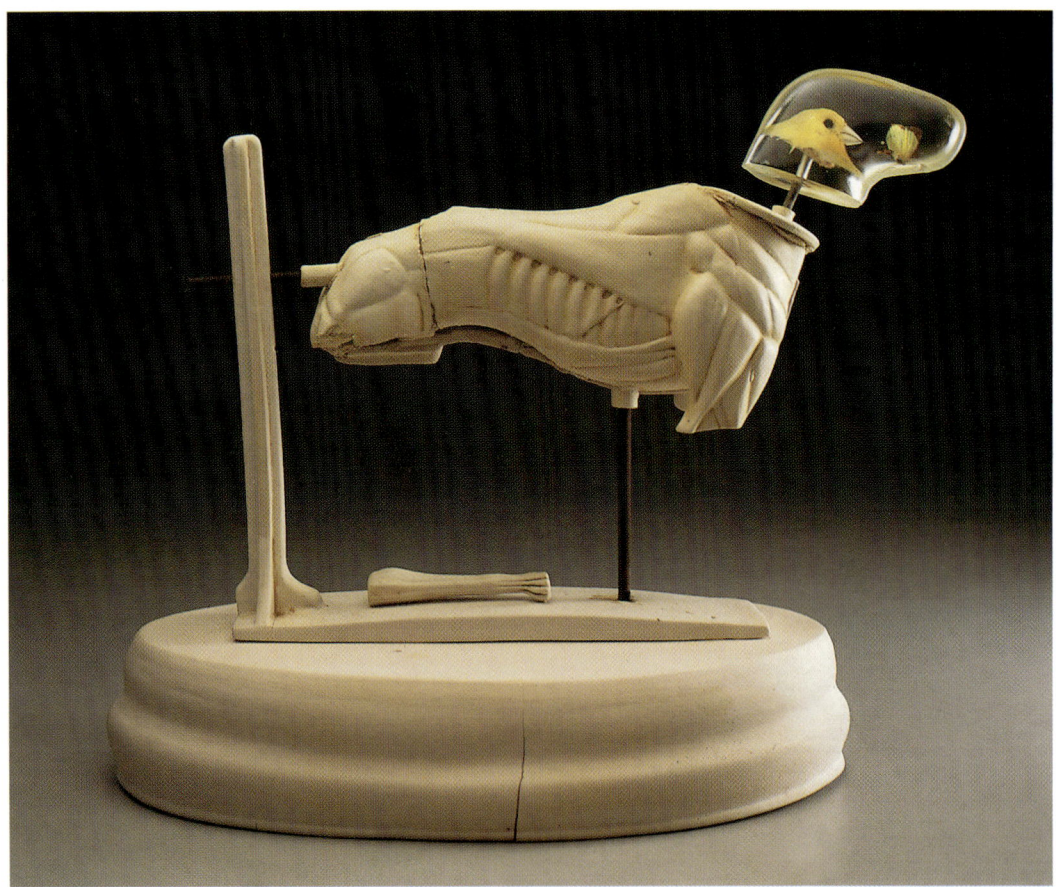

"Laika Model," 14 inches (36 centimeters) in height, clay, taxidermy, resin and metal, by John Byrd, Baton Rouge, Louisiana.

All this discussion of money may seem a vulgar recital of greed. But that is really just a superficial, simplistic criticism and usually a dishonest one. One of the old saws about the arts is: When bankers get together, they talk about art. When artists get together, they talk about money.

Before proceeding, I want to emphasize that the art gallery is not the only market; in most countries, it either does not exist or else is so small as to be immaterial. Craft shops, crafts fairs, studio sales are still the major market for the majority of ceramists.

Why the focus on the fine arts market? Is it a focus on wealth, fame and power? Seeing as I know few artists and no dealers in this field who can claim to have achieved all three of these goals, it really seems to be about something else—the reality of cultural mechanisms and how their wheels turn. The top end of the market does have a disproportionate effect on how the rest of the medium is viewed. It is the needle-sharp, uppermost point of the market triangle.

Painting is not presented to the world at large through secondary and tertiary artists. Its most public face is through primary artists. The stature of those artists, which is established for better or worse in the marketplace, in many ways determines how seriously painting is taken, how much money is spent on exhibiting that work in museums, what kind of scholarly research can be afforded, how much money can be spent on publications. If one is almost invisible in the food chain, all of these resources are impacted, reduced or even denied.

Am I saying that there is a direct causal connection between market profile and the allocation of resources to a field? Yes, I am. Ceramics has suffered from being allocated a very small part of the total pie, precisely because its top end is so small. It is this part of the ceramics world that generates most of the mainstream reviews, and the press in turn make us visible and seemingly viable. This material is seen and read by those who sit on the boards of foundations. If we do not seem to be players in the art world, we are either given nothing or fobbed off with minor funding.

"Garth's Girth," 5 inches (13 centimeters) in height, earthenware, with overglazes, by Ron Nagle, San Francisco.

There is an argument common among some ceramists, particularly those in universities, that if we push for a strong market we are "going for the money." To this criticism, I can only ask one question, "What exactly do you think that the ceramics market should do, strive for poverty?" I think we have done that for long enough and it has kept ceramists in indentured servitude. A strong market for ceramics at the top end, even for a small group of artists, lifts price ceilings, and raises the profile and the glamour of the entire field.

Those who complain most loudly about the evils of selling art are usually those who take home regular paychecks from academia. Their attitude flies in the face of universal truths for art survival. They seem determined to trap ceramics in an economic cul-de-sac, whereby they claim some specious moral higher ground. However, this group does not suggest that their friends in the worlds of painting follow the same route, and are indeed often proud of their colleagues' market success. Nor do they suggest that they be paid less than their colleagues who teach in wealthier areas of the arts.

This sackcloth market is reserved for the clay dauber. It's the throwback to Leach's hypocrisy, to William Morris' dilettantism and to the presumed ethical superiority of academia over the free market. These ideas have repeatedly failed ceramics and will continue to do so. Yet, in the face of this failure, I still hear the droning voices from the spoilers, masking with false humility their insecurities, perhaps a fear of failure if they are tested in this ruthless proving ground or, sadly, an even greater fear of success.

But this fine arts market is not for everyone. First, access is extremely difficult. Second, most ceramists do not fit. It's a very particular aesthetic, and only particular artists will survive in this world. It demands a high level of professional input from both artist and dealer. This means that to progress, ceramists have to give up their cherished culture of amateurism or what one dealer scathingly referred to as a "hobbyist-wanker" mentality. Remember there is a difference between a professional artist who takes his or her income seriously and a commercial artist who panders (and one finds the latter in every market high and low). A professional artist (perhaps "working artist" is a less loaded term) confronts the responsibility that art must sell if he or she is to afford another day in the studio.

All artists do, and probably must, feel ambivalence for the admittedly artificial mechanisms of selling art, but they still have to come to terms with being professionals. Some of them do this superbly without any compromise to their art, while others hide behind the shibboleth that artists are congenitally incapable of any kind of efficiency or direction.

Until recently, the record for a work of art made from clay was shared by Marcel Duchamp, for his 1960s remake of the urinal ready-made "Fountain," and Jeff Koons for "Lady with Pink Panther," each of which fetched $1.8 million at sales at Sotheby's and Christies respectively. But on May 15, a new high was reached when Koons' larger-than-life- porcelain sculpture "Michael Jackson with Bubbles" was sold for a staggering $5.6 million. The implications of this sale—what it says about ceramic art's new viability in the marketplace, what it means to the more traditional ceramics market (if anything) and the conten-

"Untitled Vessel," 4 inches (10 centimeters) in height, white stoneware, by John Pagliaro, Shelter Island Heights, New York.

Now that artists from other media, such as sculptors Tony Cragg and Thomas Shutte, are entering the ceramics field, and often with good and ambitious work, the market paradigm, once dominated by the specialist ceramist, is in flux. Good? Bad? It does not matter. It is happening. You are not alone in the ceramics market anymore. You are not protected in a discrete controlled marketplace. Increasingly, ceramists are being pushed out into the cut and thrust with competitors whose signatures alone give them a head start, as does their powerful marketing networks of international dealers. These artists have smashed the ceiling that once prevented claywork from achieving the same prices as works in other media.

tious issues of the artist's hand over fabrication—are all relevant, all fascinating, but indiscernible.

Whatever this new wrinkle may mean, it is clear that it is no longer business-as-usual for the ceramics artist. One needs to juggle all the issues—finding time for teaching (if that is part of your career), finding time to make the art in sufficient quantity (and with reasonable continuity) to be a player, looking into how your art can find a voice in concert with other media aside from ceramics, learning to work in the rough and tumble of a furiously competitive art market. Ceramists love tools. The time has come to acquire some new ones for the marketplace, and to learn how to use them to compete. ▲

MATERIALS AND EQUIPMENT

Build a $75 Electric Wheel

by Jolyon Hofsted

Building your own equipment can drastically cut the cost of establishing or expanding a studio. The electric wheel depicted here can handle up to 20 pounds of clay as well as most commercial wheels.

I don't claim to have invented it; it simply came to be one day in a junkyard. Twenty years ago, I had a new teaching job, with no equipment to speak of, and had gone to a wrecked auto yard looking for an inexpensive way to make kick wheels. The mechanic at the yard and I talked, and the idea for an electric wheel was born. I've been showing people how to make them ever since.

Based on the front wheel assembly of a car, this potter's wheel is compact, quite easily constructed and will give many years of trouble free use. The first step is to go to an auto junkyard and purchase a complete front wheel assembly (prices vary but the cost should be well under $50). Have them cut it just behind the mounting bracket connecting it to the car. This will be used to mount the wheel, complete with rim but without tire. Be sure the bearings in the wheel assembly are not frozen, and that they are in good condition.

Next, you'll need to find an electric motor from ¼ to ¾ hp. If, after a little scouting around you can't come up with one, a rebuilt motor can be purchased.

Then you'll need to find a heavy industrial plug, the kind with a metal clamp around the back used to secure it to an electrical cord. This will become the rubber drive for the motor. The plug's male prongs are removed either by unscrewing or just snipping them off. The plug is then slid onto the motor's drive shaft and secured in place with its own metal clamp.

Standard wooden 2×4s are used for the wheel's framework. The width will be determined by the diameter of the front wheel assembly. Plan for at least a 2-inch clearance around the wheel assembly. Once this is laid out, the frame's length is constructed from 3-foot-long 2×4s, standing on edge.

The front wheel assembly is mounted in place, using the existing brackets secured to 2×4s running across the frame. Make sure the assembly is mounted level. Next, secure two 2×4s on each end of the frame to raise the wheel off the floor. At this point, you should have a frame constructed of 2×4s with a free spinning wheel head (car wheel without tire) secured in place.

The next step is to fill the top of the tire rim with plaster. Clay can be used to plug any holes from which the plaster might leak out. The plaster provides the necessary weight, as well as a good throwing surface. Pots can also be thrown on bats attached to the plaster.

To mount the motor, secure a 2×4 across the frame directly in line with the back of the wheel assembly. Attach a 12-inch square of plywood to this cross member with the use of a hinge. Secure the motor to the plywood. Some motors come with mounting brackets; if yours has none, metal straps can be used to bolt it in place. Position the motor so that the rubber (plug) drive shaft just clears the bottom of the wheel rim. By lifting the hinged plywood, the rubber will make contact with the rim and the wheel will go around.

Speed will be controlled by a pedal. Drill a vertical hole, in line with the center of the hinged plywood square, through the right side of the 2x4 frame. With two nuts, secure a long bolt through the frame and a 3-foot length of 1x2. This should be a very loose connection so that the pedal lever has lots of play. One end of this lever will be under the hinged plywood; the other will project from the right side of the wheel. Stepping on the lever raises the hinged plywood, thus touching the rubber drive shaft to the wheel rim. Removing your foot from the lever will disengage the drive shaft, thus slowing the speed.

The last step is to build a plywood box around the frame to enable you to sit (over the motor) at your $75 variable speed electric potter's wheel, and work comfortably. ▲

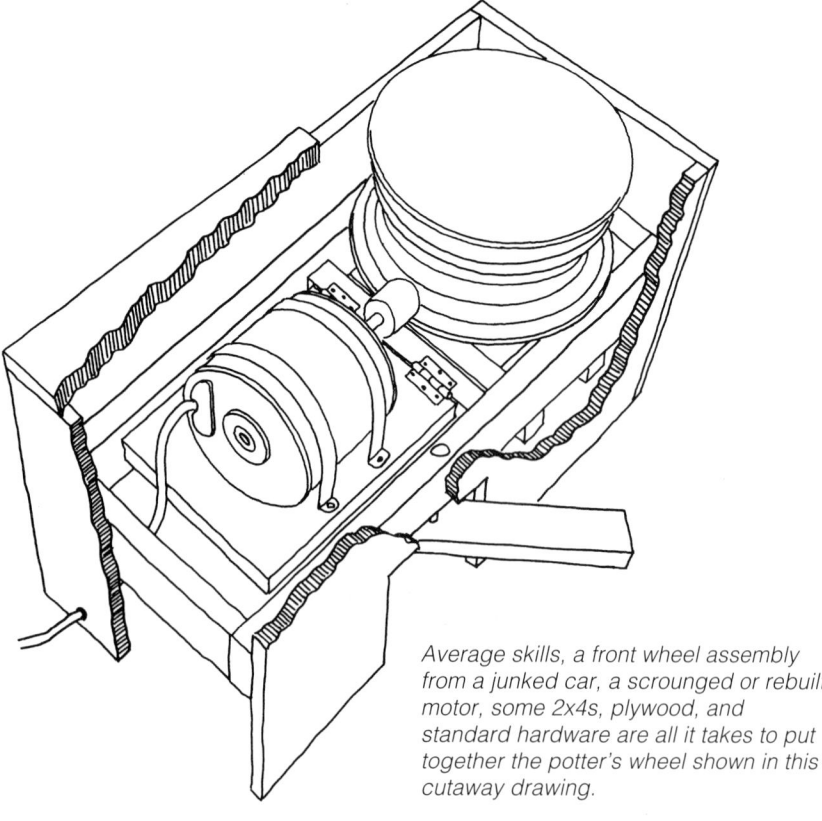

Average skills, a front wheel assembly from a junked car, a scrounged or rebuilt motor, some 2x4s, plywood, and standard hardware are all it takes to put together the potter's wheel shown in this cutaway drawing.

A Dry Clay Mixer
by Brian VanNostrand

The author (right), assistants Anita Lee and Dempsey Carpenter with a day's yield from their self-built clay-making equipment.

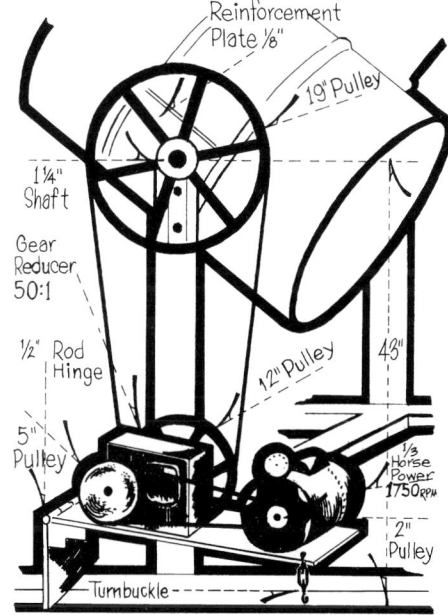

Two 55-gallon drums, mounted with their vertical axes at right angles, counterbalance each other, making it possible to use a ⅓-horsepower electric motor for power.

Our clay body preparation includes particle size reduction of crude clays, dry screening, dry mixing, wet blunging, dough mixing and pug milling. For many years all the phases, except for the dry blending, have been mechanized. A mortar hoe and large mixing box had sufficed for blending the five dry ingredients. But with the need for more clay and a concern for reducing health hazards, Loy Carpenter and I decided to construct a dry-mixing unit capable of radically reducing labor and eliminating excessive clay dust.

We wanted an inexpensive device which would be in proper scale to our other processing equipment, preferably more efficient than actually necessary for the present to allow for possible increased clay requirements in the future. The resultant design is based on two 55-gallon drums with snap-on lids.

Built for a small fraction of the cost of industrial dry clay mixers, ours was assembled from the miscellaneous parts we already had on hand. However, all the mixer's components could be considered ubiquitous and purchased at scrap prices in most salvage yards.

Capable of thoroughly mixing the body in approximately 10 to 15 minutes per batch, each drum will hold at least 200 pounds of dry materials of various particle size. By mounting the barrels on 1⅛-inch steel shaft with their vertical axes at right angles to one another, a counterbalancing is effected which makes it possible to use a ⅓-horsepower electric motor for power. The final rpm output is first reduced somewhat by two V-belt pulleys, then coupled to a 50:1 ratio gearbox to supply the torque to rotate the drums.

Critical to the design of this simple mixer are the four reinforcing plates which are first cut out square, then curved to fit the sides of the drums where the four shaft joins are located. The wall of a 55-gallon drum is not sufficiently thick to directly weld to the drive shaft, and if not reinforced in this manner would tear away from the shaft.

Also critical to the blending action are interior ⅛-inch thick baffle plates to disperse the ingredients, which have a tendency to flow almost like a liquid.

Loy and I have built several pieces of clay processing equipment over the years and have found that by hinging the power unit and using a turnbuckle as a belt tightening device we have an accommodating system for many V-belt sizes. The dry mixer utilizes this hinge design to allow the combined weight of both gearbox and motor to place tension on the V-belt driving the main shaft. The turnbuckle adds the final tension.

Having used this dry mixer a great deal, we find no drawbacks in its operation. There is, of course, dust encountered while loading and unloading, so dust masks are a must then. However, the mixing operation itself is completely dustless, and the drums are easy to fill and empty into a wheelbarrow. ▲

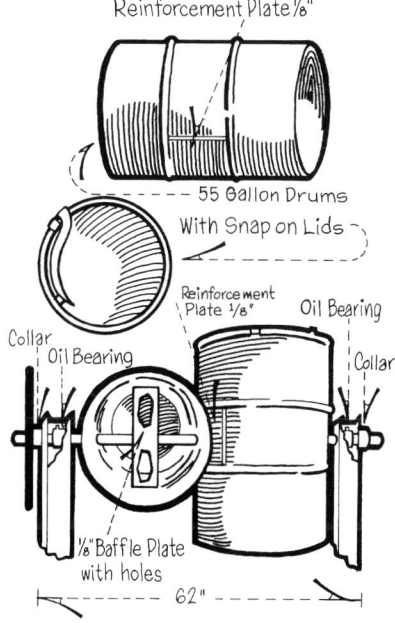

Far left The ⅓-horsepower motor is coupled to a 50:1 ratio gearbox, furnishing enough torque to rotate the drums with a system of V-belts and pulleys. Hinging the power unit and using a turnbuckle as a belt-tightening device accommodates various V-belt sizes.

Left To mount the drums on the shaft without tearing their walls, four ⅛-inch-thick metal plates are welded in place around the shaft joins. Baffle plates attached to the shaft inside each drum help disperse the dry ingredients, which tend to flow like a liquid.

Modify a Cement Mixer for Processing Clay

by Susan Nykiel and Ray Bub

As artists we need to control the entire pottery-making process, from mixing raw materials to firing the kiln; as a small business, we want to minimize expenditures. Mixing clay from dry materials helps us toward both goals. In addition, we can feel secure in knowing that each batch has been formulated and measured correctly.

The best clay processing machines commercially available to the studio pottery range from $2000-$4000. These blade mixers efficiently blend 250-300 pounds of dry materials with water to produce good quality clay, but the purchase price is often out of reach, and they do not eliminate the necessity of pugging or wedging to blend and de-air the clay for throwing or handbuilding. Buying premixed, pugged clay from a supplier will normally cost at least twice as much as buying the equivalent in dry materials and adding water, so some kind of clay processor makes good business sense.

A Sears backyard cement mixer can be altered to process clay satisfactorily. It will not mix clay as fast or as thoroughly as the blade mixers, nor will it efficiently blend clay powder with slip or dried clay chunks, but it does produce good quality clay with vastly less time and effort than hand methods. Pairing this Sears mixer with a pug mill will yield good clay efficiently. (Given the choice, it is wiser to invest in a good pug mill before an expensive clay mixer.) Of course, one doesn't have to have a pug mill too-it just shortens the time and effort required.

To adapt the cement mixer for clay processing, first unbolt and remove the four mortar-mixing blades. (Clay would cake on these and not blend evenly.) Seal the two top holes with nuts, bolts, and washers-they are too close to the mouth of the drum to help in the mixing process. Then bolt three _-inch, threaded rods through the other six blade-mounting holes with nuts and washers both inside and outside the wall of the drum; tighten the nuts securely so the rod can't rub on the drum and enlarge the hole. The drum will not leak, and we have had to replace only one rod in six years due to breakage. Experiment with the placement of the rods to find the best pattern for cutting and blending clay lumps as the drum turns. The machine can easily handle a dry measure of 100 pounds when processing the following recipe:

Above A backyard cement mixer can be altered to process clay satisfactorily. The four mortar-mixing blades are removed and the two top holes sealed with nuts, bolts and washers.

Right Three ¼-inch, threaded rods are bolted through the other six blade-mounting holes, with nuts and washers both inside and outside the wall of the drum. The nuts are tightened securely so the rods won't rub on the drum and enlarge the holes.

Oak Bluffs Stoneware Clay (Cone 11)

Custer Feldspar	10 pounds
Cedar Heights Goldart Clay	56
Georgia Kaolin (6 Tile Clay)	10
PBX Fireclay*	10
Tennessee Ball Clay (5)	10
Flint (200 Mesh)	2
Grog (20 Mesh to Fine)	2
	100 pounds

*No longer available, substitute Newman Red

Make a dust lid for the mouth of the drum and wear a respirator to dry mix the clay. Tumble for three minutes or so, holding the drum at an angle just above that where the batch would spill. Turn off the motor. Tilt the drum upright so the clay settles in the bottom. Add 25-30 pounds of water (27.5 pounds for a softer-than-throwing consistency). The water should be weighed since it won't mix in easily after the initial input-mix clay a little wet to aid in the aging process.

Adding the water correctly is the key to mixing consecutive batches conveniently without having wet clay caked on the sides of the drum. Pour the water into the center of the dry clay, taking care not to wet the metal wall. Replace the dust lid, then immediately start the motor again and ease the drum to an almost horizontal position for several revolutions. After the clay has tumbled for three minutes (or until it is thoroughly wet), you can remove the dust lid to watch the mixing process. Move the clay mass back and forth over the cutting rods by raising and lowering the handle as the drum turns. The longer the wet clay tumbles, the better, but ten minutes is normally sufficient for one batch. Soft throwing consistency corresponds with the formation of grapefruit-sized or larger balls of clay. If you do not have a pug mill, you will want to mix the batch more thoroughly.

Clay can be spilled a bagful at a time directly onto heavy plastic laid in front of the mixer. We spill the clay into a garden cart while the drum is turning, then wheel the cart to the pug mill. Although we immediately pug the freshly mixed clay to more completely blend the particles and water, hand wedging achieves the same result. After pugging or wedging, store the clay in heavy-duty garbage bags in a warm place for at least a week, or preferably a month, to age it. The warmth will encourage bacteria to migrate throughout the clay, thus increasing plasticity.

Above The ingredients are dry mixed for about three minutes with the drum mouth slightly raised. Then the motor is turned off and the drum righted. Water is poured directly into the center of the clay, the motor turned on and the drum eased to an almost horizontal position, mixing for approximately ten minutes.

Right Proper consistency is achieved when the clay forms grapefruit-sized balls.

The $1200 Studio

by Lili Krakowski

The ideal studio is 40×120 feet of solar-paneled brick and clapboard, built atop a hot spring. It is set in a pristine wilderness two hours drive from every major art gallery in the country. To the north, a rich agricultural valley sweeps up into colorfully forested and snow-capped mountains. To the east, a fish-packed river flows between forested banks. To the south, peaceful, warm sands set off the crashing rhythms of the ocean. To the west is the shimmering splendor of a night-flowering desert. The building includes a showroom, plus a kitchenette, a den and a hot tub. There is also space for an office, a shipping and storage area, and a loading dock. Everywhere, the air is filtered and temperature/moisture controlled. There is a central vacuum cleaner and a stereo, and maybe even a wine cellar.

That is the ideal studio. Most of us make do with much less—especially at the beginning, before fame and fortune, those thoughtless bloodhounds, have found us! It is a pity, therefore, that so many potters don't realize how very little one actually needs; and that those who taught American potters to appreciate Japanese aesthetics failed to instill the concomitant frugality. Examination of books on Japanese potteries reveals sparse studios that often spill outdoors. Clay is dug in one place, cleaned and mixed in another, then taken to the studio. Pots are dried outdoors, and carried over footpaths to sometimes distant kilns. None of this has lowered the quality of the ware.

Potting easily divides into six stages: clay mixing; storage; production; drying; glazing; firing. These need not happen in a single place. Indeed, there are advantages to using different spaces. Many variations are possible—especially, once one sorts the essentials from the would-be-nices. The essentials are workspace, clay, light, water, kiln. Everything else is nonessential.

Space

Despite the sarcasm that is frequently heaped on those who pot in basements, garages and chicken coops, perfect (even prizewinning) pots have originated in these workspaces. The important thing is to have a well-ventilated space that holds the equipment needed for the job one is actually doing. Equipment not used concurrently need not be together. If the slab roller and the glaze tubs are never used together, why should they occupy the same space?

It's easier if pots can stay where they are made till they go to the kiln, but they can be put on ware boards and carried elsewhere to dry. Each operation can be apart from the others. It is ironic that, while such splitting-up is the norm in large studios, it is sneered at in small, one-potter operations.

An 8×12-foot space is adequate for a wheel, wedging table, storage shelves and a small kiln. I potted for years in such a space (a wooden garden shed). While I actually gave the kiln space to a wood-burning stove—the kiln being in my basement—it worked very well. Had we insulated the shed, and put in baseboard heaters, the wood stove would have been unnecessary.

My present studio is 12×14 feet, not a huge space, and the kiln remains downcellar. Space must be limited to what can be heated affordably. (Heating costs are a major consideration in the clay economy—once-frozen pugs will fall apart and need a good rewedging but are not lost; once-frozen pots are history.)

Space for drying pots can range from a wind-free, sun-free patio to shelves above the washer and dryer. Moving half-finished pots around is a nuisance—but any time spent making pots brings that bigger, more convenient studio closer. Space costs are too variable to be included; that $1200 is limited to equipment and essential supplies. Shelves and racks built from new material will cost about $50.

The kiln can be anywhere safe—for itself and others. The two vital considerations: that no one can mess with it (or get burned); and that there is no danger whatsoever from water. As blasts of cold air are bad for the kiln (if it is hot) and can raise firing costs, a kiln should be protected; simple, even temporary, partitions will do.

Glazing space is hard to sum up, there being so many variables. The simplest, easiest method is to glaze pots when they are leather hard. This minimizes space requirements, and saves time. For several years, influenced mainly by encroaching arthritis, I have used a variety of brush- and trailer-applied slips, a transparent and a black glaze. The unexpected time/space savings have delighted me.

Clay

Unless you mine and process your own clay, the cost of your clay body not only includes ingredients, but also shipping (from the mine), preparation labor and equipment, space tied up in drying and storage, and shipping from the dealer. By the way, commercial bodies are about 25% water. For me, it is easy to make a pilgrimage downstate every year or so, load up on sacks of materials (clay, feldspar, grog, etc.) and mix in bathtubs behind my studio. After a year of aging, the clay is dried to usable consistency, then stored in two discarded freezers. The trip takes two days, with an overnight visit with a good friend. It takes one day to mix the clay up and several hours here and there to stir the slip with a hoe, to put it in drying boxes, then pug and store. With a pickup truck, some help and extra tubs, I could produce a full ton. (A bathtub holds about 250 pounds of material mixed into slip.) Living where and as I do, and having a pug mill, this makes sense for me.

For people with limited space, this is not practical. Commercially prepared clay has lots of advantages: it is neat and tidy; it can be stored anywhere (no more than a day's supply need be brought into the studio); and the supplier deals with problems caused by strikes, embargoes, or housing projects being built over the clay mines.

Clay costs: 500 pounds pre-mixed and delivered will run ±$125; 500 pounds of dry materials plus mileage and processing time, ±$70. Used bathtubs will be about $15 each.

Light

Lighting is a real drawback of underground studios. The electrician who installs the kiln can put in wiring for lamps as well. Any light is enhanced by reflection; mirrors from garage sales, mounted on selected spots on the wall, focus light where one needs it most. (Many potters, of course, have "throwing mirrors," which allow them to study the underside of pots on the wheel without cricking their necks.) Light sockets that swivel, while pricey, can eliminate the need for more lamps.

Lighting cost: $200 if an electrician is called; $50 if you can do it.

Water

Rarely does one need more than 5 gallons of water per day. This can be carried in in plastic milk jugs. A sink, salvaged from a demolition, or bought secondhand, can be set up on a scrap-wood stand and a 5-gallon bucket placed underneath to catch the waste water, as well as lumps of clay, nylon fiber, bits of plaster or bisque. Let the water settle overnight, then drain the clear water or siphon into a bucket kept for the purpose, then dispose of the grunge.

While on the subject of water, a toilet is nice to have, as trips to a distant loo can be a major mud-tracking experience. Toilets are pretty cheap bought at demolitions, salvage companies, or as slightly damaged from plumbing suppliers. If the needed drains are not in place, the project becomes too costly. Consider a chemical toilet, available from camping and mobile-home suppliers. A thrift-shop shower curtain provides privacy should a real partition prove a hassle. Water cost: sink, $10; buckets, $4; toilet, either type, $50; plywood for partition, $25; wood to support sink, $5; shower curtain, $2.

Kiln

The kiln is the biggest expense in setting up a studio. Some consideration should be given to renting kiln space at first; that's a particularly good choice for those who are likely to move within a few years, or who are not certain they really are serious about clay.

People who do hobby ceramics are not held in high esteem by potters, but they fire regularly and very carefully. While their usual firing temperatures are very low, their kilns will go higher, and some might agree to fire your work to the cone you need. Other potters, schools and recreational centers may offer firing space for a fee as well.

This article allows $700 for a kiln; $600 buys a ±3.5-cubic-foot electric kiln. Dealers often offer specials and if one watches *Ceramics Monthly* ads, one can do a bit better. The extra $100 is for transportation.

British authors Robert Fournier and Emmanuel Cooper both speak of building one's own electric kiln. I suspect things are different in Great Britain, where both live, because every time I've priced out such a project, it would have cost me more. If you have access to materials at a reduced price, building is perfectly feasible.

As to which kiln to buy: buy the nearest national brand. Shipping costs are so humongous you may be able to go one size bigger just by picking up the kiln yourself. Also, while a well-treated kiln is very durable, parts do wear out, and service from a nearby dealer saves you money in the long run.

More about electric kilns: Fuel burners dominated the U.S. pottery landscape for more than a quarter century in an interesting symbiosis of economy and aesthetics. Was it coincidental that with the de-regulation of gas and the rise in oil prices, electric kiln firing "suddenly" took the lead? Regardless of vogues and costs, electric kilns always have had their advocates, who appreciated both the results achieved and the ease with which they can be operated. Any responsible person who can read a watch and the settings on a switch can fire an electric kiln. To the best of my knowledge, nowhere do electric kilns require special permits.

An electric kiln is best located close to where the electricity enters the building. This means, essentially, near the fuse box or circuit breakers. Not only does this save on the costly lines needed from circuit breaker to kiln, but it reduces wasteful voltage drop (which lengthens firing time and raises costs).

Gas and other fuel burners can be built quite economically. It is hard work, and the advice of someone with experience is a boon. The problem with fuel-burners today isn't construction, but the time-consuming, unpredictable hassles one can encounter with "regulators"— zoning boards, fire and building inspectors, and insurance companies. Consider what regulations may be around five years from now. Some communities are now banning wood stoves. The problems of fuel-burning kilns go well beyond the usual caveat emptor.

With this said, fuel-burning kilns can be built very big, altered as necessary, and are low in maintenance costs. Many excellent plans exist; once size has been decided on, several similar plans should be priced out. The more material can be had locally, the more can be bought secondhand (angle iron, chain, brick), the cheaper the project will be. Plans for burners also are available; they, too, can be purchased secondhand.

One last word about kilns: the size must relate to production, as well as to work cycle. If there is room for only 3 cubic feet of ware in the shop, a 30-cubic-foot kiln is inappropriate. A 4- or 5-cubic-foot kiln would be okay, as pots can be stacked when dry or bisqued.

Everything Else

Before proceeding, I want to make something perfectly clear. I am devoted to recycling, reclaiming, reusing, adapting, salvaging, etc., because I abhor the wastefulness that is filling our landscape. I am as vehemently opposed to any form of theft. So whenever I suggest scrap materials from construction sites, I take it for granted that the person in charge has been asked and permission received. If that sounds formidable, I hasten to add that in a lifetime of scrounging, I have always met with generosity, which I have tried to reciprocate through gifts of mugs or cereal bowls.

Most studio equipment can be built from salvaged materials. Construction crews discard pieces of plywood (of the outdoor type you want) that are smaller than 4×4 feet. They also discard boards with knots or cracks, and 2×4s that are bowed or less than 3 feet long. Demolition crews keep only the good wood, tossing the rest into dumpsters. Cable TV companies and utilities discard cable spools that are defective. Plumbing contractors have old pipe, as do people who build and rent scaffolding.

Whether you hunt the city streets the night before the trash is picked up or attend farm auctions, you'll find the world full of excellent used tools and equipment. As the Canadian potter, Eric Ciup, likes to point out, very little actually is made just for us potters. Most of what we use is made for much larger industries, which is why we can find bargains as well as freebies at factories, garages, boatyards.

I am asked pretty regularly if all this scrounging is worthwhile. It depends on your circumstances. If you can earn the money to buy a wheel or worktable in less time than you need to scout out freebies to build one, do it. If you have plenty of time and no money, scrounge. As with renting-not-buying a kiln: the less you have invested, the less you lose if you move.

The Wheel

Hints about wheels: A wheel is a disk on a shaft; same idea as a lathe or car wheel, except there the shaft is horizontal and the disk vertical. But any such contraption could be adapted. A wheel must run steadily and smoothly. It must be in harmony with its propulsion. If the motor that turns the wheel is too strong, you could break your arm; if it is too weak, you cannot throw very big. (Gearing down most likely is needed.) A kick wheel must have a flywheel that is heavy enough to run a long time and light enough to be kicked without injuring one's knee.

Different automotive assemblies that include a shaft and bearings can be adapted for use in a potter's wheel. Several books (available at libraries) have excellent plans; you should study these before making your decision—which should be guided by materials on hand.

Whatever construction surrounds the wheel must be strong and stable. Either might make cleanup difficult. A wheel that skedaddles across the floor is a nuisance; nevertheless, before getting into an engineering frenzy, just remember a wheel need be no more than a disk crosscut from a tree trunk, centered on a straight, pointed stick, set in a cup of some sort in a hole in the ground.

Slab Roller

Slab rollers are space-eaters; a 30-inch piece of white plastic pipe, filled with shot, ball bearings or pebbles, and sealed at the ends with cork and duct-tape, does an excellent job.

In *Getting into Pots,* George and Nancy Wettlaufer include a slab-roller plan that, using second-hand materials, should cost very little; with new materials, probably about $100.

Very few potters need both a wheel and a slab roller. In the beginning, you may have to decide between them.

Wedging Table

The wedging table is *the* project to build out of scrap materials! If plywood or chipboard is used, some tape or molding should be put around the top edges, as those splinter "forever." Very solid legs (4×4s) should be bolted to a wooden box. This can be designed to hold several pugs of clay, adding weight to the table, or to be filled with cement or plaster, which makes the table cumbersome to move.

The wedging table can be replaced by a wedging board. A piece of plywood or chipboard is covered with canvas and placed on the floor. One kneels on it to wedge, protecting one's knees from the edge with a pad of burlap or a piece of foam rubber. Kneeling to wedge is easy on the back, as the distance from shoulder to wedging board is bound to be correct, and the thigh muscles help with the work.

Worktables

As a student of Frans Wildenhain, I "grew up" with knee-high worktables. When one sits, they allow one to work with the arms extended; when one stands, they allow one to look over spread-out tiles, plates, etc. For such tables, pallets cut in two are the perfect support. My best one is made of two halved pallets, topped by a "found" door.

Pallets are square, slatted platforms on which everything moved by forklift is shipped. Since no one wants to risk expensive merchandise by using bad pallets, these are thrown out at the slightest sign of damage. Pallets are hardwood and nailed together for keeps, but they can be sawed quite easily. Discarded pallet cost: $0.

The plastic pallets used by bakeries for deliveries are also thrown out when slightly damaged. Covered with newspaper for a wicking effect, they make excellent surfaces for drying large pots.

Tools

Trimming and modeling tools can be made very easily from steel strapping, such as that found in the junk pile at lumberyards and garden nurseries, as well as all over our streets. Used hacksaw, bandsaw and saber-saw blades, and Surform® blades too worn for woodworkers are all free for the asking and make perfect clayworking tools. So does the recoil spring on the electric cord of a vacuum cleaner.

Ribs can be made from any hardwood or from bamboo, not to mention old credit cards. Plastic lids can also be cut to proper shape.

Old fishing spoons and really chintzy metal spoons hammered flat, wooden spoons and spatulas from garage sales—all make wonderful tools.

The best cut-off wire I've found is uncoated leader wire purchased from a tackle shop for $4.

No matter what, brushes are costly. Reassured when I read that the great Lucie Rie used an ordinary household paintbrush to apply glaze, I have been using Chinese pig-bristle brushes bought at paint- or kitchen-supply houses. For more elaborate decorating, I use regular Chinese brushes bought at sales, or in Asian neighborhoods. Cost of brushes: $25 should get you going, but the sky is the limit.

Glaze

For many potters, mixing one's own glazes from raw materials is an intrinsic part of the process. For as many others, it is a tangential, nonessential skill. While the high-volume production potter may find glaze mixing economically worthwhile, the studio potter who makes few, very elaborate pieces may appreciate the ease and security of commercial glazes. Stick to commercial glazes if you do not have the space to store the raw materials safely or you do not know how to "fix" glaze problems, such as crazing.

If you wish to mix your own glazes, you will need to buy a scale. The usual balance-beam scale used by potters costs over $100 (look for seasonal sales) and is necessary to do glaze testing. Tests are made in small quantities (usually 100-gram batches) and most kitchen scales will not measure less than 1 gram. If you only want to mix up large batches of glazes you know about, then a kitchen scale can be had for $25.

There are also excellent recipes for glazes mixed by volume. For those, a set of kitchen measuring cups and spoons will do.

Raw materials: ±$2 average for 1-pound lots; less per pound as quantity increases; be sure to estimate shipping costs. Commercial glaze: averages $2.50 per pound dry; less as quantity increases.

One last piece of advice: Don't overinvest. If, regardless of what you have in the bank, you start with a $1200 studio, you give yourself a lot more breathing space. Fancy equipment neither guarantees better pots, nor better sales. Fancy equipment also is costlier to maintain than homebuilt.

If several friends get together to form a group studio, make sure the arrangement is truly businesslike. Countless variations are possible—the important part is that the studio can be dissolved, or one person leave/join, without ruination or bitter feelings. Settle everything ahead of time, preferably on paper, with a lawyer.

Don't buy anything in the hope of recouping costs later. While you can usually get most of your money back out of slab rollers, pug mills and electric wheels, a lot depends on where you live. A friend who had to move lost a bundle; she was in a large city where secondhand pottery equipment was plentiful. Kilns are risky secondhand—buying or selling. I would buy a second-hand electric kiln only from a trusted friend or for so little that, should all the elements and all the switches go at the first firing, I'd be "covered."

Finally, if you plan to support yourself with potting, take a few small-business courses. Over the years, I've seen many successful potters go under, even though they had everything going for them. Nothing can guarantee ongoing success, but failure is underwritten by an unprofessional approach. Business courses can teach you how to grow and expand at a proper rate; how to make decisions (Do I buy more equipment? Do I hire people?) that success foists upon you. Luck is part of it—so is hard work. But knowing how to handle business problems probably is the deciding factor in a potter's survival. ▲

William Shinn extruding a fluted/ribbed tube to be altered.

"Cantata," 14 inches (36 centimeters) in height, stoneware extrusion, carved when leather hard, fired to Cone 10.

"Brisighella Babe," 18 inches (46 centimeters) in height, extruded white stoneware on thrown base, fired to Cone 10.

The Versatile Extruder

by William Shinn

In the field of studio ceramics, the extruder generally has been thought of as a mechanical device for creating simple tubular shapes or for squeezing out straps of clay for handles. Few ceramists have really taken advantage of the extruder's ability to create original forms and, after the initial excitement of squeezing out round and square pots wears thin, often have relegated it to an out-of-the-way corner of the studio or classroom. That's too bad. With a little experimentation, they should be able to extrude a wide variety of shapes.

Shortly after retiring from teaching, I purchased a small extruder, and started experimenting with wooden dies (for me, wood was the easiest material to work with). Immediately, a new, uncharted world of ceramics was revealed. At first, simple slots were cut out of a standard round form, producing finlike protrusions on the extruded tube. This form offered so many possibilities for carving, piercing, stamping, etc., I finally had to graduate to a larger extruder, as the dies became increasingly complex.

For one series of "fin" forms, I bent the tube as it was extruded. After the extrusion was cut away, the top was pinched and paddled together to form the base. No further clay was added. When leather hard, the fins were carved extensively.

Altering shapes as they were being extruded became a two-person operation, so I finally acquired a power-driven system. Aside from solving all my handling problems, the power-drive extruder afforded phenomenal savings of energy. This was apparent after my first day-long workshop utilizing the device.

"Viking Vessels," 22 inches (56 centimeters) in length, extruded hulls, with handbuilt and press-molded additions, glazed and fired to Cone 10.

"Tourbillon Carré," 10 inches (25 centimeters) in height, extruded stoneware, center piece thrown and altered, fired to Cone 10.

Some more complex dies produce shapes that are easily altered by compressing and expanding. A metal rib attached to a stick makes a handy tool to accomplish this. Wheel-thrown, press-molded and slab-built elements can also be added.

One project was suggested by interconnecting sidewalk bricks as seen in some European countries. The challenge was in designing a die shape that would produce forms that fit one another when turned 90°. Four together would then form an interlocking shape. This has great creative potential and might be a good assignment for an advanced student. However, while the project presents interesting technical problems, the real satisfaction for me was in the discovery of new sculptural forms.

The extruder is an ideal tool for sculpture—both abstract and representational—and is particularly handy for work requiring modular elements. Dies created specifically for this purpose can produce work that can be easily bent, twisted and joined together. When the work is sliced with a wire at an angle, exciting results are sometimes revealed. The ability to quickly extrude a number of pieces in a short amount of time also encourages experimentation.

As with all claywork, timing of the various production steps is extremely important. Immediately after extruding, the clay can be easily rolled and twisted. Later, when the clay has become leather hard, designs can be carved or walls pierced.

The creation of certain representational forms is ideally suited for an extruder as well. Boats, for example, are easily made by the process. While a submarine shape was not much of a challenge, a sailing ship was much more difficult. A die patterned after the cross section of a Viking vessel produced a shape that could be easily pinched into the familiar upturned bow and stern. Filed grooves in the die produced the overlapped planking. After the firing, I was surprised to find that the piece floated.

Another more practical use of the extruder to the production potter is the making of rims for free-form-platter hump molds. Freshly extruded, the strip of clay can be bent and cut into a variety of shapes. After bisque firing, the pieces are reassembled and glued to a flat surface, and the cavity filled with plaster.

The extruded cylinder is then easily expanded, compressed or trimmed to any shape desired.

A stick with a metal rib attached to the end is ideal for shaping and refining from the inside of a tall extrusion.

Extruded ridges can be shaped to form the edge of a hump mold. After a bisque firing, they will be glued into position, and the space filled with plaster to complete the mold.

"Four-Piece XTR Vessel," 6 inches (15 centimeters) square, extruded white stoneware, with slab base.

"L'Envolé III," 22 inches (56 centimeters) in height, extruded, split and altered white stoneware, glazed and fired to Cone 10.

The extruder can also be a valuable aid in wheel throwing—particularly in creating tall forms. Centering and lifting a large amount of clay on a wheel requires a great deal of skill and effort. The extruder can quickly and easily produce the initial tall cylinder. After the extrusion is cut free, it is simply carried to a wheel and centered for shaping into any desired form, e.g. bowl, bottle, etc. Thrown forms 20 inches in height or more are easily achievable utilizing this technique.

The first-time use of a new die often produces serendipitous results. The uneven distribution of clay in the first extrusion will often twist and tear into interesting shapes before finally combining into a straight form. With ingenuity, it is possible to salvage such pieces and combine them for sculptural forms as well as pots. It is even possible to encourage such aesthetic "disasters" by purposely splitting the form at the beginning of the process. This is accomplished by fastening a wire or monofilament across the base of the die and removing it halfway through the process. The extrusion is then left hanging to become leather hard overnight. I am occasionally greeted next morning by a clump of clay on the floor (this seems to occur only on the more successful pieces). Be sure to look carefully before discarding any "accidents," though. On one such occasion, I worked an accident into a sculpture that won an award.

There are no doubt many other possibilities for this versatile tool; in addition to vessel and sculpture forms, extrusions could be used to produce lamps, fountain modules and musical instruments, to name just a few. I recommend everyone approach extruding with fresh eyes. You will not be disappointed. ▲

An Environmentally Safe Spray Booth

by Bill Campbell

No one wants to pollute the environment with glaze overspray, but most spray booths designed to catch airborne particles leave something to be desired. One solution is an environmentally friendly booth that uses ordinary tap water to "scrub" exhaust air.

This scrubbing action is quite simple. Water from a reservoir at the bottom of the booth is pumped by a submersible pump (A) through a 1¼-inch-diameter plastic pipe (running up the exterior of the booth) into another 1¼-inch-diameter pipe (B)-horizontally mounted through the walls on either side of the booth and along the top of a sheet-metal backdrop (C). This horizontal pipe has _-inch-diameter holes drilled along its top, so that water sprays up toward a second backdrop (D) of curved sheet metal. (Any commercial roofer or metal shop should be able to do the sheet-metal work for a reasonable price.)

When glazing, some overspray simply falls through the expanded metal floor of the booth, but air drawn up and over the primary backdrop (C) must pass through water falling from the curved secondary backdrop (D) toward the primary backdrop. Any particulates that are not caught by this waterfall must then pass through water spraying from the horizontal pipe (B), then through a second waterfall directed by the bottom of the secondary backdrop toward the back of the primary backdrop. The particulate-laden water simply flows to the reservoir below.

Almost all glaze overspray is stopped by that first waterfall. At my studio in Pennsylvania, an inspector from the Department of Environmental Resources found that there weren't even enough particulates coming through this system to require a permit.

A drain at the bottom of the tank facilitates the removal of the settled glaze materials from time to time. Drained into a bucket, this scrap can be recycled (if you are spraying only one glaze) or left to dry completely for disposal. Contact your local environmental safety agency for complete information on proper disposal.

Exhaust power for the booth is provided by a tubeaxial fan-often found for less than retail wherever used industrial equipment is sold. This type of fan has an aluminum (sparkless) blade, and its motor, drive belts and ball bearings are protected from any debris moving through the air stream. A shutter over the exhaust opening in the studio wall will keep cold air from coming in when the fan is not in use. To avoid any special lighting, keep light fixtures outside the booth.

Caution: Despite the fact that virtually no glaze particles make it to the outside, you should still wear a respirator when spraying. Remember, air at the front of the booth is just entering the filtering system, and you only have one set of lungs. ▲

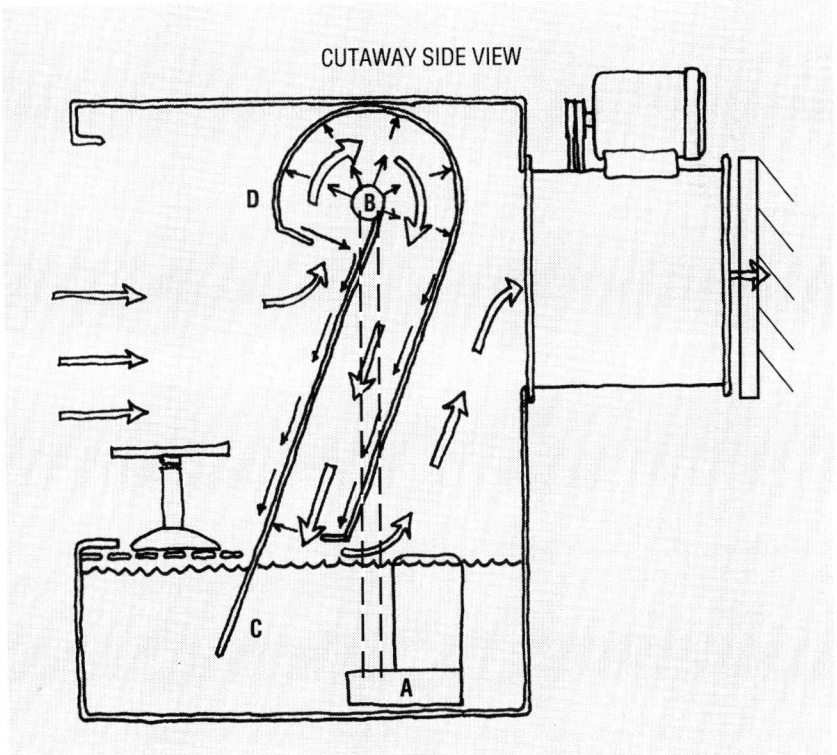

In this environmentally friendly, sheet-metal booth, glaze overspray is "scrubbed" from the exhaust air by water falling from the front edge of the curved secondary backdrop (D) toward the primary backdrop (C), by water spraying upward from pipe B and by a second waterfall at the bottom edge of backdrop D directed toward the rear of backdrop C.

A Utilitarian Booth Display

by Carol and Jim Gross

For over 20 years, we've sold ceramics at outdoor/art craft shows. During this time, our booth has evolved through several phases and we'd like to pass along the design for the "highest form" so far. Even if it doesn't suit your needs exactly, we hope there are some ideas here that you could adapt, as well as some lessons you won't need to learn the hard way.

In the "early days," we simply took two cartons full of work and a solid-color blanket to spread on the ground. Our display eventually became two cone-shaped peach baskets (packed with ware) and a stained board; the baskets were easier to carry than the cartons, and they supported the board at a comfortable height for viewing/handling by customers. The addition of hanging pots to the product line led to a display pole, initially lashed to crossed sticks.

The next generation-the first booth we designed-was composed of three 1×10-foot shelves supported by 2×2-inch uprights. Drilled holes (angled downward) in the uprights held dowel rods on which planters or wall plaques could be hung. This design lent an air of professionalism, but still had drawbacks.

We finally decided that the ideal booth should:

1. Provide for attractive display of various forms: bowls and casseroles on shelves; plaques and mirrors on vertical "walls"; and wind chimes and planters suspended from above.
2. Serve as containers in transport-like the old peach baskets.
3. Fit inside a medium-sized station wagon-booth and ware-with nothing tied onto the roof or loaded in the passenger's seat. (We had to bend this criterion a little; the poles in our final design can interfere with normal opening of the passenger's door.)
4. Require little or no hardware. (That first booth design bolted together and was always a hassle to screw and unscrew; there were even times when a critical nut was lost.)
5. Be suitable for uneven turf as well as flat concrete, and be very stable in gusty winds. (Both of these criteria were added through unfortunate experiences.)
6. Invite the viewer to "come on in and browse" among the wares. (We prefer to sit at one side or walk around the space rather than set up a counter/cashier situation.)
7. Be easy to store between shows.

What emerged from these criteria is a walk-around, pedestal-like booth. It consists of four large boxes on the bottom supporting four smaller boxes. Above these are vertical boards or pegboards. Enclosing all is an octagon of wooden rods from which hanging wares are displayed. Shelves in both the large and small boxes are adjustable.

The booth works well on level or uneven ground, requires no hardware, and can be loaded in a station wagon. The separate boxes making up the structure can hold wares on the way to the show, then nest compactly on the way home and between shows.

Though we usually use it in the pedestal-in-the-center form, the boxes, boards and linkages lend themselves to a straight-line display as well. In fact, a number of creative arrangements are possible with the "unit block" concept.

For a standard configuration, the shelf support rods and shelves are installed as the boxes are unloaded. The four large boxes are then set up with their corners touching. The small boxes span the large boxes so that the pole holes line up. Next, the poles are slid in from the top-long ones to the outside, short ones to the inside. The last steps include installing the pegboard around the four inner poles and suspending rods with S-hooks between the outer poles.

For construction, we were able to fine $\frac{7}{16}$-inch plywood in which the center of three plies was thickest. This is a good weight and provides enough hold for wood screws. If that size is not available, $\frac{3}{8}$-or $\frac{1}{2}$-inch plywood can be used. Be aware, however, that with overlap construction, the dimensions of most pieces will have to be adjusted slightly. For economy, some composite board could be used, but then it would need to be glued together, which means a closer fit is required. With respect to quality, let aesthetics and cost by your guide. We were satisfied with A-C grade.

Quarter-inch pegboard is used for the shelves and the vertical panels. Shelves could, of course, be solid Masonite. The vertical poles are closet rods, shelf supports are $\frac{1}{2}$-inch dowel rods, horizontal hanger rods are $\frac{3}{4}$-inch dowels and the small pegs they hook onto are $\frac{1}{4}$-inch dowel rods.

The vertical pegboard panels are transported and stored as a four-panel folding screen. Instead of hardware hinges,

Materials

Lumber
Three 4×8-foot sheets of $\frac{7}{16}$-inch plywood
One 4×8-foot sheet of $\frac{1}{4}$-inch tempered pegboard
One 2×4-foot sheet of $\frac{1}{4}$-inch tempered pegboard
80 lineal feet of 1-inch diameter clothes rod (eight 7-foot poles and four 6-foot poles)
11 lineal feet of $\frac{3}{4}$-inch dowel rod (four 19-inch long hanger rods and four 11$\frac{3}{4}$-inch long hanger rods)
30 lineal feet of $\frac{1}{2}$-inch dowel rod (eight 26-inch long shelf supports and eight 18-inch long shelf supports)
2$\frac{1}{2}$ feet of $\frac{1}{4}$-inch dowel rod (eight 4-inch long hanger support pegs)

Hardware
150 1$\frac{1}{2}$-inch long flathead wood screws (#5 or #6)
16 screw eyes (outer loop diameter approximately $\frac{3}{4}$ inch)
16 S-hooks (loop approximately 1 inch in diameter)
Pegboard hooks as needed

Miscellaneous
Sandpaper
Glue (optional)
Cord or rawhide thongs for pegboard hinges
Stain (and/or waterproof finish)

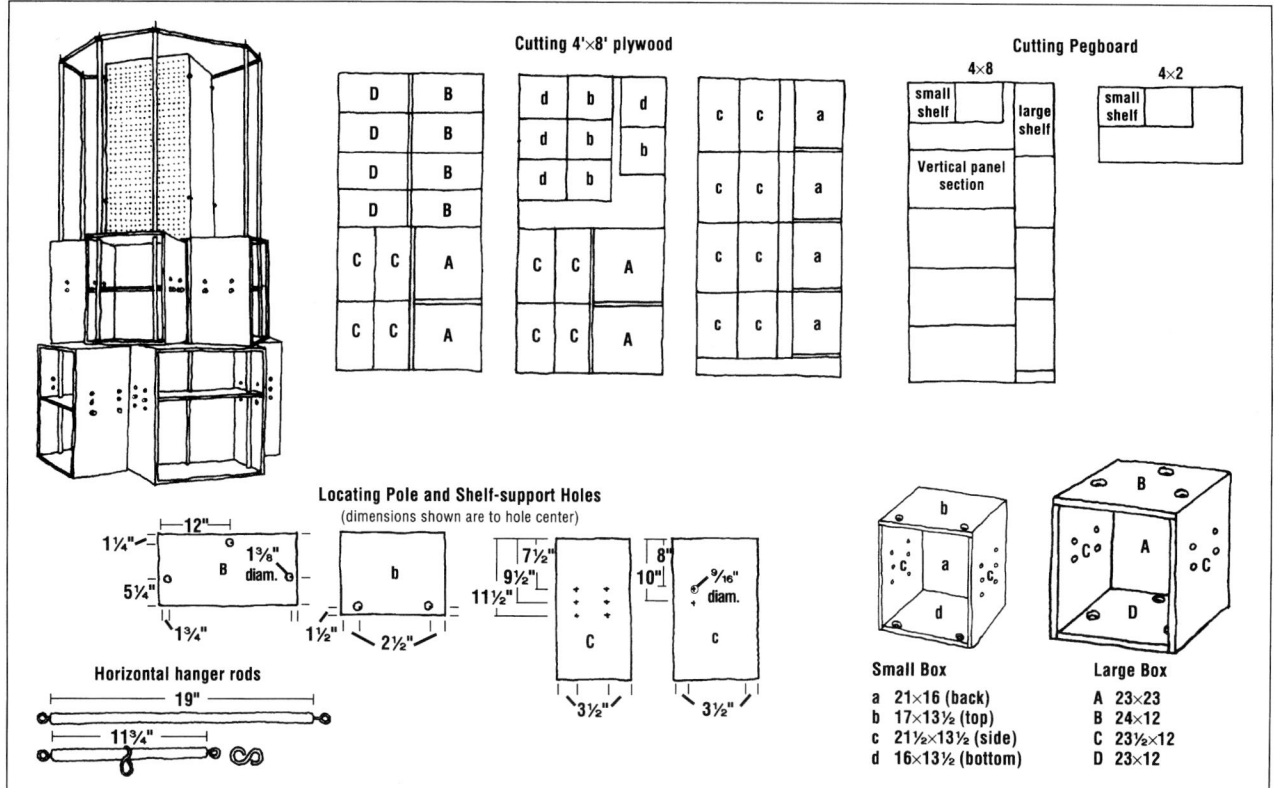

thongs are laced through and tied. When putting up the booth, the open joint is similarly tied to form the closed box.

The hardest part of the project is laying out the cutting of the plywood and pegboard to minimize waste. Before starting, it's important to note that sawing removes some material. You can't mark all the lines then cut things out. Start at one edge, measure, mark and cut. Then use the new edge as the start of the next measurement. Also, while some dimensions are fairly critical for gap-free construction, others (like shelf sizes) can be less exact. In fact, considering our fifth criterion, it is good to have some looseness to accommodate any misalignment caused by uneven surface.

Once the pieces are cut, sand the edges, then predrill holes to avoid splitting the plywood when screwing the boxes together. Since these are pretty deep holes, it is important that they be perpendicular. The top of the box will overlap both sides and the sides will overlap the bottom, while all four overlap the back panel.

Next, drill 1⅜-inch diameter holes in the tops and bottoms of the boxes for the vertical poles. You can then drill holes in the sides of the boxes for the shelf-support rods. We drilled shelf-rod holes at two positions in the small boxes and three in the large for flexibility in displaying our work.

The shelves must have holes along the edges to accommodate the vertical poles. These could be rectangular or square cutouts. But circular holes add rigidity to the whole structure and keep the shelf from tipping forward, even if the circles go off the shelf edge. The box bottom can be used as a guide to establish hole positions in the shelf.

Finally, the rods are cut to length. The clothes-rod uprights have short pegs force-fit or glued into the top end to anchor the screw eyes at the ends of the hanger rods. We used ¼-inch dowels about 4 inches long with 2 inches sticking out.

Finishing consists primarily of painting or staining the plywood. We used a fairly dark oil stain so that the boxes and poles are nearly the same color as the pegboard. If you expect long-term exposure to rain, perhaps waterproofing would be in order. While there are some interesting painted surfaces available from upscale spatter to wood graining, we decided against paint because that would scratch or chip in transporting or assembling.

As we indicated earlier, this booth can be transported inside a station wagon. The large boxes usually ride open-side up, thereby carrying wares, smaller boxes or other necessary items like a cashbox or lunch.

The only problem pieces are the poles, which have to lie alongside the passenger door; this means the passenger either climbs over top of them of slides in from the driver's side. Neither is very troublesome, and having the whole thing safe from theft and weather is a substantial plus.

The rods for hanging items often serve as rollers to help slide the large boxes forward from the tailgate, and the holes (through which the poles are inserted) are handy for hooking a finger while lifting or sliding boxes. At times, when a designated booth space is far from where we can park, we even suspend one or two boxes from a pair of poles and carry them litter-fashion.

This arrangement has worked fairly well for us. Even if it does not meet all your needs, the design may help you avoid some of the mistakes we made previously. Of course, there's still room for improvement; recently we've thought about sun and rain protection. It should be possible to support some type of covering with an X-shaped frame of 1×2s fitting over the pegs at the top of the vertical poles. There are no doubt other improvements to suit particular needs. ▲

Bamboo Tools

by Mel Malinowski

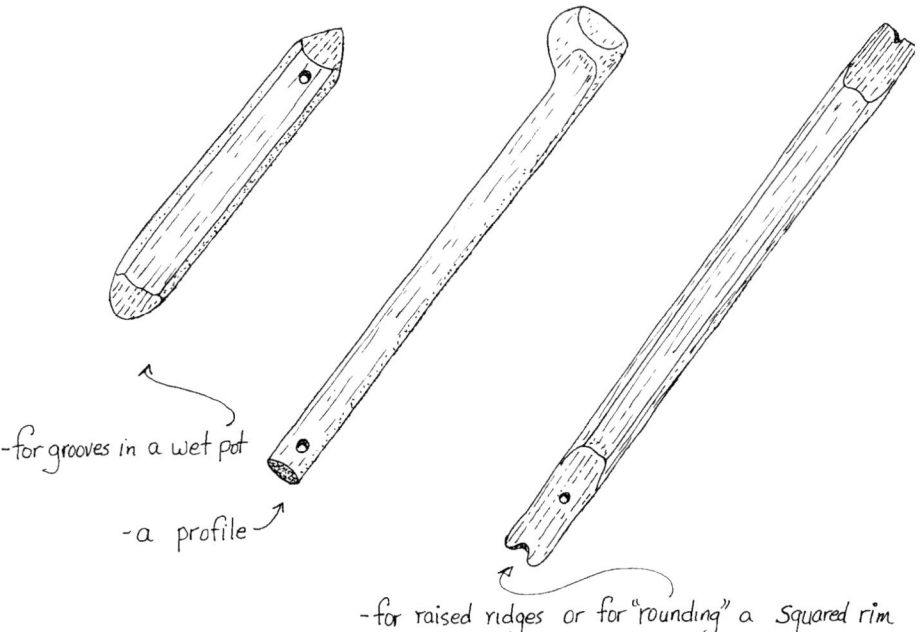

- for grooves in a wet pot
- a profile
- for raised ridges or for "rounding" a squared rim

Most potters, I suspect, are drawn to their craft because of the inherent simplicity of taking a piece of nondescript, unformed clay and making from it any one of infinite possibilities of shape and function. There is something pleasing in that those possibilities never go away, never lessen in spite of the passing of the years, or the intricacies of glaze recipes, firing schedules, kiln repairs and tax forms. Simply put, it is good to work with basic things with basic talent to make basic things.

This is increasingly true in our modern age as more and more become hands-off—at a distance, remote and too often machine-made and machine-controlled. There is a nostalgia in handmade things that causes one to want to reach back into the past for the simpler tools and the simpler ways of getting things done. It was this feeling that drew me to handmade bamboo tools.

I've always been attracted to the Japanese traditions, in pottery, philosophy and martial arts. In my studies, I often encountered the Japanese high regard and universal appeal of humble bamboo as a tool. It is used for everything from chopsticks to fans to scaffolding rivaling skyscrapers in lashed-together height. In many books and films on Japanese potters, I often saw bamboo tools being put to use. Thus, about a year ago, I thought that it was time for me to give bamboo a try myself.

There is an inherent danger in reaching back into the past for traditional ways and tools. Often, these old items,

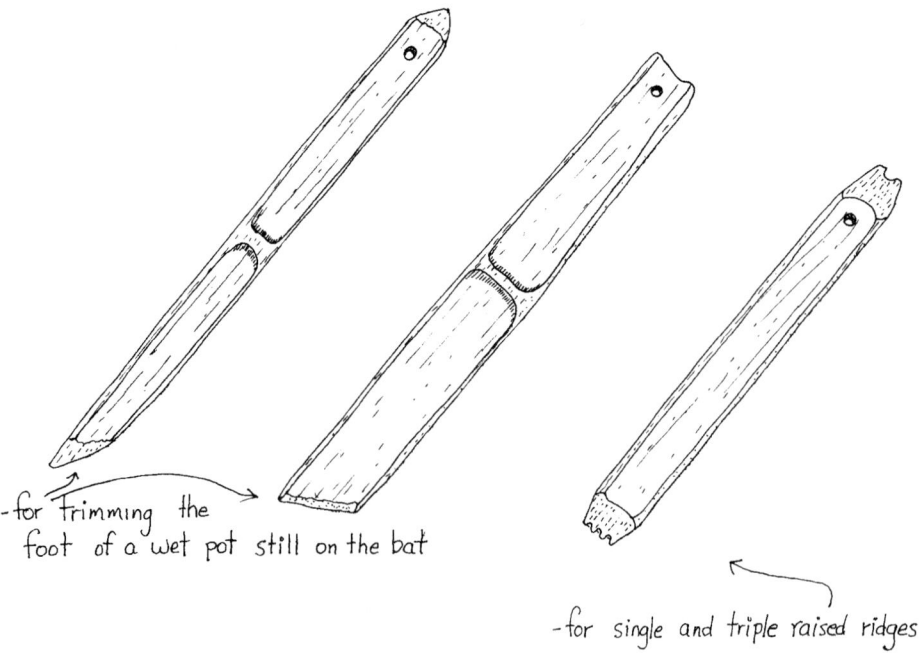

- for trimming the foot of a wet pot still on the bat
- for single and triple raised ridges

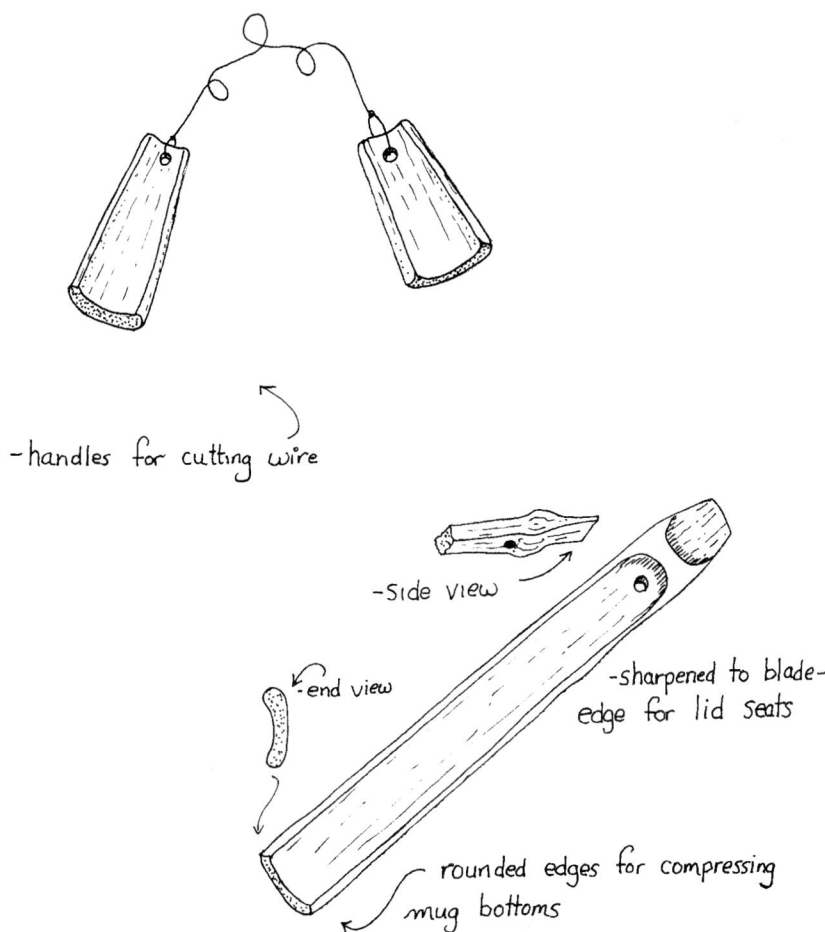

while warmly nostalgic to use, are simply not up to the standards of modern materials. In other words, there is often a very good reason for change and that reason is usually improvement or greater ease of doing things. Beethoven, you can be sure, would have used a synthesizer if he had had one. And how about Shakespeare? I am sure that he would have loved to use my computer. Still, I liked the idea of using bamboo, and gave it a try. I'll never use anything else. So far, all my basic tools have far exceeded my hopes and expectations.

Bamboo is actually a grass and, as a result has a long, running "grain" that makes for an incredibly durable and flexible material. With a sharp knife, bamboo can be readily shaped and will hold an edge that stands up to heavy usage far beyond most woods. It is also far superior to wood in terms of its water-resistant features. I have often left these tools standing in my water bucket, sometimes over holidays for weeks at a time, and they never become soft, waterlogged, cracked or warped.

One final point: Bamboo isn't as readily available as most woods. There are, however, a couple of sources you can try. For smaller tools, at least, check at a local greenhouse. You should be able to find thin bamboo in lengths of 5 to 6 feet and with a diameter of ½ inch or so. A better source, one which I have used, is your local *kendo* (Japanese fencing) teacher. Kendo practitioners use swords made of four tapered and smoothed strips of bamboo lashed together. The strips are resilient, flexible and absorb incredibly quick and hard blows that the fencers inflict upon one another. They used to use swords made from one length of solid wood. Even though they do wear armor, this practice, unfortunately, resulted in high numbers of deaths.

Due to the vigorous nature of the art, the bamboo swords, the *shinai,* can become damaged. I traded a bowl for the remains of three, and both the teacher and I came away happy.

Thus, with bamboo in hand, I fashioned the tools illustrated here. You will, no doubt, find other uses once you have tried this marvelous, traditional material yourself. ▲

Mining with the Potter in Mind

by David Hendley

In the world of clay mining, Blackjack Clay is a small operation. Forget about photographs you may have seen of clay pits encompassing dozens of acres, going down hundreds of feet. Most of Blackjack's clay pits are an acre or less in size and go no deeper than 20 feet. These deposits would be too small to be considered commercially viable to a big mining operation, but on the more human scale of hand-thrown pottery, an acre of clay is a lot of material.

Typically, Blackjack clays are dug only a few weeks of the year, then stockpiled next to the pit to weather. The wind, rain and sun help to wash away any residual soluble salts and to dry the clay so it will break down more easily into small chunks.

Just as potters using dry bagged clays from the major mining companies combine different types to create a good clay body, Blackjack works with several different clays, each with different characteristics, such as particle size, good workability and color. "Our clays are mined and processed with the potter in mind," explained owner John Morrison. "We control every step of the process, from digging the clay in our own pits to putting the de-aired pugs in plastic bags."

"The studio pottery market is a very small percentage of the business of the large clay companies," he continued. "They mine and process their clays as heat-dried, air-floated bagged clays for their larger customers. Any contaminants found naturally in clays, such as small rocks, lignite (a type of coal) and soluble salts, are all processed and bagged with the clay. Probably the most damaging part of the processing is the drying, as heating robs the clay of its natural plasticity."

Morrison started Blackjack Clay, Inc., in 1970 in the tiny East Texas town of Murchison. No, he's not a gambler; he named the company after the nearby and even smaller community where he grew up. Although his company sup-

A former clay pit is now a small pond for watering cattle. The mounds of clay dug from the pit are weathering as they await processing at Blackjack Clay.

To begin a typical 5000-pound batch, the crude clay is loaded into a crusher hopper mounted above the blunging tank.

plies clay to all the major industrial potteries in East Texas, Morrison is also interested in addressing the needs of studio potters/artists. He will sell one 25-pound bag of clay if that's all the customer needs.

All of the clays used in Blackjack's clay bodies are mined within a 20-mile radius of the clay-processing facility. Some of the sites are on privately owned land that is leased for clay rights, and some are on land owned by the company. Morrison likes to point out that he treats his sites, either leased or owned, with a deep sense of environmental commitment. "When removing earth from an area, we always have a contingency plan in place to reclaim the land," he says. "We work with the landowner to create a stock tank or a lake. We know that environmentalism is a part of expert and responsible manufacturing."

Karla Wagner, a ceramics engineer with extensive experience in clay body and glaze formulation, is responsible for quality-control testing of current production, and for designing new clay bodies. Currently, she is working on finding nearby sources for clay body additives, such as fluxes, feldspar and silica. It's not just a matter of looking for closer and therefore less expensive materials, but part of the philosophy of using local materials whenever possible. "If we can't get what we need locally, we would at least like to make an 'all-Texas' product," says Morrison.

Once all the raw material bays at the Blackjack plant are filled with clay transported from the clay pits, it takes about 24 hours to transform the crude, hard chunks into pure, smooth, ready-to-use potter's clay. First, the various clays are measured and dumped by a front-end loader into a crusher hopper mounted above the blunging tanks. A typical batch calls for about 5000 pounds of clay. The high-torque, slow-moving mixer blades of the crusher break the raw clay into fist-sized or smaller pieces, and slowly feed the batch into the water-filled blunging tank. Bagged materials, such as feldspar and 200-mesh silica, are added by hand. The batch is then blunged in excess water using high-speed, low-shear agitation until it is a smooth, creamy slurry.

Next, the slurry is cleaned by a double screening process. Impurities, such as rocks and roots, are caught in the first sieve; the slurry is then passed through a fine 60-mesh sieve to remove any remaining impurities. From there, it is sent, via 2-inch pipelines, to one of six filter presses. Using compressed air, the filter press squeezes excess water from the slurry until it is about 20% water, or plastic clay. The water dripping from the filter press looks clean enough to drink; in fact, it is recycled back to the blunging tank to mix the next batch.

The filter press room is a good place to be on a hot Texas afternoon: fans blowing across all that dripping water lower the temperature by at least 10° or 15°F. After about three hours in the press at 120 pounds-per-square-inch of pressure, plastic clay, in the form of "filter cakes," is removed. Each pressing yields 68 1-inch-thick, 30-inch-diameter filter cakes, or about 2800 pounds of throwing-consistency clay.

Much of the output is destined for the industrial potteries, so most of the filter cakes are stacked on pallets, in heavy pallet-sized plastic bags, ready for shipment. Clay for studio potters/artists is sent to the nearby pug mill room, where it is de-aired, extruded and packaged in 25-pound blocks.

There's no denying that this clay is a pleasure to work with. Any experienced potter will tell you that blunging, then removing the extra water to produce a plastic body, is the best way to make clay, as this kind of processing allows each platelet to be thoroughly wetted for maximum plasticity. The result is a clay body that's smooth and responsive, yet plastic enough to be stretched without collapsing—a clay made with the potter in mind. ▲

Once smooth and uniform, slurry from the blunging tank is pumped over a vibrating sieve to remove impurities, then into the slip tank.

After three hours under pressure in the filter press, the 40-pound "filter cakes" of plastic clay are stacked inside a heavy plastic bag on a pallet.

The Perfect Clay Body?

by Jeff Zamek

Is there a perfect clay body? No. Are some clay bodies better than others? Yes, but first I should define what is meant by the term "clay body." Today, a combination of clays, fluxes and fillers form most clay bodies. In the past, only one or two elements made up a clay body. Natural clays were simply dug from deposits, then possibly sand or another temper materials was added to the mix. With a scientific understanding of raw materials came increasingly complicated clay body compositions.

One method of understanding clay bodies is to think of the total mixture as having three basic parts-clay, flux and filler. Each serves as least one function: enhancing forming characteristics, surface texture or color, and/or reducing drying shrinkage, fired absorption rate of fired shrinkage. Many different materials can be used to fulfill these requirements. For example, if the recipe requires flux, there are many frits and feldspars that could be used. The best clay body recipe will have the correct ratios of the appropriate clays, fluxes and fillers to achieve the desired result.

Clays are grouped depending on their refractory qualities, particle size, oxide composition, loss on ignition, shrinkage rates, absorption rates and other defining characteristics. The basic clay groups found in clay body recipes are fireclays, ball clays, kaolins, stoneware clays, bentonites and earthenware clays. Within each major group are subgroups that further define a particular clay characteristic, such as plastic kaolin and nonplastic kaolin-Grolleg is a plastic kaolin while English China Clay is a nonplastic kaolin. Each group and subgroup contains many individual "brand names" of clay. For example, among the many individual brands of ball clay are Tennessee ball clay #9, Taylor ball clay, Kentucky ball clay (OM 4), Kentucky Special and Thomas ball clay.

Each group of clays (fireclays, stonewares, ball clays and earthenwares) contributes specific attributes to the clay body. Such clay qualities can be particle size, green strength, fired strength, fired color, shrinkage, plasticity, texture, forming abilities, and low amounts of warping in drying and firing.

When a particular clay is not available, a substitution can be made from the same group or subgroup. By choosing a clay within the same group, most of the clay characteristics will remain consistent. For example, in throwing bodies, Thomas ball clay can be substituted for Kentucky ball clay (OM 4). Other factors, such as degree of desired plasticity, green strength, particle size distribution, and metallic oxide content should also be considered to "fine tune" the clay body.

Fluxes help lower the melting point of heat-resistant clays and fillers in a clay body. Increasing the amount of flux also increases the glass formation with the clay body. A primary goal of a flux is to cause the clay body to melt at a predetermined maturing range. In functional pottery, the maturing range occurs when absorption, shrinkage and fired color are compatible with the glaze, producing a dense vitreous body.

For every temperature range, there are appropriate flux materials that will work correctly. Using the wrong flux can have serious consequences. If a low-melting flux is used in a high-temperature body, overfiring can result. Conversely, when a high-temperature flux is used in a low-temperature clay body, it will not melt. In such cases, the flux acts like a filler.

Moreover, the correct amount of the appropriate flux must be used. An overfluxed clay body can bloat, slump, shrink excessively and fuse to the kiln shelves. When increasing the flux component of a clay body recipe, always make test pieces and place them in a regular production kiln on top of an old kiln shelf. Be aware that firing clay and glazes in small test kilns can produce inaccurate results, because the smaller kilns have faster firing and cooling times, as compared with larger production kilns. Ceramic materials need end-point temperatures to melt, but they also need the time to reach that end-point temperature to reach maturity.

In choosing the flux for a clay body, the minimum and maximum amounts that can be used are fairly wide-2% to 3% variations will not make a significant difference. An exception occurs when frits are used, as they will shorten the maturing range of the clay drastically. Frits are a combination of oxides that have already been fired; they are fast-acting and potent fluxes. A low-fire dense clay body with 7% to 10% frit might be underfired at Cone 06 and overfired and melted at Cone 05. (All temperature references to cones in this article are based on large Orton pyrometric cones heated at 270°F per hour.) Also, some frits are slightly soluble and break down when wet, causing the moist clay body to become extremely hard or rubbery soft, depending on the particular frit used.

Talc (magnesium silicate) is a common insoluble raw material that can be used in low-fire bodies from Cone 06 (1830°F) to Cone 04 (1940°F) for several reasons: It helps reduce dry and fired shrinkage. It also reduces warping while increasing the chance of a good glaze fit. Many low-fire clay bodies are composed of 50% talc and 50% ball clay; however, high-talc bodies are not very plastic. When talc is combined with frit or nepheline syenite, the combination can cause the clay body to become vitreous at low-temperature ranges. When talc and iron are present in high-temperature bodies, a warm brown color is possible in reduction atmospheres.

In the mid- to high-temperature ranges, Cone 6 (2232°F) to Cone 10 (2381°F), feldspars are the best choice of flux in a clay body. To illustrate their melting characteristics when used alone, they melt at Cone 6 and by Cone 10 are semiopaque glasses. Soda feldspars melt at approximately 100°F lower temperatures than potash feldspars, while lithium feldspars are the most refractory. Within these three groups, many individual feldspars are suitable for a clay body formula.

The main reasons for using feldspars are their ability to go into a melt easily and slowly over a wide temperature range. The most successful functional stoneware bodies have a range of two to three cones at which they will be dense and vitreous without being overfired or underfired. Feldspars are the ideal group of fluxes to promote this situation.

Fillers reduce clay body shrinkage and warping in the drying and firing stages. Flint, silica sand, sawdust, mullite, calcined kaolin, calcined alumina and grogs of various sizes are the most widely used fillers. While flint can be called a glass former, it needs very high temperatures (3200°F) to go into a melt by itself. It is only when flint is combined with a flux that the melting temperature is decreased. As a filler, flint reduces dry shrinkage and warping in the clay body.

If the amount of filler is too high, the clay body's plastic qualities are decreased. Clay bodies designed for slab building and tile work usually have more filler or nonplastic materials than throwing bodies. Less warping and shrinkage in tile bodies are a higher priority than plasticity.

A perfect clay body is a subjective term, but the chance of obtaining this ideal mixture increases when the correct amounts and ratios of clay, flux and fillers are present. When designing a clay body, take into consideration the forming method, drying shrinkage, firing temperature, kiln atmosphere, glaze interaction, fired color, fired shrinkage and fired density.

After testing many combinations and having students try out the most promising results, I developed the following clay body:

ZAM Super Clay Body
(Cone 6-10, oxidation or reduction)

Material	Parts
Custer Feldspar	7 parts
A.P. Green Missouri Fireclay (28 mesh)	15
Cedar Heights Goldart (200 mesh)	40
Hawthorn Bond Fireclay (35 mesh)	10
Old Hickory Thomas Ball Clay	15
Sheffield Clay or Cedar Heights Redart	3
Flint (200 mesh)	10
Maryland Refractories Grog (48/f)	8
	108 parts

A good throwing body, having a wet-to-dry shrinkage rate of 6%. It fires a medium brown in reduction and to light cream in oxidation. Total fired shrinkage is 12.0% at Cone 6, and 12.5% at Cone 10. The absorption rate is 2.6% at Cone 6 and 0.5% at Cone 10.

Composing a clay body is based on theory, experience, current materials and personal choice. Listed here are the clays, fluxes and fillers, along with my reasons for choosing each material. A perfect clay body may not exist, but it does help to know what considerations are made when a recipe is developed.

Fireclay

Fireclays are the weakest part of any clay body because of poor reliability. In fact, if the clay body contains fireclay, eventually a problem can be traced to this marginal performance clay. The problems with fireclays can range from excessive and small-size silica (causing cooling cracks); high organic content, lignites or coal (causing black coring); calcium nodules (causing lime pops); and sand (causing excessive grittiness). Other impurities that have been found in fireclays are tree branches, metal bolts, paper, rocks and cigarette butts. Based on reports of poor quality control, many potters simply choose not to use any fireclay in their clay bodies.

Overall, the negative aspects of fireclay can be mitigated by spreading the risk and using two different fireclays in the recipe. Inspecting the dry clay before the mixing operation will help prevent large and obvious contaminates from entering the clay mix. Some pottery supply companies will even screen the fireclay, which is a significant step in improving the quality. The screened clay costs more but if it saves one pot, it is worth the extra price. Using fireclays should be calculated on a risk-versus-reward basis. Each potter must decide if the good qualities are worth the risk.

Why use fireclay? The coarse or large particle size makes it ideal for adding "tooth" or stand-up ability in throwing and sculpture bodies. Fireclays also lower drying and firing shrinkage, and the warping potential of a clay body. Their refractory or heat-resistant nature allows for a high-temperature clay body.

Why aren't good-quality fireclays mined and sold to potters? Economics. Potters buy less than one-tenth of a percent of all the clay mined. And the fireclays that are currently being mined already meet or exceed the major users' requirements. Such industries as steel manufacturing, casting and ceramic refractories control the market, and the quality of the fireclay. Potters and ceramics supply companies do not have the economic purchasing power to demand a better grade.

While it does appear that fireclays contribute many potential problems to the clay body, they do serve a useful function in their ability to add large particle sizes to the total mix. Some of the best clay bodies have small, medium and large clay platelet sizes. The variation in platelet sizes (large platelets in fireclays, medium platelets in stoneware clays, small platelets in ball clays) mechanically interlocks the moist clay, resulting in greater surface areas touching, which increases plasticity.

Excess fireclay can make the fired clay too porous, nonplastic and decrease the fired strength of the pots, but too little fireclay will lower the maturing range and yield a soft body with little "tooth." Clay bodies with no fireclay component often feel and throw like cream cheese. The amount of "tooth" required is a subjective decision that has to be decided by the individual potter.

Stoneware

Cedar Heights Goldart stoneware is the backbone of the recipe, as it is the major material by weight. Stoneware clays are relatively clean, medium-platelet-size clays and, as their name implies, they can be fired to stoneware temperatures (Cone 6 to Cone 10). While Goldart had high concentrations of sulfur in the past, that has been kept under control for the last 15 years.

Stoneware clays have greater plasticity than fireclays, but they are not as plastic as ball clays. As a group, they are reliable and adapt well to other clays in the recipe. Low amounts of stoneware clay will cause an unbalanced mix. Conversely, too high a stoneware percentage will detract from the qualities of the other clays in the body.

Ball Clay

While ball clays contribute plasticity to the clay body, they also increase the rate of shrinkage during the drying and firing stages. Achieving a balance of greater plasticity and minimum shrinkage must be considered when choosing the amount of ball clay for the recipe. Low amounts of ball clay will produce a "short" body that will crack easily when bent in the forming process. On the other hand, too much ball clay can lead to excessive shrinkage, and warping of the clay in the drying and firing stages.

Flint

The addition of flint (silica) to a clay body yields several benefits: It decreases warping and shrinkage in the drying stage; however, high amounts of flint can make the clay less plastic. It reacts with feldspar during the firing to augment the development of glass formation within the clay body. It also promotes a better glaze fit and decreases the chances of glaze crazing defects.

In Cone 6 to Cone 10 throwing bodies, the amount of flint should generally be kept below 14%, the exception being porcelain bodies, for which flint can be as high as 25%. While clays and other materials, such as talc, feldspars and frits, also have a silica component, the amount of silica is usually not enough to achieve optimum vitrification.

Clay bodies generally use 200-mesh flint and glaze recipes frequently call for 325-mesh flint, but either mesh size is suitable for a clay body; however, for consistent results, it's important to use the same mesh size every time the body is mixed.

Flux

Feldspar is the major flux or glass former in the clay body. If too much is incorporated, a pot can slump or attach itself to the kiln shelf during the firing. In extreme overfluxing, the clay body can achieve the "Chernobyl effect," a molten mass on the kiln floor. Overfluxing caused by excessive amounts of feldspar can also darken the fired clay color if any iron is present in the body, or cause it to bloat or become brittle.

Too little feldspar in the clay body will lower the amount of glass formation within the fired clay, which can lead to improper glaze fit and the possibility of moisture seeping through the fired clay form. One method of fixing a clay body that does not hold liquid is to tighten up the body with increased amounts of flux. Once the correct amount of flux is added, the absorption rate of the fired clay will decrease and it will hold liquids. Most stoneware functional pottery should have absorption rates of 3% or lower. A glaze should never be considered as a "sealer" or waterproof coating, as water will always seep through any small imperfection in the glaze. The only reason for using glazes on functional objects made from properly formulated stoneware are for aesthetic purposes and to provide an easily cleaned smooth surface.

Generally, potash feldspars (such as Custer or G-200) are preferred over soda feldspars (Kona F-4 and nepheline syenite) because, as a group, potash feldspars are less soluble. Over time, soda feldspars can sometimes break down in the body, causing the moist clay to become thixotropic or rubbery in the forming process. The clay can also feel soft and have a Jell-o consistency when being worked on the wheel. As water is applied to form the pot, the clay becomes very soft and loses its ability to hold a thrown curve. In time, the clay cannot support its own weight and the form usually slumps or cannot be pulled higher.

Sheffield clay is a low-temperature earthenware mined by Sheffield Pottery Supply Company in western Massachusetts. It serves more than one major function in my clay body. When a raw material can offer more than two functions, it should be strongly considered for inclusion. Besides contributing different clay platelet sizes to the mix, Sheffield clay has a high iron content, which causes a brown clay body color in reduction and a medium cream color in oxidation atmospheres. Being a low-fire clay, it also promotes fluxing action in the clay body. Cedar Heights Redart, another low-temperature clay, can be substituted for Sheffield clay.

When a darker color clay body is required, it is always better to incorporate high-iron-bearing clays rather than adding straight red iron oxide. Additions of metallic coloring oxides to the clay body for color will make the moist clay take on water very fast during the throwing process, causing the clay to become too soft. Also, metallic oxides can easily overflux the clay body, especially in reduction atmospheres. If metallic oxides are added to the clay body, they should be limited to 2% or less. A better solution is to find a metallic-oxide-bearing clay. Again, having one material cover several purposes will produce greater stability.

For color, platelet size and minor fluxing properties, small amounts of earthenware clay can be incorporated into clay bodies formulated for stoneware temperatures; however, earthenware or other low-temperature clays should not be used in amounts of more than 10% in stoneware bodies, as their fluxing action may then cause bloating, warping and excessive fired shrinkage.

Filler

Grog is manufactured from virgin deposits of alumina/silica refractory material. It is then calcined or fired to high temperature. Grog can also be manufactured from ground-up firebrick. As a rule, particle-size variation is preferred when choosing grog due to the mechanical advantage of interlocking grog sizes and shapes. Different size grog particles touch and combine, yielding a cohesive clay body. Grog also decreases dry and fired shrinkage in the clay body; however, high amounts of grog can make the moist clay less plastic.

Since the grog is already fired, for every 10% of grog added to a clay body, fired shrinkage is decreased approximately 1%. Little or no grog in the clay body decreases the amount of "tooth" when the clay is being formed on the wheel. The moist clay has difficulty standing up and will slump during throwing. In most stoneware throwing bodies, grog amounts of more than 15% negatively affect the plasticity and handling qualities. Too much grog in the clay body will produce a "gritty" moist clay that will be "short" or nonplastic.

Grog is classified by particle size. The lower the number, the larger the grog particle size. Grog 8/12 mesh size looks like small pebbles, while grog 100 mesh is a fine powder. Grog 48/f ranges from 48 mesh (about the size of beach sand) with varying smaller particles to powder size; it gives good particle size distribution to the clay body.

The Plasticity of Clay

In the past, Japanese potters used to mix and store moist clay for future generations of potters. By this process, the clay was "aged," becoming more plastic. Today, other methods are available to increase a clay body's plastic qualities. Two important factors determine the moist clay's plasticity: the ingredients and the amount of time the clay body spends in the moist state. Different clay body additives can be used to accelerate the plasticity process, but the length of time under the right conditions is still a critical factor in the development of good throwing bodies.

The unique characteristics displayed by clay/water structures contribute to the plastic qualities of moist clay. Under magnification, clay particles look like flat plates, which makes for ideal surfaces when brought into contact with water. The colloidal action of the water attracts and holds the clay platelets. A good example of this action can be shown by tearing paper into small pieces. The paper represents dry clay, which does not bond or stick together at this point. Now add just enough water to moisten both sides of each piece of paper. The pieces of paper will stick together and can even be bent or shaped.

Increasing Plasticity

The natural plasticity of clay/water structures can be enhanced by several methods. As mentioned earlier, additions of bentonite or ball clay can improve plasticity; however, bentonite should be limited to no more than 2% to avoid "gummy" clay, and ball clay should not exceed 25% to avoid excessive dry shrinkage and warping. Too much ball clay can also cause handles to crack at joints, and any thin area (such as an overtrimmed pot bottom) is likely to crack. Such drying cracks occur because of the shrinkage stress induced where a thin cross section of clay meets a thicker cross section.

Starting mold growth in the moist clay can also improve plasticity. Mold increases the binding action or attraction of the clay platelets. When mixing a 100-pound batch of clay, add to the water ½ cup beer, coffee or apple cider vinegar, or 3 ounces yeast. Any one of these agents will start mold growth.

Stoneware clay bodies seem to successfully accept wider variations of mold growth than porcelain clay bodies. Green mold seems to offer the best plastic qualities to the moist clay; black mold growth can cause problems due to its lack of blending in with the surrounding clay body. Some types of black mold can even cause voids in the moist clay. Always wedge moldy clay before beginning the forming process.

Adding 3-5 ounces Epsom salts (magnesium sulfate) per 100 pounds dry clay ingredients can increase plasticity on another level. Epsom salts will increase the attraction of clay platelets in the moist clay state, causing the clay to become flocculated. To disperse uniformly throughout the body, add Epsom salts to the water used in mixing the clay. The clay platelets are then drawn together in a manner similar to the attraction of the poles of magnets. The overall effect is a tight, plastic body with good throwing properties.

Additive A is a blend of lignosulfonates and other chemicals manufactured by Lignotech USA (Post Office Box 582, Lavonia, Georgia 30553) for use in the paper-manufacturing process. When Additive A is added in amounts up to 0.75% based on the dry weight of the clay, it can increase the moist clay's plasticity without changing its fired shrinkage, absorption or color.

Additive A is produced in several versions, some of which (types 1, 3 and 4) contain barium in a safe, nontoxic form; these can be used to eliminate the scumming common on clay bodies where soluble salts are present. When included in a clay body, it has the advantage of increasing the plastic properties of the body while not causing excessive shrinkage rates in the drying and firing stages.

Methods of Mixing

Simply mixing the dry ingredients

and adding the correct amount of water are all that is really required to achieve a plastic mass of usable clay. Hand mixing will accomplish the goal, but when larger quantities of moist clay are required, machines are labor- and time-saving necessities. The goal is simply to surround each clay platelet by a film of water. Achieving this will ensure the greatest plasticity.

Combining the use of a clay mixer and a pug mill is the most efficient method of mixing clay. Ceramics supply companies use both machines in the production of stock clay bodies as well as custom-mixed clays. The dry clay and water are blended in the clay mixer, then the moist clay is transferred to the pug mill and compressed by mechanical screw. It then goes through a chamber where the air is removed and is extruded from the pug-mill nozzle in usable condition. Clay compaction can also make for a denser fired clay body, as compacted clay platelets fuse faster and more completely during the firing than noncompacted platelets. Pug-milled bodies can run 0.25% to 0.5% less in fired absorption than the same recipe not pugged.

Hand-wedging the clay before use should increase plasticity and can help avoid potential problems caused by the pugging process. The tube or block of clay that is extruded from the pug mill can have weak spots or shear lines. Sometimes fine-particles within the moist clay body are rubbed by the pug mill auger blade and separated from coarse particles, causing two separate clay bodies. As the clay is augered through the mill, fine-particles clays are moved up against coarse-particles clays in a concentric ring pattern. When the body is extruded, there will be a seam line between the fine-particle and the coarse-particle clays. If visible, this seam will look much like the circular pattern of a sliced jelly-roll cake; however, because the extruded clay is moist and compacted, the seam might not be apparent, especially through a plastic shipping bag.

To find out if a pugged clay has such a weak area, slice 2 inches from the extruded face and place this slab in water overnight. If the clay shows "jelly-roll" cracking patterns the next day, be sure to hand wedge thoroughly, particularly before attempting to throw

One method of understanding clay bodies is to think of the total mixture as having three basic parts-clay, flux and filler. Each serves at least one function: enhancing forming characteristics, surface texture or color, or reducing drying shrinkage, fired absorption rate or fired shrinkage.

wide-based forms, such as plates. Otherwise, upon drying, the clay seam separates, causing a crack.

Another method of mixing clay requires the use of a filter press. Dry clay is mixed with excess water to form a slurry. It is then pumped into a series of absorbent bags, which are subsequently compressed to remove the excess water. The resulting "leaves" of moist clay can then go onto the pug mill for further mixing and de-airing. While filter pressing is expensive and labor intensive (and not frequently used by commercial clay-mixing operations), it produces greater plasticity than other mixing methods because each clay platelet is surrounded by water in the slurry stage.

Whatever the mixing method, the best results are obtained when the moist clay is allowed to "rest" or "age" for several days before forming begins on the wheel. After mixing operations, the moist clay is pliable and can be bent into shapes; however, each clay platelet is not thoroughly wet (with the exception of filter-press clays), resulting in a lack of plasticity. The same moist clay a few days or weeks later will have most of its platelets surrounded by water, yielding an increase in plasticity.

The Perfect Recipe

Is there a perfect body that can accomplish miracles and overcome bad technique or improper firing cycles? No. Can the Zam Super Clay Body do well in salt, soda and wood firing, as well as reduction and oxidation atmospheres? Yes. Does it throw well? I think so. It has proven itself over the years with many potters; however, anyone interested in using it should still begin with a small test batch before getting out the old mixer and making a ton.

Choosing the correct clay body is a subjective decision. If this recipe does not meet your needs, I hope it at least provides a starting point for your own research. While it is true one clay body cannot do everything, certain combinations of clay, flux and filler work well under many different conditions.

It is always a good idea to first mix up a small amount of any new clay or glaze recipe, then test fire it on an old kiln shelf to prevent any possible damage to the kiln. If the result is good, mix up a larger batch and continue to test until the new recipe has proven itself over a couple of firings.

A super clay body or glaze recipe will not lessen the time and effort involved in producing, good, honest pots. The magic recipe is in the potter, not the clay. A good potter can go into any studio, anywhere, scrape the clay off the floor and still make pots. ▲

Clay Body Absorption and Shrinkage

by Jeff Zamek

What is meant by clay body absorption and how does it affect our pots? We all know that, as clay is fired, it becomes harder and denser. We also know that clay shrinks in the drying and firing stages. What we may not realize is how these changes can impact our work.

At some point, we have all seen a vase or cup leave a watermark on a table. Body absorption indicates the amount of water that can leach through the fired clay, regardless of the glaze coating. It is false to assume a glaze will seal a clay body—that is, prevent water from penetrating and eventually moving through the clay.

A glaze has two functions: one is aesthetic in nature, and the other is to provide a smooth surface for easy cleaning. The idea that a glaze can keep water from penetrating the underlying clay body seems reasonable, as glass is often used as a container for liquids. But while the glaze may look as smooth as glass to the eye and feel solid to the touch, there can be microscopic imperfections in the surface.

If the clay body is porous, it can actually wick or draw moisture to itself. The water eventually moves through the cross section of clay, leaving moisture on any object the pot is resting on. The same action can be observed when wetting one end of a dry sponge; in time, the water moves throughout the whole sponge.

When clay bodies are fired, mechanical or "free" water is driven off during the first stages, from 100°C to 200°C (212°F to 392°F). The chemically combined water begins to leave the clay in the 450°C to 600°C (842°F to 1112°F) range. As the temperature increases, organic matter is oxidized or burned off, and the clay body begins to sinter or enter the first stages of melting. The glass phase, or vitrification, starts when the primary flux (frit or feldspar) begins to react with silica (either in the form of flint or silica tied up with other materials in the clay body; many frits and/or feldspars found in clay bodies contain silica). As the temperature increases, more silica is drawn into the flux, causing increased amounts of glass formation.

Most stoneware clay bodies have a maturity range of two or three cones; for example, Cone 6 to Cone 9. This means they will be nonabsorbent within this range. When a clay body does not reach its maturation range, it can leak, be structurally weaker and possibly cause delayed crazing in glazes.

The glass phase in a clay body is also influenced by the time it takes to fire the clay to maturity. A clay body placed in a kiln and fired to its endpoint temperature in three hours will not be as dense, hard and vitreous as the same body fired over a 12-hour period to the same temperature.

In addition to the firing cycle, the rate at which any clay body becomes vitreous also depends on several other factors, including the specific clay body components, particle size, preparation (pugged clay can result in lower absorption rates because the clay platelets are physically packed tighter, causing greater melting action than unpugged clay, which has a looser platelet arrangement) and atmosphere.

An absorbent clay body is often best described as a porous body with a high absorption rate, which means it will absorb moisture and eventually leak. It can also cause glaze crazing, due to the glaze contracting upon cooling more than the underlying clay body. In some instances, the glaze can look intact, but develops delayed crazing when exposed to moisture in the atmosphere or in normal cleaning.

A porous clay body with a high absorption rate is also not as physically strong as a dense, vitreous clay body with a lower absorption rate. With porous clay bodies, handles can easily break off cups and the lips of pots can frequently chip or crack under normal usage. Since the clay body is permeable, it is also an ideal medium for growing mold or showing penetrating stains from food or drink. For sanitary and aesthetic reasons, this condition in functional pottery is not recommended. Keep in mind, though, that low-fired porous pottery can offer many different aesthetic qualities, particularly the bright glaze colors that can be elusive at higher temperatures.

Absorption Measurement

The absorption factor of a fired clay body is expressed in percentages, as with the shrinkage rate of the clay. There is a direct relationship between increased firing temperature, causing greater glass formation within the clay, and greater amounts of clay shrinkage. Vitrification (glass formation) also causes a lower absorption rate, making the fired clay denser and more durable. However, if the clay body is overfired, the greater amount of glass formation can cause warping, bloating (voids or bubbles trapped within the fired clay body), and the eventual melting of the clay body onto the kiln shelf. If the kiln can be fired high enough, it is possible to turn any clay body into a glaze.

The greater the amount of vitrification, the lower the absorption and the higher the shrinkage. When fired to Cone 06, red earthenware averages absorption rates of 12% to 14% and shrinkage rates of 6% to 8%. When fired to Cone 9, porcelain bodies have absorption rates of 0% to 0.5% and shrinkage rates of 14% to 15%. With stoneware bodies (Cone 6 to Cone 9), absorption ranges from 0.5% to

3% and shrinkage from 11% to 13%. Stoneware bodies fall between the two extremes of earthenware and porcelain, but if properly formulated and fired, they do not shrink and warp from excessive formation of glass within the clay, and should hold liquid.

Moisture in the fired clay can come from water in the atmosphere or from cleaning. Moisture can also accumulate in clay bodies during use (i.e., when holding liquids). As stated, if a clay body contains the appropriate materials and is fired to maturity, it can have low or 0% absorption and will not subsequently leak. Neither a glaze nor any of the commercially available "sealing" materials will take the place of a dense, vitreous clay body.

Typically, absorption rates are derived from clay that is rolled into bars, placed in a kiln and fired to the recommended maturation temperature. One method involves placing the fired bars in boiling water for two hours, then removing them from the water, patting dry all sides and weighing. The following formula is used to calculate the absorption percentage of fired clay:

$$\frac{\text{Saturated weight} - \text{Dry weight}}{\text{Dry weight}} \times 100 = \text{Percent absorption}$$

Usually, several bars are used for the absorption test, with an average of the results for all bars determining the absorption percentage rate for the clay.

Another method that can be used to obtain practical information on a clay body's absorption characteristics is to make several pinchpots and place them unglazed throughout the kiln. Because many kilns do not fire evenly, placing several pots in different sections of the kiln will offer the widest range of test results. The pinchpots are then fired along with the glazed pottery. Once the pots are removed from the kiln, fill each with water and let it stand for 24 hours on a nonabsorbent surface. If there is moisture under the pots the next day, the clay is absorbing water and leaking. Among the options for correcting the problem are firing the clay to a higher temperature, firing the clay over a longer period of time, or adjusting the clay body recipe by adding more flux materials, such as feldspar or, in some cases, frit. The amount of additional flux and type of flux will depend on the firing temperature of the clay body.

Shrinkage Measurement

As soon as the moist clay is taken out of its plastic storage bag and comes into direct contact with the atmosphere, it begins to shrink. Water is drawn from the clay until it reaches the moisture content of the surrounding studio atmosphere. Some potters mistakenly believe that if they let the clay dry for months, it will be thoroughly devoid of water; however, at this point, there is still mechanical water (moisture in the studio atmosphere) and chemical water (water tied up on a molecular level within the clay) contained in the "bone dry" clay. If the clay is heated too fast, steam will develop, causing it to crack or blow up in the kiln. Clay also shrinks during the process of glass formation within the clay body as it reaches higher temperatures.

To determine the amount a clay body shrinks, mark a 10-centimeter line on the moist clay, then measure the length when the clay is thoroughly dry; the difference between the wet and the dry divided by the wet length will indicate the wet-to-dry shrinkage of the clay. Fired shrinkage is measured the same way, after the marked bar is fired to its maturity.

How to Interpret Absorption and Shrinkage Percentages

The manufacturers of prepared clay bodies publish the shrinkage and absorption percentages for the indicated firing temperature of each particular body in their catalogs. These percentages are best used as a comparison with the shrinkage and absorption rates of other clays listed in the catalog. There is no universally accepted method to determine absorption and shrinkage, and the different suppliers do use different methods; therefore, their results will vary. If ceramics supplier A uses one method for determining a clay body's absorption and ceramics supplier B uses another method, the results can be quite different for the same clay body. Also, results could vary between kilns. Remember, the published absorption and shrinkage percentages indicate only how the clay reacts when fired in the ceramics supplier's kiln. Firing in a larger kiln and at a slower rate of temperature climb could cause more melting and a lower absorption rate. The moist clay test bar could also have a different percentage of water than premixed clay, which could result in an increase or a decrease in the shrinkage rate.

It is best to use the ceramics supplier's published figures as "ball park" estimates, with an accuracy of plus or minus 1%, when relating them to studio needs. Greater accuracy is achieved by doing your own shrinkage and absorption testing in your own production kiln(s). A small test kiln contains less thermal mass and generally will heat and cool faster than a larger production kiln, all factors that can produce an inaccurate test result.

Absorption and shrinkage characteristics of clays are often overlooked factors when we develop clay body recipes or even when we buy a premixed moist clay from a ceramics supplier. Nevertheless, to produce functional ware or weather-exposed tilework or sculpture, it is always important to know the actual absorption and shrinkage rates. When used for sculpture, a slightly porous clay body might be an advantage, in that the clay will not shrink or warp as much as clays with low-absorption rates; however, durability may become a concern, especially when the fired clay is to be placed in outdoor freeze/thaw conditions.

Clay bodies that have extremely high shrinkage rates can contain a high percentage of fine-particle clays, such as ball clays. This type of clay body can warp or crack in the drying stages. It is also possible for handles or added sections to crack where they are joined to the main body of the pot.

The most noticeable defect in high-absorption-rate clay bodies is their porous quality and inability to hold liquids. They can also be structurally weak and induce crazing in glazes.

Choosing the appropriate clay body for a particular forming technique, function (sculpture/functional pottery) and temperature range must be balanced with the clay body's shrinkage and absorption factors. ▲

KILNS

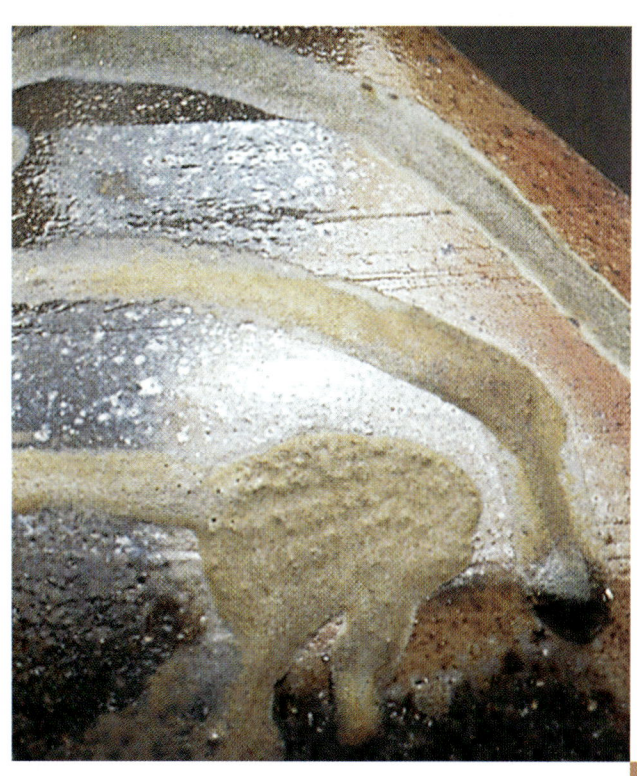

To test the effectiveness of protective coatings, a salt kiln was built from a variety of new and used refractory materials.

Salt and Refractory Coatings

by Mel Jacobson

One of the most destructive forces in firing is salt. It melts bricks, collapses arches, destroys flues and ports, and is generally a killer of kilns.

During a conversation at the 1998 NCECA (National Council on Education for the Ceramic Arts) conference, Feriz Delkic, owner of International Technical Ceramics, assured me that his "products will resist the effects of salt corrosion in a kiln." I was skeptical.

After several days of discussion, he came up with the idea of building a kiln at my farm in Wisconsin to test the effects of salt on ITC refractory coatings. But it seemed to me that the only fair test would entail the sharing of expenses, so I would not feel obligated in any way to give answers that were not proven. Feriz agreed and said he would supply several small fiber modules, some scrap fiber materials and the coatings. I would supply a variety of brick, steel support, shelves and posts, a new stack with thermal liners and a shelter to house the kiln.

Feriz asked for "design" rights, to which I agreed, as long as we used the Nils Lou double-venturi downdraft system and propane burners. I also wanted my long-time friend, potter/educator Kurt Wild, to be brought into the project.

Originally, we wanted a kiln that would be a changeable updraft/downdraft combined in one kiln. That became a venting nightmare for us and was disregarded. The idea still has merit, as an updraft kiln will generally fire faster than a downdraft, but speed was not our most pressing issue.

One of Feriz's most emphatic requests was based on the theory that a kiln must breathe air on all sides; in his words, "Do not build it on a solid concrete or block base."

This was a challenge, and the final solution was to build a loose concrete block base with expanded metal on top of the block, anchored with ⅛-inch steel strap. The hardbrick base leveled very well on this system. We sandwiched a course of softbrick between two layers of hardbrick.

We proceeded to build a standard flat top kiln, 36 inches square by 34 inches high (inside dimensions), with a doorway of 9×27×34 inches. The capacity of nearly 32 cubic feet is in keeping with other kilns that Kurt and I have been building—small, compact and easy to fire, with very fast turnaround time.

Laying the floor brick on expanded metal over a loose concrete block base to allow the kiln to "breathe."

The brickwork was framed with ¼×4×6-inch angle iron.

Raising the roof, a folded-fiber module.

All exposed surfaces were sprayed with ITC 100.

A cast-iron wheel at the bottom corner of the angle-iron framed fiber door helps support the weight, and facilitates opening and closing.

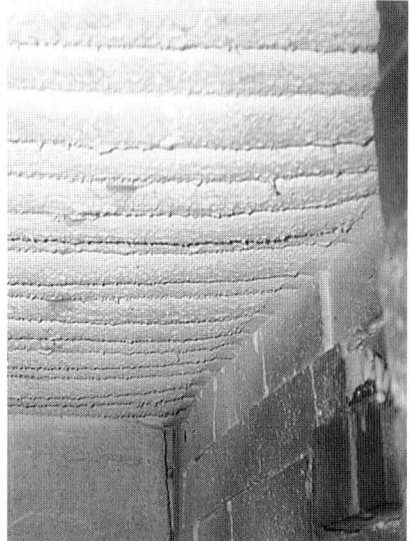

Ceiling module after six firings; the refractory coating not only provided protection from the corrosive salt, but prevented fiber fragments from becoming airborne.

Kurt wanted to use a variety of brick inside the kiln so we could see which kind did or did not fail. We had several hundred used softbrick from Thermal Ceramics, and purchased K2300 and K2600 softbrick from A. P. Green. The silicon carbide shelves were used: eight 14×16 inches and four 4×16 inches.

The roof module was 56 inches square, made of ceramic fiber folded onto itself to 10 inches thick, supported by rebar and wired together. It was very wet when delivered, and because of spring storms, did not dry, so it was another challenge to put the roof in place because of the water weight. Finally, we (six strong people with one person underneath for support) just "picked it up" one day, then simply walked it into place and set it down.

A ¼×4×6-inch angle iron frame was placed around the kiln. A similar frame was built for the door module and hinged to the kiln frame; a cast-iron wheel was also added to the lower outside corner of the door frame to help support the weight and facilitate opening and closing.

ITC 100 HT was applied to all inner surfaces of the kiln, using a sandblaster gun with about 60 pounds of constant pressure. We followed the normal procedure of cleaning and wetting all surfaces. Feriz also advised us to give extra heavy coatings to the modules.

It had been decided that the back wall of the kiln was to be laminated, so we used 1-inch fiber blanket soaked in ITC 100 HT and pounded it lightly onto the already wet wall of brick coated with ITC 100 HT. Only the hot faces of the modules were sprayed.

We also took care to spray the entire length of the stack riser sleeves with ITC 100 HT. The stack was built of two lengths of 24-gauge, galvanized 10-inch pipe, 5 feet long, joined with sheet metal

After four firings, corrosion on the flame way wall was patched with fiber soaked in refractory coating; the patch held perfectly during the next two firings.

After six firings, one salt port showed some corrosion on the lower edge.

screws. The risers were from Fire Brick Supply of St. Paul, Minnesota. The completed stack was placed on the standard flat top flue-box with its double venturi. Trowel-eze mortar was used to assemble the flue box.

Next, the kiln was fired empty to about 2000°F to dry the coating materials and set it against the brick and modules. I then sprayed the kiln inside with a second coat of ITC 100 HT, giving heavy applications to the lamination and modules. I used at least five coats on the fiber surfaces. All kiln shelves and posts were also sprayed with ITC 100 HT, and after the initial glaze firing, I sprayed the entire kiln with an even layer of ITC 296A top coat.

The first salt firing was amazingly fast; we used our Nils Lou propane burners with about 18 pounds of pressure. A 25-foot copper line from the 500-gallon tank and 20 feet of high-pressure rubber hose from the connector to the burners were used. We reached reduction temperature of 1800°F within two hours from a dead start, and Cone 9 was down in four hours. We began salting with about 15 pounds of salt and completed it in less than an hour. Cone 11 was flat over.

We cracked the door the next morning at 6 o'clock, and the results were wonderful, perfect light salt and not a reject pot in the entire load.

We unloaded at 8 AM, began reloading at 10 AM and lit the kiln again at 11:30 AM. The second load fired in less than five hours.

We continued this schedule for six straight days. On the fourth firing, we noticed some melting of brick in the flame way wall. I decided to make a patch in the area with ITC 200 EZ fill material and ITC 100 HT, laminating a 4-inch by 12-inch piece of rigid ¼-inch fiber soaked with ITC 100 HT. The patch held perfectly and this hot spot did not recur during the final two firings.

The fourth, fifth and sixth firings were almost identical, with heavy salt buildup on the pots. We were more than pleased with the results. There were no rejects from the hundreds of pots that were fired, and the kiln fired to near perfection, in record time, with an amazing 50% savings in fuel.

Our old salt kiln fired in about 7 hours, with the same burners and pressure, and was about 40% smaller. The K2500 bricks in it started to deteriorate badly on the first firing, and were unusable after only 30 firings—the inner layer of bricks had mostly melted, with some turning to dust.

Kurt and I insisted on firing the new kiln fast, wide open, with heavy salting—throwing in a mixture of three quarters rock and a quarter table salt. In the final analysis, the kiln held up amazingly well—in fact, far beyond what we expected. There was no damage to the modules or the lamination; however, there was some small melting at the fire port walls, which were later patched. One salt port had some brick melting on the lower edge, and we lost the face of one brick in the doorway. The kiln shelves did not gather salt where they were sprayed with ITC 100 HT ("smart pills" just fell off) and did not need cleaning between firings; no posts stuck to shelves.

Six firings gave us a great deal of information, but 60 more will give us an answer. I am sure that heavy salting will ultimately break down this kiln, but the ITC products have slowed this process considerably.

Wheel-thrown stoneware bowl, 7 inches in height, mixed glazes with heavy salt, by Tara Simpson, Minneapolis; fired in a test kiln protected by refractory coatings.

Small stoneware vase, 5 inches in height, glazed and salt glazed, by Kurt Wild, River Falls, Wisconsin.

Salt-glazed tumbler, 6 inches in height, underglaze brushwork, by David Hendley, Rusk, Texas.

Materials and Costs

Altogether, the kiln used nearly 800 bricks. We estimated used insulating firebrick (IFB) at $1 each. New IFBs were about $4 each (three cases of 24 were $290). The hardbrick were worth about $0.50 each.

Floor: 3 courses (2 hardbrick, 1 soft) = 216 bricks

Three walls: 14 courses × 34 = 476 hardbrick

Flue box: 96 hardbrick

Riser sleeves: $83

Galvanized stove pipe: $30

Shelves (used): $400

Posts (new and used): $150

Metal and welding (we did our own): $300

Fiber modules: $1000 each ($100 per square foot, plus shipping)

ITC spray: $450 (3 gallons at $150 per gallon)

Pole building: $1200 (includes slab)

Strontium-green-glazed teapot, 10 inches in height, salt glazed, with handmade handle, by Dannon Rhudy, Paris, Texas.

Teabowl, 4 inches in height, wheel-thrown stoneware, with Shino and orange glazes, salt glazed, by Mel Jacobson, Minnetonka, Minnesota.

I have since sprayed refractory coatings on six kilns that I own, including a small electric kiln that is 35 years old. In all cases, I have experienced fuel savings, faster firings and better pots. None of the coatings have spalled off the kilns. Additionally, ITC 100 HT stabilizes the surface of fiber and does not allow the small fragments to be airborne. This attribute alone makes fiber kilns stronger and safer to use.

Without question, we have built a good kiln, but it was not a bargain kiln; in fact, it was expensive, but well worth it. Kurt and I feel that this kiln will serve us well for many years to come. ▲

Teapot, 7 inches in height, with thin Shino glaze, salt glazed, by Doug Gray, Florence, South Carolina.

ITC-coated kiln 2003

We have fired the salt kiln coated with ITC products now nearly 70 times. We have had small failures in the coating, but each is very repairable. Usually scraping the corroded spot out and painting ITC 100 on the damaged area.

The roof and door fiber is in perfect condition. The back wall with the soaked in ITC 100 has come loose, but we see that we did not install it the right way. It still works. It should be installed with 12 inch squares of tile, soaked in ITC 100 and pressed into the brick face. Overlap the tiles and make sure they are tight together.

If we were to build this kiln again we would:
- Use hard brick in the flame way and the first three rows of brick.
- Dip the entire K23 brick in ITC 100. We discovered that the salt gets behind the brick face and corrodes from the inside out.
- Make sure the stack is well coated with ITC 213 metal coating and Kaowool sleeve liners soaked in ITC 100. Stacks take a very big beating with salt.

All in all, this kiln has performed very well. We know that if we would have built this from hard brick or insulated fire brick the kiln would be ready for destruction. We anticipate at least a hundred more firings. Then we will repair and keep firing it.

Insulating Existing Kilns

by Regis C. Brodie

There is a simple method of upgrading and improving the thermal efficiency of an existing kiln, which only requires mortaring a ceramic-fiber insulating material to the hot or interior face of the kiln's brick wall. By doing this you can reduce fuel consumption by 8 to 30 percent, depending on the thickness of the fiber you choose. But you will not only realize a reduction in fuel costs by "veneering" your kiln in this manner, you will also extend the life of your kiln, improve its insulating quality, shorten your firing cycle (stores less heat), improve its thermal-shock resistance, and enhance temperature uniformity.

The modular method uses ready-made fiber modules, which are made by cutting ceramic-fiber blankets into strips and then stacking the strips one on top of the other. A gauze netting is used to hold the strips together into a module-12×12 inches are standard. The width of the strips-usually 2 to 12 inches-and determines the thickness of the module. Nearly all the ceramic-fiber companies manufacture a variety of veneering modules, with different densities and temperature ratings.

Another type of module, manufactured by the Unifrax Corporation, formerly known as the Carborundum Company, for cone 9 and 10 applications, is the folded module. Cutting strips of fiber blanket, folding the strips, and stacking the folded strips one on top of the other, form these. A 3-inch module would be made up of eight strips 1×6×12 inches. When the 6-inch strips are folded and compressed (16 to 12-inch), they make a 3-inch thick 12×12 inch module. The folded modules are manufactured and sold in this assembled form and are available in a variety of thicknesses, from 3 to 12 inches. The modules are adhered to the wall by the use of a high-temperature, air-setting mortar.

The following companies manufacture 12×12 inch ceramic-fiber modules that may be used to insulate an existing kiln.

- Thermal Ceramics, formerly Babcock & Wilcox Company, Cerachem® Veneering Modules, 8-pound density, 2 inches thick. Standard sizes available 2, 3, and 4 inches.
- Unifrax Corporation: Fiberwall® Bonded-26 Modules, 9.3 pound density, 3 inches thick. This is the smallest thickness listed but indicated that a 2-inch module could be provided.
- Vesuvius USA Corp, formerly Premier Refractories Inc., Cer-wool® HTZ 2600. Veneering Module 4 inches thick. This is the smallest thickness available.

1. The interior of the Big Mama kiln prior to insulation.

2. To remove the unwanted kiln wash, the walls are sanded with a 7" disc sander equipped with a tungsten-carbide disc (24 grit). This process generates irritating dust and therefore proper protective clothing and equipment must be worn. CAUTION: This picture was taken in 1982. Since then, more and recent studies have found that a much higher standard of safety must be employed when working with and around airborne ceramic dust and fiber particles. (See the last paragraph of this article).

3. The mortar (the consistency of thick pancake batter), the plywood fiber holder, and two metal tools are used to trowel on the mortar. Each wall module requires 2 to 3 lbs. of mortar for proper adhering; each roof module requires 3 to 4 lbs. of mortar. Moisten the brick wall just before applying the mortar, to prevent the mortar from drying prematurely.

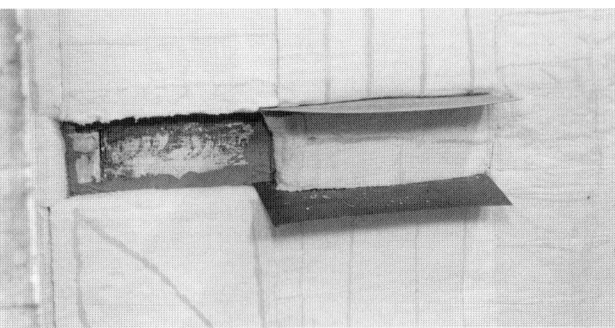

4. The veneer modules are applied to the back wall in a parquet pattern. To piece in a small section, two thin Formica sheets may be used; sheet metal will also work.

5. Burner-block holes are cut into the modules after the fiber has set overnight.

6. After the front and back wall are veneered, the sidewalls may be covered. The sidewall modules are all applied in one direction, rather than in a parquet pattern, which turns out to be the best orientation because it leaves fewer and smaller gaps.

I recommend a 2-inch thickness of insulation having a density of 8 pounds per cubic foot. This is suitable for temperatures over 2250°F and up to 2400°F. You should keep in mind that the lining, once installed, will cut down on the amount of interior kiln space-3 inches would increase your fuel savings, but it would also decrease your stacking space. Two inches seems to be a reasonable compromise, unless you have a large kiln and would not miss the lost stacking space. The modules are available in different thicknesses, but 2 inches is what I recommend.

Several financial considerations should be made before you decide to veneer your kiln. First get an estimate of the cost of materials. Labor is not a factor, as it is very easy to do. Second, consider the potential fuel savings you can obtain by using modular linings. The 2-inch edge-stacked Kaowool ST Modules reduced fuel consumption by 19.6%.

Cost Analysis of Insulating
(Using today's products and costs)

Skidmore College's Big Mama car kiln has 27 cubic feet of stacking space. The cost for installing 2 inches of Cerachem® Veneering Modules was:

50 Modules
@ $20.01 each $1000.50
6 square feet Cerachem® blanket
@ $8.37 per sq ft) $50.22
150 pounds K-Bond Mortar®
@ $38.50 per 50 lb) $115.50
Total $1,166.22

The cost of firing Big Mama to cone 9-10 before the lining was installed was $32.30 (4,600 cubic feet of natural gas). After lining, the cost was reduced by 19.6 percent, a savings of $6.33, for a total cost of $25.97 (3,700 cubic feet of gas).

The payback period using natural gas would be:

52 firings multiplied by
$6.33 = $329.16
$1,166.22 (cost of lining)
divided by $329.16 = 3.5 years

If the kiln was fired with propane to cone 9-10, the payback period would be even shorter. Before the lining was installed, the cost of firing was $82.40 ($1.60 per gallon × 51.5 gallon). After lining, the cost of firing was reduced by 19.6 percent to $66.25, a savings of $16.15.

52 firings multiplied by $16.15 (fuel savings) = $839.80
$1,166.22 (cost of lining) divided by $839.80 = 1.4 years

Fuel costs will continue to increase dramatically in the future, which is an even more compelling reason to insulate your existing kiln, and the payback time will be even shorter. In addition to saving fuel, you will have an improved kiln that will fire better and last longer-an excellent opportunity for energy conservation.

For the potter who cannot afford to build or buy a new kiln, insulating an existing kiln is the next best thing to do. An existing kiln that still has years of good service left, but is consuming fuel in an inefficient manner, can be made fuel efficient by insulating. Not only will you be able to reduce your fuel consumption by an additional 5 to 10 percent by accelerating your firing cycle. The low heat-storage capability of ceramic fiber makes this possible. A fiber-lined kiln will reduce fuel consumption, extend the life of the kiln, shorten firing cycles, improve thermal shock resistance and enhance temperature uniformity. With so much to gain, the studio potter can ill afford not to take advantage of this option.

CAUTION: Since 1982 when this article was originally written, more and recent studies have found that a much higher standard of safety must be employed when working with and around airborne ceramic dust and fiber particles. Ceramic fiber products can be used safely providing that the proper protective clothing and equipment are utilized. Contact the Product Stewardship Program representative of the Refractory Ceramic Fibers Coalition, RCFC, Unifrax Corporation (800-322-2293); Vesuvius USA Corp. (800-355-1100 ext. 1975) and or Thermal Ceramics Inc. (800-722-5681). Either company will provide you with a Material Safety Data Sheet (MSDS) on ceramic fiber and detailed information on the proper protective clothing and equipment that should be used for this project application.

Excerpted from *The Energy-Efficient Potter*, 1982 by Regis Brodie, published by Watson-Guptill Publications. ISBN 0-8230-1614-5. Company names, products, and prices are current as of August 2003.

7. Remember to apply mortar to both the module and to the area of application. Using the plywood holder, the module is pressed firmly to the surface, moved slightly back and forth, and then positioned tightly up against the adjacent module where it is held in place for 10 to 15 seconds. CAUTION: Again, new findings require proper protective clothing and equipment must be worn. (See the last paragraph of this article).

8. The finished interior before firing.

9. Detail of the interior after several firings. This shows the advantages of using edge-stacked modules that are installed under compression, i.e., very few shrinkage gaps develop.

The Mysterious Hole
Determining Correct Burner-Orifice Size
by Marc Ward

It's such a simple thing. It's just a hole. But the burner orifice is, perhaps, the single most misunderstood and mysterious item in a gas line. Every year, I speak with hundreds of people about their kilns or the kilns they plan to build. Most have a "feel" for the general workings of a gas kiln, but when it comes to the burner orifice, many haven't had the chance to develop a "feel" for exactly what's happening inside their burners.

Maybe one of the things that keeps potters in the dark about orifices is math. Some people are so put off or frightened by math that they will stop reading this article at the mere mention of the dread subject. Hang in there. If you can use a calculator, you can figure out the exact Btu (British thermal unit) output of a burner or determine what size orifice is needed.

A burner orifice is simply a hole that allows pressurized gas to escape and mix with air to form a burnable mixture. Natural gas and propane will burn if not mixed with air, but the flame will be yellow and sooty, and will not produce the maximum Btu's possible. With excess air, the flame will be blue, clean and cool. This can be just as wasteful as a yellow, sooty flame. So, the trick is to provide the correct proportion of air and gas.

In venturi burners, the shape of the burner and the size of the orifice help bring about this proportional mix. Without getting too complicated, this proportion at sea level is 10 cubic feet of air per 1000 Btu's. As any mountain climber can tell you, there's less oxygen at higher altitudes. This decrease in oxygen will not affect burners until you get to 5000 feet above sea level. After this point, the orifice needs to be downsized to produce a higher air-to-gas ration-typically one orifice size smaller at 5000 feet and one orifice size smaller for every 2000-foot increment over 5000 feet. With forced-air burners, this works out to a 5% increase in air at 5000 feet and a 5% for every 2000 feet thereafter.

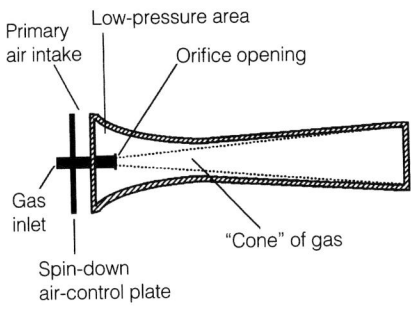

Illustration 1: Venturi Burner Cross Section

To draw air, venturi burners depend upon their shape and the orifice to create a suction of sorts. In Illustration 1, you can see how the cone of gas released by the orifice follows the shape of the venturi tube. When this happens, a low-pressure area develops behind the orifice. Air rushing into this area is pulled along, then is mixed with the gas. As the kiln temperature climbs and draft increases, even more air is pulled into the mixing end of the burner. When you turn the gas up, more air is pulled in, the temperature rises, draft increases, and so on. It all works well as long as things are in balance.

Too small or too large an orifice in relation to the venturi tube can throw your burners out of whack. In Illustration 2 and 3, you can see what happens with an incorrect orifice size or a burner that is either too large or too small for the orifice you want to use. Whether it is the burner or the orifice that is the wrong size, the result is the same. The low-pressure area behind the orifice is changed so that the wrong amount of air is pulled into the burner. Now this doesn't mean that there is only one size orifice for a particular burner. It means that there is one recommended orifice for *optimum* performance. I've found that a range of 20 orifice sizes per burner, 10 larger or 10 smaller than optimum, will still work well with venturi burners. If your burner does not have numbered orifices, this works out to be about plus or minus $\frac{1}{32}$ of an inch. Because different manufacturers make burners with slightly different lengths and tapers, you'll need to follow their recommendations on optimum orifice size.

If you don't know who made the burner or can't find any reliable information to go by, it's going to take trial and error. When the burner produces a nice tight blue flame and can also be put into a heavy reduction with a soft yellow flame, it has an orifice that will work well. A burner that just can't seem to get a good clean blue flame probably has an orifice that is too large. On the other hand, if you're having trouble reducing, the orifice is probably too small for the burner.

Illustration 2: Orifice Too Large for Burner

Illustration 3: Orifice Too Small for Burner

Orifice-size relations are not the only variables. Gas pressure is another. Imagine that the gas is a liquid and you can see what happens when you increase the pressure-there is an increase in speed. Even though you increase the pressure (speed), the cone of gas leaving the orifice doesn't change shape much. This velocity increase will strengthen the low-pressure area behind the orifice and help draw in more air. Lower the pressure and the reverse happens-less gas and less air.

Now, there's a practical limit to raising the pressure to increase the burner output. As the speed of the gas increases, it enters and leaves the kiln faster. The less time the burning and heated gases are in the kiln, the less time they have to transfer their heat to the ware. Specially designed high-velocity burners can overcome this limitation, but most venturi burners cannot. For this reason, I recommend keeping gas pressure at 3 psi (pounds per square inch) or less.

While the orifice size and gas cone shape are very important to the functioning of venturi burners, forced-air burners (with blowers) are more forgiving. With forced-air burners, the air is pushed into the burner and mixed with the gas as shown in Illustration 4. There's not as much of a balancing act, and the chimney need not provide draft to help pull air into the burners. Because of their structure and operation, forced-air or power burners should be operated on low-pressure gas (½ psi or less). The stream of gas does not pull in the correct air ratio, as in the venturi burner, so the blower and the resulting turbulence mix the gas and air. If the gas is injected with too much speed (pressure), it can stay "bundled" together and not mix properly with the air stream.

When dealing with low-pressure gas, which is considered anything below 1 psi, you'll see the term inches of water-column pressure, or just WC. This term is based on the amount of pressure it takes to raise a column of water a certain number of inches. There are 27.7 inches of water column pressure in 1 psi. That means that 7 inches WC is equal to about ¼ psi. This pressure, 7 inches WC, is the normal pressure at

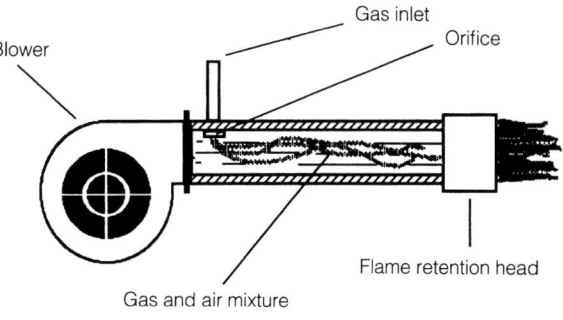

Illustration 4: Forced-Air Burner Cross Section

which natural gas is delivered. Propane for household use (water heaters, stoves, etc.) is generally delivered at 11 inches WC. With propane, you have the option to change your working pressure with the use of pressure regulators. With natural gas, you get what they give you: 5-8 inches WC. Because of the low pressure and Btu value of natural gas, you may have to use forced-air burners on large kilns.

Whatever gas you choose, determining your orifice size is basically the same procedure. If you can't find an orifice chart that is applicable to your situation, you're going to have to use that math I warned you about earlier. Most orifice charts are based on a set pressure or only one type of gas. This is the formula I use for determining Btu output per hour:

$$\text{Btu's} = V \times A \times \overline{K} \times 1655 \times \sqrt{H \div G}$$

I know seeing that will make a few eyes cross and palms sweat, but you don't have to be a rocket scientist to use this formula. It's easy if you take it one step at a time. Once you know what the letters stand for, and plug in the numbers for them, it's simple. V is the Btu-per-cubic-foot value of the gas. If you are using natural gas, V = 1000. If you use propane, V = 2500.

A stands for the area of the orifice hole in square inches. When using numbered orifices, you'll have to refer to an orifice chart, your gas company or someone who sells burners to determine the area. When using regular drill bits, figure the area the same way you would any circle πR^2. Remember that π = 3.14. To determine the radius (R), divide the diameter in half.

Now, I know you're thinking, "This is way too complicated." Don't give up. Grab a calculator and work through this example. To find the orifice area made by an 1/8-inch drill bit, we need to know the diameter. Simple-divide 1 by 8. What does the calculator say? The diameter is 0.125. The radius is half of that, se we divide 0.125 by 2. The radius is 0.0625. The R^2 symbol means the radius squared or the radius multiplied by itself (0.0625 x 0.0625 = 0.00390625). All we do now is multiply π (3.14) by R^2 (0.00390625) and we have the area, A = 0.012265625. Pick any other fraction and work out the area. Try several till you get the hang of it.

$\overline{K}$ stands for orifice coefficient. Anytime gas passes through a restriction such as an orifice, there is friction loss. So, think of K as a percentage of the full flow of gas. Standard orifice plugs run around 0.80 (see Illustration 5). An orifice drilled in the side of a pipe or in a pipe cap runs about 0.75 (see Illustration 6). Looking back on our Btu formula, we see the number 1655. Think

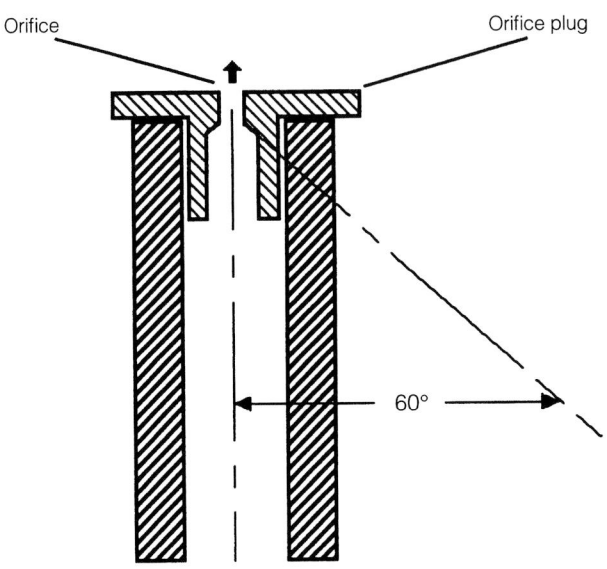

Illustration 5: Cross-Sectional View of Mixing Pin and Orifice Plug

of this number as the full flow of gas. Our orifice is only going to give us 75%-80% of this flow. For our purpose, K = 0.75 or 0.80 depending on the type of orifice you're using.

H is simply the pressure in inches of water (WC). Remember, if you're using pressure based on psi, you need to convert to WC inches. For instance, if you're using 3 psi, multiply 3 × 27.7 (27.7 inches WC in 1 pound of pressure).

G represents the weight of the gas (specific gravity). Regular air is the standard weight and is expressed as 1. If you're using natural gas, which is lighter than air, the specific gravity is 0.65. Using heavier-than-air propane means you would use the number 1.52 for G.

Here's what we want to know: How many Btu's per hour will we get using an _-inch orifice in a venturi burner on natural gas (7 inches WC)? Plug in the numbers and this is what our formula looks like:

$$\text{Btu's per hour} = 1000 \times .0122654 \times 0.80 \times 1655 \times \sqrt{7 \div 0.65}$$

To the calculators! Since you have a square root function, we'll start with that so the calculation is one smooth operation: 7 ÷ 0.65 = 10.76923. Now, simply hit the √ button. The number 3.2816504 appears in the little window. Just keep multiplying back through the equation. 3.2816504 × 1655 × 0.80 × 0.0122654 × 1000. You now have 53,292-the Btu's per hour that the burner is capable of producing.

To see what a change in pressure and type of gas can do, let's hook up this same burner with its ⅛-inch orifice to a high-pressure propane line operating at 3 psi.

$$\text{Btu's per hour} = 2500 \times .0122654 \times 0.80 \times 1655 \times \sqrt{83.1 \div 1.52}$$

Time to push those buttons again. As before, start with the square root side of the equation. 83.1 ÷ 1.52 = 54.671052. Hit the √ button and we get 7.3939875. Keep multiplying; 7.3939875 × 1655 × 0.80 × 0.0122654 × 2500 = 300,185 Btu's per hour.

The same hole, made by an ⅛-inch drill bit, has yielded two completely different results. The next time you grab your drill to ream out that pesky orifice or walk out to the propane tank to crank up the pressure, remember that small actions can cause large changes.

Have you gotten it right? Well, the ultimate test is to fire the kiln. Does the temperature climb evenly and at a good rate? Can you reach temperature in reasonable time? Can you adjust the atmosphere as you desire? Of course, the answers to these questions are going to give you some idea of whether you have gotten it right, but there are other variables (such as kiln design, stacking, bag walls, flue and firebox size) that can affect how the kiln performs. To truly test the efficiency of your burners, you'll need to check the atmosphere. This can be done with either an oxygen or a carbon dioxide probe. These instruments will tell you if your burners are producing complete combustion.

Checking your burners' Btu output while firing is easy if you are using natural gas. To do this, you'll need a stopwatch. Your gas meter should have a ½- or 1-cubic-foot hand. Simply time how long it takes for the kiln to use 1 cubic foot of gas while all the burners are on high. If it takes 3 seconds, you know you're using 20 cubic feet of gas in a minute (60 seconds ÷ 3 seconds); 20 cubic feet a minute × 60 minutes = 1200 cubic feet an hour. Remembering the value of natural gas from our formula, simply multiply the value of the gas by the amount used; 1200 cubic feet × 1000 Btu/CF = 1.2 million Btu's. If you're using six venturi burners, you know each is producing 200,000 Btu/hour (1.200,000 ÷ 6 = 200,000).

Determining Btu output for propane is a bit more complicated. You buy propane by the gallon (liquid) and use it by the cubic foot (vapor). In our formula, the vapor value of propane is 2500 Btu/CF; but you'll know better how many gallons you've used. A gallon of propane has about 92,000 Btu's. Since you probably can't measure vapor flow during the firing, you'll have to check how many gallons you're using per firing and estimate how much of that usage took place at the burners' highest setting. Then figure out the per-hour usage. You're making an educated guess. The only way to actually measure propane-gas usage is with a flow meter. They are very expensive and have to be installed in-line as part of the gas manifold. This brings us back to math.

If you've double checked your figures and feel comfortable with them, you can depend on them. Humans have been to the moon by depending on math (trajectories, ballistics, thrusts, etc.). Armed with nothing more than a little determination and a calculator that has a square root button, you can figure out any burner orifice size and its Btu output. ▲

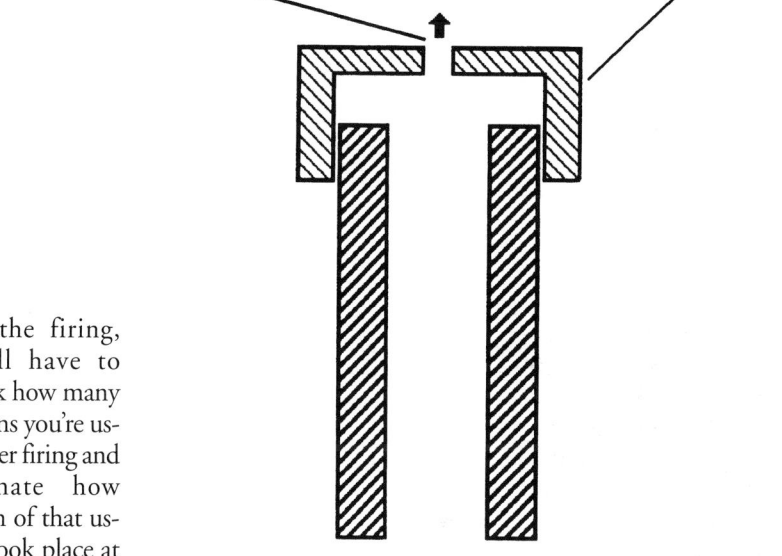

Illustration 6: Cross-Sectional View of Pipe with Pipe Cap

A Castable Venturi Burner

by W. Lowell Baker

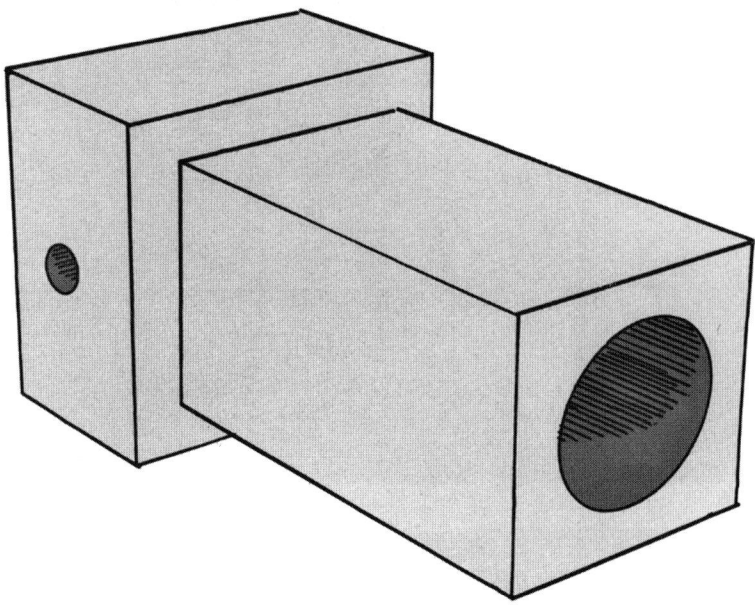

This castable refractory burner has a venturi-shaped interior, which originated as a wheel-thrown form. A gas pipe with sidewall-drilled orifice is inserted through the lateral hole of the burner block; air may be regulated with a metal flap at the rear of the burner. As illustrated on the opposite page, fabrication allows consistent production of multiple burners.

If I stacked all the burners I ever built, one on top of the other, the pile would probably be long enough to reach from here in Alabama to Don Bendel's pile in Arizona. Some people are just compelled to mix air and fuel in every conceivable way to find out how much heat comes out.

A venturi burner is very efficient, and yet it has been almost impossible for a potter with limited equipment to build a set of them in the studio. I've spent a lot of time with pipe fittings, trying to throw efficient venturi burners, then attaching the metal parts. Most of these failed simply because they did not provide a smoothly mixing flow of gas/air.

Years ago, while teaching a workshop at the Appalachian Center for Crafts in Smithville, Tennessee, I was introduced to a cast refractory venturi-type burner (with a spark plug igniter) called the Appalachian Burner. This design works well, but it requires a complicated set of wooden molds and cores to cast. So again it was out of my reach, since it was not entirely practical to cast in limited numbers. Mulling over the design, I eventually came up with a refractory burner cast in any quantity using an easily reproduced and disposable wax core.

First, a solid clay venturi form is thrown on the wheel. A pipe or dowel inserted through the clay provides empty space so the gas line can be passed through the finished cast burner. Then a two-part plaster mold is made of the clay prototype. After cleaning, the plaster mold is soaked in water to prevent wax from sticking to it, and melted paraffin is poured in and allowed to stand until a ¼-inch-thick shell forms; the remaining wax is poured off. Removed from the plaster, the wax core is then placed into a box mold for a block designed to fit into a 5×4½×9-inch burner port in the kiln. The core may be filled with water to prevent it from floating when pouring castable refractory (such as one of the following recipes, suitable for kilns and burners including those firing in a salt vapor atmosphere) into the mold.

Castable Refractory I
Lumnite Cement .... 2 parts by volume
Kaolin 2
Grog 4
                                        8 parts by volume

Castable Refractory II
Lumnite Cement .... 2 parts by volume
Alumina Hydrate 1
Grog 4
                                        7 parts by volume

One to one and a half part Portland cement may be substituted for the two parts Lumnite.

When the castable has set up (12-24 hours), the venturi core is melted out with a hand torch; its wax may be saved for the next core. A ½-inch gas line with a drilled orifice in its sidewall is added. The orifice diameter will vary according to the gas pressure and the burner size: low pressure would require 3/32-⅛-inch; high pressure, less than 3/32 inch. Estimate the appropriate diameter; if the hole proves too large, simply fill with solder and redrill the orifice. Gas pressure at the orifice causes a refrigeration effect, making it the coldest part of the burner, so there is little chance of the solder melting. A butt hinge welded to the gas line allows the easy connection or removal of a blower or a primary air control.

Relatively simple to make and affordable, the castable venturi burner may be installed in existing or new gas kilns.

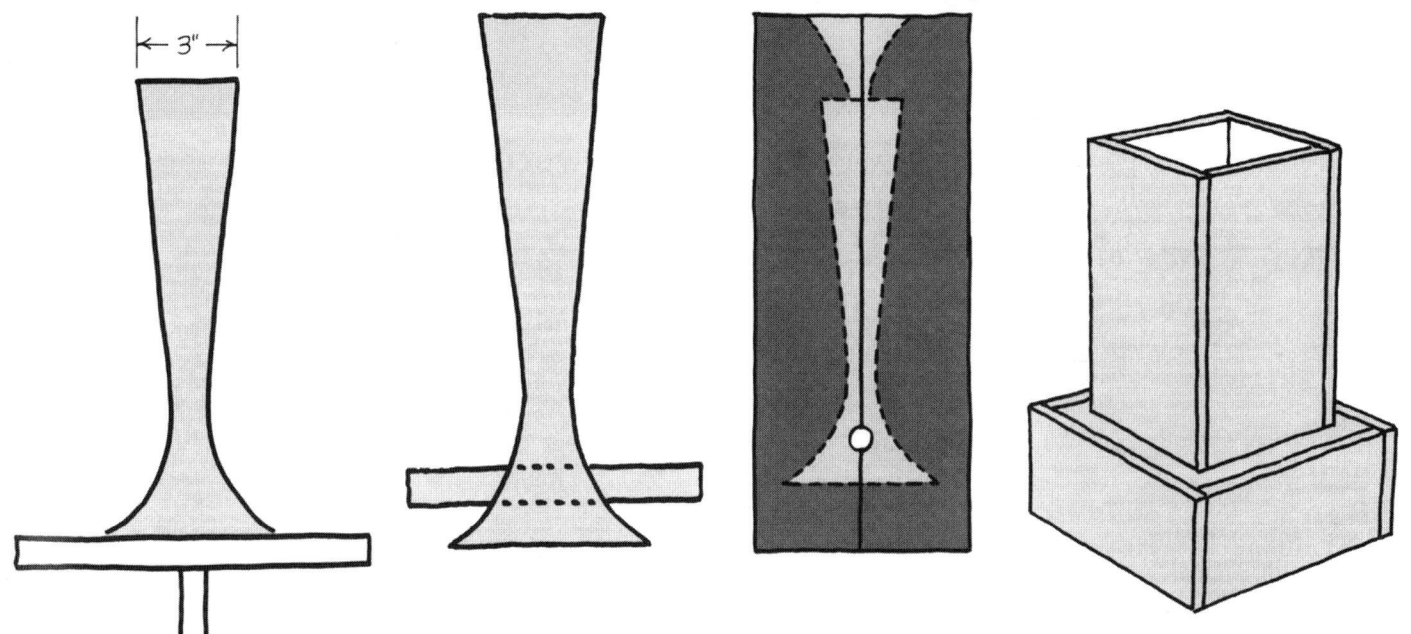

To fabricate a castable venturi burner(1), throw a sold clay form on the wheel(2), then insert a pipe or dowel to provide space for the gas line. A two-part plaster mold is made of the clay prototype(3), and after curing, the mold is soaked with water, and a ¼-inch thick wax model cast. The wax burner shell is then placed in a box mold(4), designed to produce a clay block that will fit into a 5×4½×9-inch burner port. The box mold is filled with castable refractory(5), and when this has set up, the wax venturi core is melted out with a propane torch.

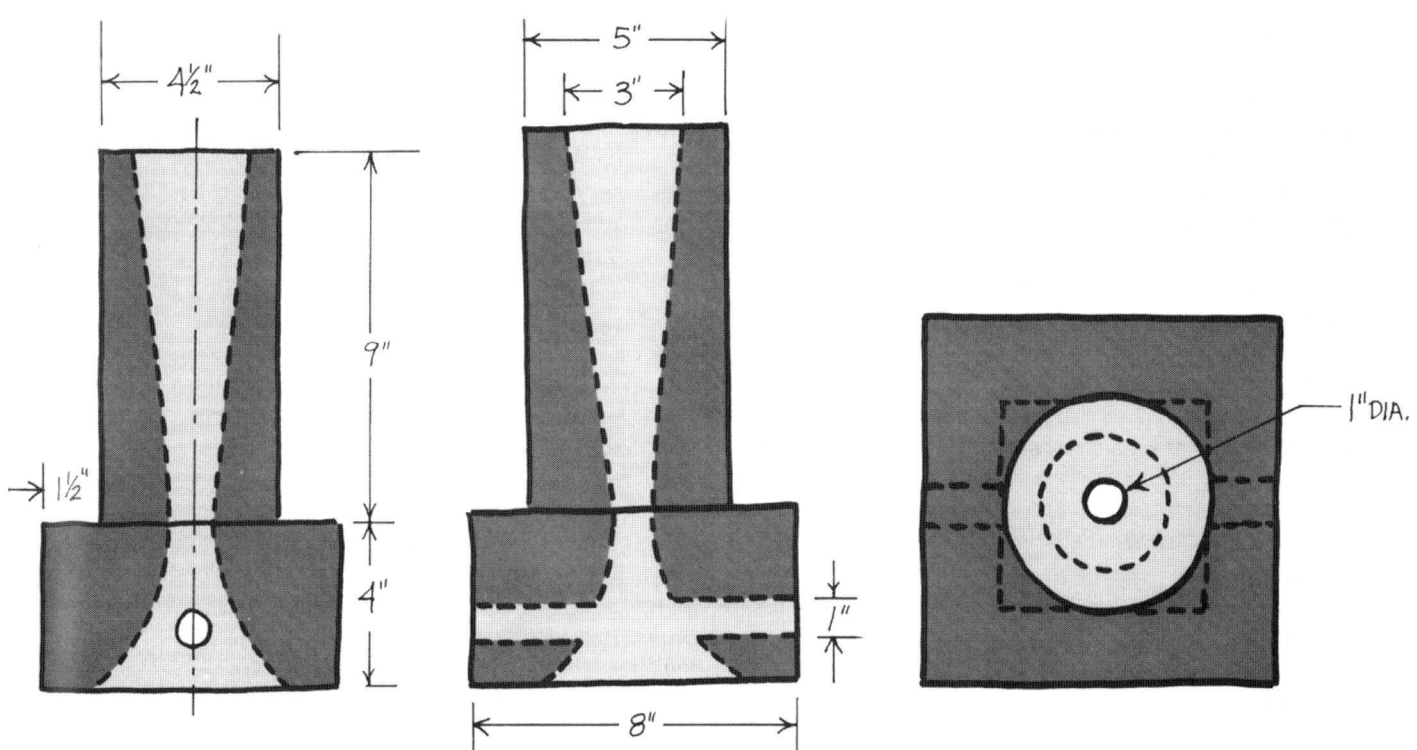

After fitting with a ½-inch interior diameter gas line with a sidewall orifice, the burner block may be installed in the burner port. The end flap of a butt hinge may be welded to the gas line inside the burner block; the other end flap to a blower, and the two hinge sections united to hold a small blower forced-air combustion.

The Oxygen Probe: A Potter's Tool

by Nils Lou

In roughly the past two decades, use of instrumentation to determine the chemistry of kiln atmospheres has increased to where significant numbers of serious studio potters and university ceramics programs are using oxygen probes to develop efficient firing protocols and to achieve more accurate determination of firing atmospheres. The initial cost for such an instrument is readily offset by fuel savings and the ability to repeat specific firing conditions, as well as the resultant knowledge of kiln operation that one gains from observing the flame, sound and smells relative to the digital information provided by the instrument.

The individual I credit with developing a simple, cost-effective potter's probe is Maxwell Murray of Melbourne, Australia. In the late 1970s, his company Architectural and Industrial Ceramics (AIC) placed an advertisement in *Industrial Ceramics* for his new potter's oxygen probe. I called him and, as he was planning a trip to introduce the probe to the U.S., invited him to visit with me. Subsequently, I placed ads for their sale in CM and other potters' journals.

In the years since, others have imported the original AIC probe to market in the U.S. Healthy competition in the marketplace has produced at least one other low-priced oxygen probe. Howard Axner of Axner Company developed and now markets a U.S.-made OXYprobe™ that utilizes the same sensor as the AIC probe. In the U.K., a similar oxygen probe is marketed by Glendale Controls, Stoke-on-Trent.

How does the oxygen probe work and what is measured? Today, almost anything designed to operate efficiently using combustion technology employs oxygen sensing to help regulate the fuel/air ratio. The oxygen probe potters use is simple in design and concept; it uses a sensor not unlike those that monitor combustion in all newer cars. The sensor itself is a mineral compound that, when heated to red heat, is sensitive to oxygen atoms. Many such compounds exist. The one used in the potter's probe is made of zirconium/yttrium oxides. It is a simple pellet sealed eutectically in the end of an alumina tube, one half in the tube and one half exposed.

To provide information about oxygen content in the kiln atmosphere, the probe is inserted through the kiln wall so the sensor is about 1 inch inside the kiln, similar to conventional thermocouple placement. Once the atmosphere is heated to red heat, the exposed end of the sensor pellet in the kiln "sees" a certain oxygen content in terms of free atoms of O_2. The other end of the pellet, sealed in the alumina tube,

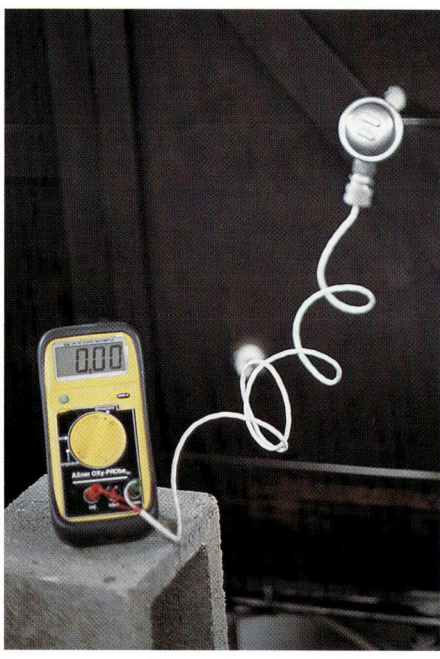

An oxygen probe provides invaluable information when firing fuel-burning kilns.

senses, as a reference, the O_2 in room air—approximately 21% of the ambient air, normally. The comparative difference of O_2 sensed on each end of the pellet produces an EMF (electromotive force) or voltage potential, not unlike the voltage potential between battery terminals. The greater the differential in O_2 sensed between one end of the pellet and the other, the greater the voltage reading (in millivolts) on a digital multimeter. For instance, at 1650°F (900°C), a neutral reading would be 0.1 to 0.15 mV, indicating an O_2 content in the kiln atmosphere of approximately 0.5% to 0.05%. Increasing reduction to a reading of 0.3 mV, the O_2 content is reduced to approximately 0.0001%.

It remains only to figure out how to effectively connect to each end of the pellet so a circuit can be completed and read by a meter. Murray solved this by simply wrapping a wire (platinum) around the exposed sensor end and connecting it to a terminal, where a meter connection could be made. To complete the circuit, the sensor end inside the alumina tube had to also connect to a terminal. This was ingeniously accomplished by inserting a thermocouple (R-type) inside the tube with a small compression spring to keep the tip pressed against the sensor (see drawing). One leg of the thermocouple was (is) used to complete the circuit when the digital meter is switched to read millivolts (mV). Temperature is expressed in milliamps (mA) as the two legs of the thermocouple connect to that switch on the meter. (Note: in addition to atmosphere information, a highly accurate temperature reading is provided, eliminating the need for a separate pyrometer.)

The original AIC multimeters were simple Radio Shack devices (since improved). The O_2 sensor expresses oxygen content relative to a reference standard (room air) in millivolts. By switching the meter to milliamps, current flow (temperature) is expressed. As the multimeter doesn't have a converting circuit built in, it is necessary to check the amperage reading in a temperature conversion chart to convert to temperature. Each type of thermocouple, such as K, R, S, will have a different reference chart for converting amperage readings to temperature. There are meters that have internal conversion circuits for K- and R-type thermocouples (Fluke, as one example), but the only inexpensive ones with both conversion circuits and a millivolt readout potential (for O_2 differential) are designed only for K-type thermocouples. The K-type is not as accurate at high temperatures as R-type and S-type that use noble metals. Both the AIC and Axner oxygen probes use the R-type thermocouple for accuracy and reliability. One leg is pure platinum and the other an alloy of 87% platinum/13% rhodium. The S-type, commonly used in Europe, is similar, having platinum and 90% platinum/10% rhodium legs.

It is important to mount (install) the probe through the wall of the kiln where the sensor will obtain a representative sample of the combustion atmosphere. Usually, this depends on the kiln design and burner placement(s). In an updraft kiln, this might be in the center of the door or back wall, providing there is no burner directly beneath the sensor. In a downdraft kiln, the center of the roof might be considered. To obtain maximum information from the instrument, record hourly readings of temperature and atmosphere. In addition, I like to record initial conditions of weather, such as high or low pressure, wet or dry. After several firings, this record will provide insight and real knowledge of your kiln's operation. You will note that, as you make small adjustments of air, gas and damper, significant changes take place in the combustion atmosphere. You will see that adjustments on burner settings and damper are not the same on high-pressure days as on stormy, low-pressure days. You will also realize, perhaps surprisingly, that if you adjust burners and damper for smoky, black carbon atmospheres, the numbers on the meter will indicate little or no reduction. This is simply because the extreme excess fuel creates free carbon, and this condition interferes with the production of carbon monoxide (CO).

Is the purchase of an oxygen probe a viable investment for you? It is if you answer one or more of the following questions with a "yes": 1) Are you a production potter wanting reproducible results? 2) Do you spend more than $500 a year on fuel? 3) Are you serious about your work and want to understand the chemistry of firing atmospheres and operation of your kiln?

With an oxygen probe and a record of a successful firing in hand (including stacking volume and placement), subsequent firings replicating the original readings should reproduce the desired results, regardless of changes in weather. The cost of an oxygen probe is offset by losing only one marketable load.

Close monitoring of combustion conditions, moving away from neutral only at times demanded for reducing or oxidizing, and then only to the percentage necessary, will generally reduce fuel consumption by 20% and more. For those routinely firing to black smoke conditions, savings might approach 40%.

The probe provides information invaluable to understanding firing conditions. Small changes in kiln settings can make large changes in atmosphere. A movement of just ¼ inch of the damper can be a 10% change in efficiency from neutral to reduction. How often does one see someone move a damper that little? Often, it is an inch or more. A well-designed flue damper is an extremely subtle control, especially at high temperatures. For students, the oxygen probe is a marvelous tool for instruction. It confirms firsthand what is going on when an adjustment is made.

A word on maintenance and handling: If the probe is mounted through a door, remove it to safe storage between firings, as it is easily broken. For permanent installation, choose the back wall or roof; again, make sure it is not directly over a flame path from a burner. Don't try different placements each time you fire; you will not get consistent readings. Make sure the installation is secure and tight. I have seen instances where the probe was put in a peephole, and the flame and radiated heat melted the cables and fried the terminal contacts.

The thermocouple and the exterior wire of an oxygen probe use almost 4 feet of platinum wire. That's a serious amount of platinum wire at about $10/inch. Both AIC and Axner provide alumina tubes to protect the sensor tube and the exterior wire. Handle gently, and reasonably long life is assured.

The most common repair is replacing the end of the

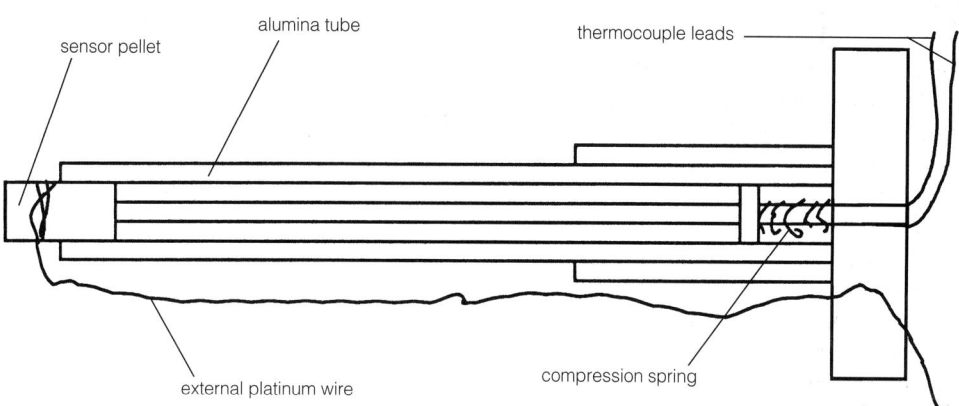

exterior wire exposed to the heated gases. Reduction causes the wire to become brittle and eventually break. Atmospheres high in zinc can break down the wire more rapidly. On average, I see probes needing repair after about 60 to 100 firings. Normally, the repair costs are about $70, so one can figure it costs roughly $1 a firing.

Information provided by the probe is invaluable for diagnosing firing problems. If your kiln takes too long to fire or fires unevenly, the probe is immensely helpful in figuring out potential fixes. When the probe is first installed, it is best to fire a normal protocol, carefully recording and charting time, temperature and atmosphere. There will likely be a surprising revelation.

Finally, as more and more potters incorporate the oxygen probe into their firings, atmospheres can be standardized relating to exchanges of glaze information. Already, glaze recipes are being published with recommended atmospheres specifying probe readings instead of just generalizing with "reduction fired," whatever that means. With the potter's oxygen probe, your kiln can be fired more precisely, with repeatable firing conditions, and with significant savings in fuel efficiency. ▲

Firing with Vegetable Oil

by John Britt

The oil-drip burner is made of channel iron welded together to form three steps. The oil temperature increases as it drops onto each step, until it vaporizes and ignites inside the kiln.

Many potters consider themselves environmentalists, yet they fail to consider the effects of their craft on the environment. As we take part in the demand for electricity, minerals and petroleum, we also share the responsibility for their environmental effects. One of the most common rationalizations is that we are only using the scraps of industry and are therefore not the primary cause. For Sam Clarkson, this rationalization was unsatisfactory, and he decided to take some positive action to reconcile his love of pottery with his concern for the environment.

As a production potter, Clarkson wanted to minimize both the cost and the detrimental effects of burning hydrocarbons while pursuing his passion for high-fire pottery. For a time, he experimented with wood firing, using scrap wood from a molding factory. He reasoned that the wood was waste and would have been burned in an incinerator anyway. This solution worked well for a while, but wood firing is extremely labor intensive and can produce large amounts of soot emissions.

While searching for another solution, Clarkson heard a story on NPR (National Public Radio) about a car that runs on biodiesel, a mixture of 80–90% vegetable oil and 10–20% ethanol alcohol. It is produced from a chemical reaction that is catalyzed by the introduction of lye into the vegetable oil. He thought that if it was possible to run a car on vegetable oil, surely it would work as fuel for a small kiln. So, while in graduate school at Penn State, he experimented with vegetable-oil fuel in a 7-cubic-foot kiln. After some initial success, he longed to experiment with a larger kiln to test the viability of this method in a production setting.

His chance came in the fall of 2001 while team-teaching an eight-week concentration at Penland School of Crafts in North Carolina. Although the focus of the course was functional dinnerware, he and fellow teacher Alleghany Meadows persuaded the 20 students to take on the experimental project of firing Penland's noborigama with used vegetable oil.

Other people who fire such kilns use wood to reach Cone 8, then finish off with diesel fuel. Switching fuels allows them to quickly and easily reach the final temperature, while eliminating fly ash at the upper end of the firing. Clarkson and Meadows decided to adapt this method of a wood/fuel/salt firing, but substitute vegetable oil for the diesel fuel. The plan was to start the kiln with wood until it reached approximately Cone 1, thus allowing enough time for some early ash deposits while establishing enough heat to ignite the oil.

One advantage of burning used vegetable oil is that it is a waste product of the massive fast-food industry. Some major restaurants and fast-food chains have contracts with companies that process their waste oil for use in cosmetics, livestock feed, pet food, heating, etc. Yet there are thousands of smaller restaurants across the country that simply dispose of their waste oil. This means there are millions of gallons of vegetable oil that could potentially be available as fuel.

Aside from being readily available and free, the most important reason for using vegetable oil is that the hydrocarbon, soot and nitrogen emissions are very low. Tests show that biodiesel emissions are substantially lower in carbon dioxide, carbon monoxide, sulfur dioxide, nitrogen dioxide

Far left: Plumbing for the water and oil was installed to conform to the shape of the kiln, out of the way of the stokers.

Left: Oil is gravity fed from a 50-gallon drum on an elevated platform.

and a host of other emissions than petroleum diesel emissions. In fact, the amount of carbon dioxide emitted is about the same, theoretically, that is absorbed from the atmosphere by growing the next crop of soybeans or corn.

Canola and corn oil are probably the most popular vegetable oils used in fryers across America. Canola oil has one of the highest yields of any of the oil crop, around 200 gallons per acre. The Penland kiln consumed approximately 20 gallons per firing.

Most of the oil used for the first two firings was new, as it seemed unwise to collect and store a lot of used oil until it was established that it would work. For the next firing, 25 gallons of used canola oil were acquired from the Penland kitchen fryer, thanks to the generosity of the head chef, "Big John" Renick. After the oil was screened, it worked just as well as the new oil, although it did have the familiar smell of french fries.

A reconditioned 50-gallon drum barrel was then purchased to store the used vegetable oil. It should always be stored in dark containers in a cool, dry location. It is also a good idea to keep the container as full as possible to minimize contact with air and moisture. This is important, as the oil may become very smelly from the growth of microorganisms.

With the help of the studio assistants, Steve Schaeffer and John Arsenault, I set out to construct a burner and oil-delivery system that was efficient enough to fire the kiln to Cone 10. The 50-gallon drum was elevated to approximately 6 feet by a stand made of 2×4s. The drum had both a 4-inch and a 2-inch female-threaded opening, which were placed at the bottom. This allowed us to easily attach threaded pipe for the delivery system. It also allowed the oil to be fed by gravity and kept our delivery pipes overhead, out of the path of workers. With an acetylene torch, we cut a 6-inch hole in the top of the drum where we poured in the vegetable oil. This hole remained open.

The burners were constructed from 5-inch-wide I-beam metal that had been cut into 12-inch lengths, then welded together in a stepped configuration. The three "steps" extended about 15 inches into the firebox, so that the heat of the firebox would be conducted to the metal burner. As the oil drips down the burner steps, it becomes successively hotter and hotter, until it vaporizes and ignites. A shut-off valve is used to control the flow of oil.

Another supply line feeds water onto the burner. This serves two purposes: it causes the oil to dissipate and flow down the metal burner channel, and it creates hydrogen reduction in the chamber. Hydrogen is far more reactive as a reducing agent than is carbon. When water combines with red-hot carbon, it produces carbon dioxide and hydrogen. This carbon hydrogen is also known as "water gas."

The Chinese have used hydrogen reduction since the Han dynasty in the production of gray bricks. It is still used today in some wood-fired kilns in Jingdezhen. The water is either dripped down the interior walls of the kiln or introduced through channels in the kiln as it reaches peak temperature. The kiln is then shut off and sealed.

Our water delivery system was constructed from a standard water hose that was reduced in diameter with a fitting and connected to ⅜-inch copper tubing. We controlled the water with a shut-off valve at the hose and a needle valve at each burner. This had to be adjusted often because the water pressure fluctuated frequently. During the firing, it sounded a lot like water dripping into a hot frying pan—with the accompanying smell of cooking pancakes.

After several attempts, we determined that we needed four oil-drip burners. In order to have more control of the flame, we placed two oil burners in the front of the main firebox and two burners in the stoke holes of the main ware chamber. Each had separate feed lines to maintain equal pressure. Through patience and perseverance, Clarkson and the students were able to find a good blend of fuel, water and air. The kiln reached temperature and was well reduced throughout.

Firing kilns with used vegetable oil has great potential as an alternative energy source. It requires only a small investment in burners, supply lines and storage drums. The oil is easy to obtain, inexpensive (or free) and produces sufficient heat to fire to Cone 10. However, more research and experimentation is needed to perfect this method. One area to explore would be a stainless-steel injection burner system that would spray in the vegetable oil with compressed air.

The use of waste vegetable oil and other alternative fuel sources could help potters address the impending shortfalls of petroleum fuel, as well as its associated pollutants. ▲

Salt-glazed cup, 3½ inches (9 centimeters) in height, wheel-thrown porcelain, with black slip and celadon glaze, fired to Cone 10 with wood and vegetable oil, by Alleghany Meadows, Carbondale, Colorado.

Salt-glazed teapot, approximately 6 inches (15 centimeters) in height, thrown, stamped and altered porcelain, with celadon glaze, fired to Cone 10 with wood and vegetable oil, by Sam Clarkson, Sewanee, Tennessee.

George Wright
Oregon Potters' Friend and Inventor Extraordinaire
by Janet Buskirk

George Wright operating his 100-year-old pug mill.

George Wright has been involved with clay in Oregon since 1945. Over the years, his knowledge and skills have had a significant impact on studio pottery in the region. In tribute to his contributions, the Oregon Potters' Association recently recognized him as "Inventor Extraordinaire; Helper to All; Teacher First Class; Friend Above and Beyond the Call of Duty."

George's association with clay began when he came home from World War II and, with a friend, bought a brickyard in Molalla, Oregon. They had no brickmaking experience, but the brickyard's previous owner agreed to stay for a year and teach them how to run it. They produced flowerpots and bricks from 1945 until the mid 1950s, when George left Molalla and moved to Forest Grove, Oregon, to run another brickyard. While there, George and his wife Pearl took a pottery class with Dave Frank. Pearl went on to become a well-known potter; however, George "never quite got the hand of making pots."

At that time, the clay sold to studio potters in Oregon came from outside the state. Dave noticed George's old pug mill and suggested that they produce pottery clay. George's initial response was, "I don't know about clay; all I know about is bricks."

By the late 1950s, small brickyards that produced drain tile, flowerpots and various other earthenware items were having a difficult time competing with the plastic products entering the marketplace. With Dave's prodding, George retooled and soon was making clay for most of the schools in the area, as well as for local potters.

George then bought an electric kiln and built a gas kiln. Within a short time, the facility was full of pottery students (including Pacific University classes), and many other potters began to work there.

In the 1960s, George bought 30 acres in Manning, Oregon. Although he did not build his own house there until about 1975, a few potters settled on the property. Jim Sloss was one of the first. He had been a student at Pacific University and had worked in George's studio. Jim and George had spent many hours together bricking up the door of George's kiln. While they worked, they would talk, and these talks taught Jim a lot about clay.

When Jim moved to the property in Manning, he lived in a trailer George had built as a portable pottery studio (an idea that did not work out). While living there, Jim did all his firings in a wood kiln that George designed, and continued to sporadically fire his work in George's kilns until 1977, when George decided it was time for Jim to "leave the nest." At the time, Jim was devastated, but he now credits George with forcing him to take his work seriously, set up his own studio and become a full-time potter.

When George moved to Manning, he continued making clay; built various kilns, small homes and studios to rent to potters; and, with Pearl, opened the Pearl Wright Gallery, which featured pots made by the people who lived on the property, as well as works by other local potters. When the gallery opened, there was only one other in the area that sold quality pottery. By the time the Pearl Wright Gallery closed in 1983 (running it had become too time consuming), several other area craft galleries had been established.

Building the Korean wood-fired kiln.

The clay body that George originally made in Manning was 75% commercial ingredients and 25% local clay, which was blunged in a 50-gallon drum, screened wet, then pumped to the dry ingredients. Using local clay cut costs, but processing it was time consuming; the clay that George currently makes contains no local clay.

One of the things that George has always been proud of is that he charges 15¢ per pound for his clay. Whether a person buys a bag or a ton, everyone pays the same price.

At 79, George still uses the old pug mill, making several tons of clay per week for local potters and schools. His pug mill, from the old brickyard, was built in the late 1800s. It was originally run by a belt turned by a tractor engine, but the tractor's magneto wore out. Now he turns the belt on the bare rim of the back wheel of an old pickup truck.

Covering the finished kiln with earth for insulation.

Over the years, about 25 potters have lived on George's property. In addition to Dave Frank and Jim Sloss, the list includes Bill Creitz, Barbara and Dale Rawls, Andy and Pat Balmer, Ed and Diane Swick. George has also provided space for a woodworker, a glassblower, a stained-glass artist, a weaver and a painter or two. Several of these people started families or were married while living there. All of them helped build and used a large variety of kilns and other equipment while they lived and/or worked on the property.

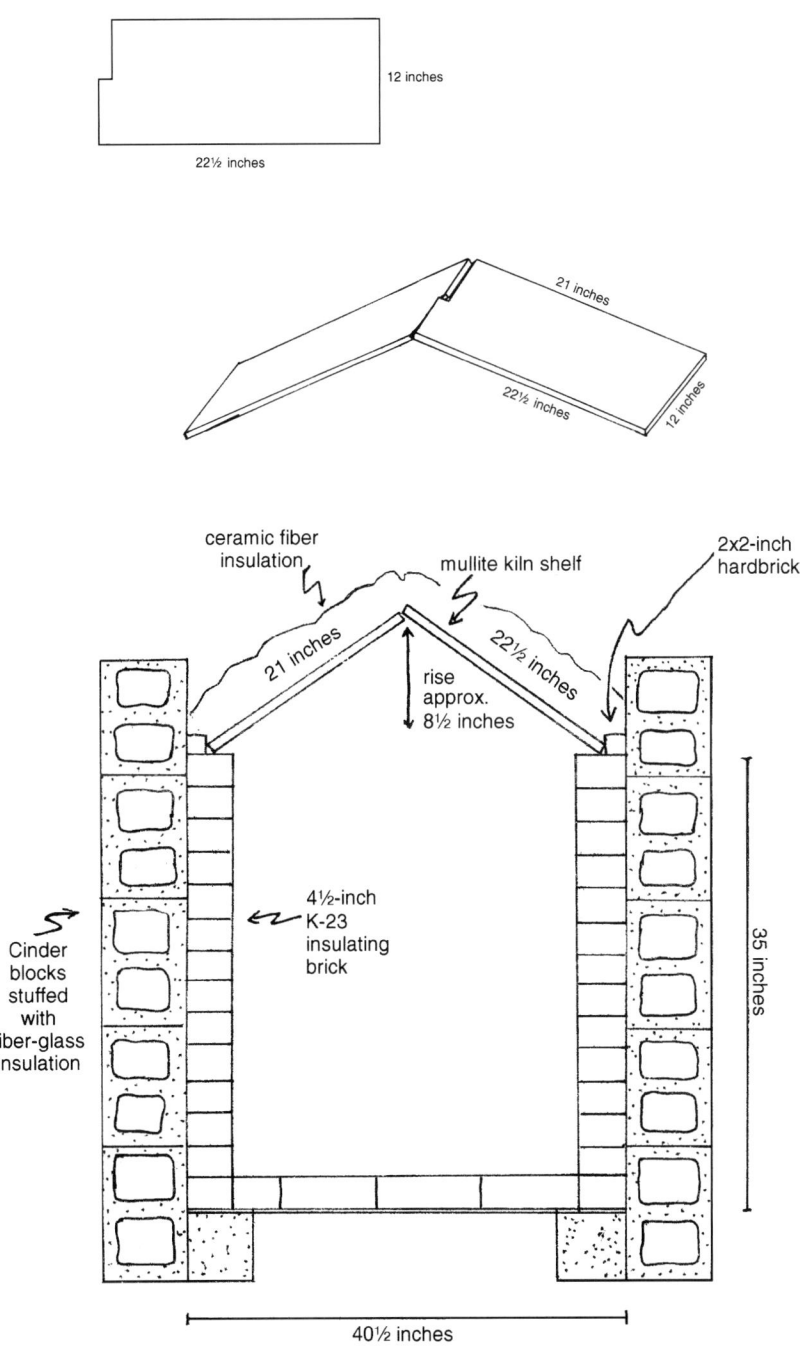

A "cathedral arch" kiln using notched mullite kiln shelves to form the peaked roof; to keep construction costs to a minimum, the firebrick is backed by cinder blocks filled with fiber-glass insulation.

In the late 1960s, George took a job with the Tektronix (an oscilloscope and computer company) ceramics department. He described this job as the easiest thing he had ever done; "you just walked around all day turning up switches." He worked there full time for a few years, then spent several years trying to quit, each successive year being asked to stay just one more year.

About 1984, George sold the clay business and announced to everyone that he had retired. Within a short time, though, he began to experiment with a high-grog, high-nylon-fiber clay that he thought could be useful to sculptors. By 1985, he was making small quantities and inviting local potters to try it out. Judy Teufel brought me and a few friends along one day. We made pots, glazed them immediately, fired them to Cone 10 in four hours, cooled them in two hours, and unloaded them six hours after we had made them. Amazingly, only one piece cracked; the rest came out whole.

That new clay was tough. Word got around, and soon George was back in the clay business. A few weeks later, when cutting off a chunk of this clay, Portland potter Gail Pendergrass looked at the nylon fibers that stuck to her wire, and asked, "What is this, dog hair?" George, a teetotaler, named the clay "Hair of the Dog." Soon he had orders for many tons. Most people use it for large sculptural pieces, but Joel Cotter, a potter in Hillsboro, has used Hair of the Dog to make hot tubs, as well as tables and chairs.

George is also known throughout the Northwest for his interesting and innovative kiln designs, many of which incorporate inexpensive, simple materials, and he has always been willing to share his plans with others. At least 25 area potters and several schools use his salt and raku kilns, as well as his various wood-fired kilns.

Currently, there are three propane kilns; one high-temperature, propane-fueled salt kiln; one low-temperature salt kiln; two high-fired wood-fueled kilns; one lower-temperature wood fueled Korean tunnel kiln; numerous electric kilns; an above-ground brick "pit" kiln; and a raku kiln on his property. All are fired regularly.

One of the things that amazes people is George's willingness to lend a hand. At the Oregon Potters' Association tribute to George, we heard many stories of times when he had helped with difficult projects; e.g., laying out the floor of one kiln, putting together a burner system for another. Dale Rawls described the time he had blown up a propane kiln. While Dale was in his house calming down, George unstacked the kiln, resprung the arch, restacked the kiln, then came inside to tell Dale he could fire anytime.

A few years after that incident, Jeanne Charles, Tony Hackenbruck and I started building our kiln. We were always busy and were taking years to finish it. One day, George drove up with a truckload of lumber and said that he noticed we didn't have a kiln shed, so he was here to build one.

When the National Council on Education for the Ceramic Arts (NCECA) conference was held in Portland in 1987, a group of Koreans came to Oregon to build a traditional Korean wood-fired kiln to be fired in conjunction with the conference. Frank Irby, the Portland liaison for NCECA, called George and asked if the kiln could be built on his property. George agreed. Partway through the kilnbuilding, it became clear that the sponsoring foundation was running low on money, so George called his old friends at refractory companies, found some discounted supplies, then paid for them himself. George's connections and his generosity made it possible to finish construction, and the kiln is still fired regularly by local potters.

George's kilns are designed to make the best use of whatever materials are available. One of his interesting, cost-effective methods of building kiln walls is to back an inside layer (4½ -inch-thick) of K-23 insulating bricks with a layer of cinder blocks filled with fiberglass insulation. The cinder blocks with fiberglass cost only a dollar or two each, compared to at least $10 for enough bricks to cover the same area.

Most of his recent kiln designs have used his "cathedral arch" design. Instead of using bricks, he cuts notches in mullite kiln shelves, then leans them

George Wright demonstrating the construction of a small cathedral arch kiln; total cost for materials, including a propane burner, is around $800.

against each other to form a peaked roof, and covers it with a few inches of fiber insulation. Every few hundred firings, the mullite shelves will sag and should be turned over. Doing this takes two people about half an hour.

He recently designed a small gas kiln with which to demonstrate his kiln-building techniques. It uses cost-effective and time-saving materials, including the cinder-block outer walls and the kiln-shelf arch. He can take the kiln apart and completely rebuild it in a mere three hours. The cost for all of the materials, including the propane burner system, is around $800.

In the Northwest, you cannot enter a gallery displaying claywork without seeing work made from George's clay, fired in one of his kilns and/or fired in a kiln of his design. In fact, his influence is felt throughout the country, since so many people have built the kilns he designed (for which others are often given credit). With his willingness to share his time and expertise, George is everyone's "friend above and beyond the call of duty."

Original Throwing Body
(Cone 10)
Custer Feldspar .... 50 lb.
Kentucky Ball
 Clay (OM 4) 200
Local Clay* 375
Mason's Blend Fireclay 700
Silica Sand (70 mesh) 100
                                       1425 lb.

*High in iron and bauxite.

Hair of the Dog Sculpture Clay
(Cone 10)
Custer Feldspar .... 50.0 lb.
Bentonite 10.0
Kentucky Ball
 Clay (OM 4) 200.0
Lincoln 60 Fireclay................ 500.0
Silica Sand (70 mesh) 200.0
A.P. Green Grog (20 mesh) ... 300.0
Nylon Fiber 0.5
                                     1260.5 lb.

A very tough, open clay body, which is useful for large, heavy or thick sculptural work. To prevent lumps of nylon, separate the fiber with wool carders as it is added to the batch. The fiber will clog screens in de-airing pug mills. ▲

Neil Tetkowski in his New York City studio, where installing a combustion kiln in compliance with strict regulations proved to be costly and time consuming.

Lessons from a City Kiln

by Marc Leuthold with Sarah G. Wilkins

When I came to New York about five years ago, I knew life would be hard for a ceramics artist in The City. Just getting work done while eking out a living there is a daily challenge—not to mention the limited studio space and availability of kilns. I resigned myself to multiple part-time jobs while making sculpture in my spare time, and resolved to apply to residency programs elsewhere in the country for more productive and intensive work phases. I also learned how to stretch a penny.

Though I shudder to think of it now, I actually worked as a "penny stretcher" for $6 an hour on the 86th floor observatory of the Empire State Building. For a dollar, I would take a tourist's penny, drop it into a machine and, by hand-cranking vigorously, squeeze the soft copper into an oval stamped with the Statue of Liberty, the Empire State Building, the New York skyline or the generic "Good Luck Penny." It was possible to turn about $100 into stretched pennies per day. Or 1000 pennies into dollars, depending on your perspective. That's a lot of cranking.

That was absolutely my worst part-time job to date. One of the best was working as an assistant for ceramics sculptor Neil Tetkowski.

Neil and I both taught ceramics classes at Parsons School of Design, but I had had little contact with him before calling about the job. I identified myself as "a part-time teacher at Parsons." As I expected, Neil didn't want to hire a "colleague," and I had a hard time persuading him to give me a chance. Then, when he finally agreed, I actually dreaded the first day of work. I'd heard horror stories about how some artists treat their assistants, and I steeled myself for the worst.

Neil had just moved into a new workspace, a block away from his apartment in Chelsea. The studio is spacious—1800 square feet with windows on opposite sides. It is on the second floor, with parking on the ground level. I could only dream of such a wonderful setup for a ceramist in New York City. I was envious.

Neil immediately set me to work painting shelves in the studio. Then together we arranged the equipment. He often asked for suggestions and seemed to really value the input—hardly the arrogant prima donna I had dreaded.

In planning to install a gas kiln, Neil knew it would be a challenge to comply with the city's complicated and strict combustion regulations. New York requires that all combustion equipment be certified for use within the five boroughs. Commercial producers of boilers, stoves and water heaters go through an expensive procedure to have their equipment certified. Afterward, identical equipment can be sold without question. However, for one-of-a-kind industrial equipment, such as a kiln, certification can cost upwards of $6000 for independent laboratory testing.

Regulations dictate that one must hire an engineer to assure that plans are filed and codes are properly carried out. The engineer Neil hired determined that the floor of the 100-year-old building would not collapse when the 6800-pound kiln was delivered to the second floor. The engineer's fee was $2500, and the filing fees an additional $300.

A certain kind of chimney was specified as well. It was required to extend beyond the roof line of the top

Because the weight of the kiln was too much for the old freight elevator, professional riggers suspended it from two I-beams and hoisted it up by hand.

Hoisting the kiln—1 centimeter per pull.

story. Fortunately, the building is small by New York standards and only goes up four floors.

For the combustion system, a $600 filing fee was submitted to the Department of Buildings, Materials and Equipment Acceptance Division. In order to avoid testing fees, the kiln manufacturer went to great lengths to help us, assembling laboratory reports for each component of the burner system to prove safety claims. Combinations of components are used in the design of burner systems, from gas valves to computer controls, and since the manufacturer purchases parts for burner systems from several other manufacturers, the compilation was a complex task.

Once the plans were approved by the city for a total of $4900, a licensed plumber was hired to install a 2-inch gas line from the street to the kiln, approximately 180 feet away. Because Manhattan has very low gas pressure, no one could guarantee that the kiln would reach temperature. Anxiety was somewhat alleviated by the news that boosters could be added later—for thousands of dollars more, of course.

Delivery of the new equipment had to be thought out very carefully. Although the width of the kiln was determined by the width of the freight elevator door, the actual weight was just too heavy for the old elevator. Professional riggers were hired for $3000 to deliver the kiln to a specific location on the second floor.

It proved to be a day's work for four expert movers. Two I-beams were suspended from the third floor inside the elevator shaft. The kiln hung from them in a sling of massive chains, then hand-powered winches moved the kiln upward at a snail's pace—1 centimeter for each pull. Once in place, the kiln was made fully functional, and has worked well ever since.

It took us a whole year to complete the renovation of the studio, which includes a large workspace near the kiln site, a spray room for the application of terra sigillata, and a clean room for office work and visitors. With assistance from Boyd Johnson and myself, Neil removed dropped ceilings, plywood paneling and crumbling linoleum—peeling away layers of ugliness to reveal the building's structural elements. During all these Herculean labors and the endless details of kiln installation, Neil's eternal optimism and focus on "the big picture" never failed to impress me. He kept telling me, "Now that I have the kiln, things are going to happen...just wait."

Two weeks later, Neil called to say that he was going to have a solo show at the Myung Sook Gallery on Broadway in SoHo. The show was a turning point for him. He had set out to become a working and exhibiting New York artist, and managed to do so about a year and a half after moving to the city.

Neil's show was also a turning point for me. While he was setting up his exhibition at Myung Sook, I left to prepare for a residency at the Kohler Company in Wisconsin. During my time with Neil, I had learned how an artist must have complete faith in the practice of art and in his own creativity, and must be flexible when facing obstacles, calmly nurturing his vision into reality. One must be prepared to reason with an irate contractor on the same day that one sells three large pieces. ▲

KAZEGAMA

by Steve Davis

The four burners welded to the gas manifold have their own ball valve controls and blower motors, but move together as a unit between the upper and lower ports for maximum ash delivery.

During the firing, ash from a bucket is fed into the kiln through the air intake of each blower.

Since 1997, I have been developing a gas-fired kiln that achieves wood-fired results without the use of wood. I named this kiln "kazegama" (which is Japanese for wind kiln), because the kiln obtains anagama results through the use of blowers; they disperse ash throughout the chamber, depositing it onto the surfaces of the wares.

Construction

When designing a kiln, I always start with the dimensions of the shelves that will be used. The framework is then designed to accommodate the type and dimensions of the insulation to be used. My kazegama started out as a small test kiln and has changed little in the way it delivers ash. What has changed, however, is the construction of the kiln. Originally, I used castables to withstand the chemical attack of the ash. However, these castables were not up to the task because they are very heavy, dense and inefficient. I currently use Thermal Ceramic's 2-inch 2600M board for the hot face, with 2-inch ceramic blanket as backup insulation. This combination is lightweight and flexible, allowing for trailer transport of the kazegama to workshops.

The M board will last up to ten firings, perhaps more, depending on its exposure to heat and ash. Prior to installation, it is fired to at least Cone 5 to preshrink the board, thus reducing additional and unwanted shrinkage in future firings. A high-alumina kiln wash will greatly extend its life as well.

The M board is anchored with porcelain buttons and Nichrome wire every 6 inches onto an expanded-metal or safety-grate backing; special attention is paid to the roof, because heat and gravity create tremendous stresses on the Nichrome wire. (Stainless-steel anchors are available, but I have not tried them.) The space between the walls and the lid is then sealed with a 4-inch-wide length of 1-inch fiber.

After installing the board, holes for the burner ports and peep holes are cut. The burners are positioned and the tips traced onto the kiln wall to mark the ports. It is best to use a ceramic sleeve in each burner port hole to reduce wear from removing ash or sealing up the kiln upon completion. The best tool for cutting clean holes in fiber products is the cut-out mid section of an aluminum soda can. After securing the mid section around the ceramic burner port sleeve, the can is pushed and twisted through the fiber wall. Leather gloves are worn to avoid cut hands. Most importantly, I always wear a face mask when working with fiber products.

For portability, the Kazegama was constructed on a trailer.

Two exit flues are cut at the back of the kiln to spread out the flow of ash. The openings are cut with a rounded butcher knife by simply rocking the knife back and forth while pressing down through the fiber and board.

The chimney is constructed from a 2-inch layer of ceramic fiber blanket placed inside an expanded metal frame. Again, the blanket is held in place with ceramic buttons and Nichrome wire. To reduce leakage caused by the shrinkage, the fiber is overpacked where it comes into contact with the flue wall.

One note about the framing of the kiln: steel exposed to heat needs to be at least $3/16$ inch thick. The 1-inch fiber seal will compress after one or two firings, exposing the frame to high temperatures. Heat exposure also exists in the areas around the burner ports and the flues.

Loading the Kazegama

Clay bodies, glazes and flashing slips used in wood firing work equally well in the kazegama. Wares are loaded in the same manner as in a wood firing. A target brick is placed in front of each burner in order to disperse the ash throughout the kiln. The shelves are placed 3 inches from the back wall so heat and ash can move through all sections of the kiln. Placing shorter pieces toward the front of the kiln allows more ash to reach the back. Pieces loaded closest to the burners will get the biggest hit of ash. Those in the back are likely to exhibit flashing, as will any surface which is in close proximity to another surface. The ash buildup can be quite

The roof of the kiln raises slightly and slides back over the exit flues for loading and unloading.

heavy, so wadding placement and size is important. Enough wadding should be used to keep pieces ½ inch off the shelf. Wadding should also be placed inside of foot rings to avoid ash flows.

Firing the Kazegama

The burner system is the heart of the kazegama. It is composed of four burners welded to a gas manifold. Each burner has its own ball valve for the propane gas and a

Dayton #4C440 blower motor for the air supply. This blower motor has an air flap that opens and closes to adjust the air/fuel ratio. Because the burners produce such a tremendous amount of heat, only one middle burner is used during the first hour of the firing. When the front kiln posts start to develop some red heat, all the burners are turned to full, and the main gas valve turned down to match the Btu output of the one middle burner. With all the burners firing, the pressure is gradually (over one and a half hours) turned up to full. Depending on the density of the load, Cone 9 can be achieved in two and a half hours.

When a witness cone placed on the top front shelf indicates the temperature is nearing Cone 9, it is time to start introducing screened wood ash. Mesquite, fruit and hardwood ashes work best; they should be screened to remove large chunks that could damage the blowers. Once the cone starts to bend, the air-intake flap of the left burner is opened to maximize the amount of air being drawn. The blowers are mounted so that the air intake is underneath the blower.

Ten handfuls of ash are then fed into the blower intake. The blower blows the ash toward a target brick 18 inches into the kiln. After the ten handfuls of ash have been introduced, the air intake flap is returned to its original position. Ash is fed in the same manner through each of the blower burners. It takes about 45 minutes to introduce 15 pounds of ash into a 35-cubic-foot kiln. Halfway through this process, the burners are moved up to the second level in order to disperse ash throughout the upper part of the kiln.

During the feeding, ash will start to clog the burner tubes and must be removed. With the gas turned off but the air still on, I remove the burner assembly with the burner tips pointed downward, tap the tips on the ground, then return the burner assembly to its mounts, and turn the gas back on to its original setting. After all the ash has been thrown into the kiln, I repeat this process to ensure the burners are firing properly.

At this point, it's time to soak. The temperature usually climbs during the introduction of the ash and can reach Cone 10 or more, which is why feeding the ash must start at no higher than Cone 9. Soaking takes 20 minutes to an hour. I determine the duration by observing the ash melt through welder's goggles.

When the desired melt is achieved, the gas is turned off and the burner assembly removed. Then the burner ports are plugged, and the dampers closed. The kiln can be unloaded the following morning. The entire firing takes five to six hours and reaches temperatures as high as Cone 12 at the front of the kiln.

From very subtle blushes to heavy ash flows, wares from the kazegama are remarkably similar to those fired in five-day wood firings. Introducing ash at the end of the firing but not soaking also creates the crusty surfaces of the firebox of a wood kiln; however, the results are not quite the same, due to the particle size and low volume of ash.

Aesthetics and Tradition

The firing process of a wood kiln or a kazegama is seductive in and of itself, and is an integral part of the final results. More importantly, however, it should lend aesthetic support by complementing form, gesture and surface qualities through the natural coloring and layering of the ash.

The kilns we fire and the types of wares we produce spring from a long history dating back many centuries. Over time, kiln designs have changed with the introduction of new technologies and demands. In this sense, the kazegama is just another tool that contributes to the ongoing tradition of the wood-fired aesthetic. ▲

Target bricks, which double as shelf supports, are placed directly in front of the burner ports, 18 inches inside the kiln, to help spread the ash around the kiln.

A Fast-Firing Test Kiln

by Rich Childs

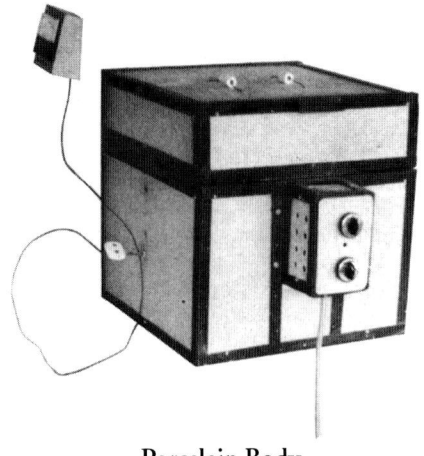

Have you ever used a test kiln to quickly assess the value of a newly acquired glaze recipe, only to find that the results could not be obtained all that quickly? Several years ago I became interested in producing crystalline glazes; however, the available kilns were slow and inefficient, so testing revolved around a frustrating three-day cycle. To facilitate temperature control, speed and efficiency, I designed a test kiln that is relatively inexpensive (about $136 new materials cost) and easy to build. Insulated with 6 inches of refractory fiber blanket, it is capable of reaching Cone 12 in 70 minutes on regular 110-125 volt household current.

For the 20×20×14-inch frame and the 20×20×6-inch lid, angle iron is welded together in overlapping butt joints. (As an alternative, the frame can be bolted together with zinc-plated nuts and bolts.) Transite, galvanized sheet metal, expanded steel or stainless steel (depending on your budget) is then cut and bolted to the framework to form the kiln's shell. If using Transite, be sure to take every health precaution for working with asbestos.

Next, make a 5×5×8-inch switch box in the same manner to bolt on the front of the kiln. Expanded metal works great; otherwise small holes must be drilled in the sides of the box to keep the switches cool.

Twelve porcelain tubes (6 inches long with a ⅝-inch inside diameter after firing) serve as conduits for the elements, peepholes and part of the insulation anchoring system for the lid. Also approximately 80 tiles (1¼×½ inch, each pierced with two holes) are required to construct the refractory fiberboard kiln chamber. I used the following Cone 10 body for the tiles:

Porcelain Body
(Cone 10)
Custer Feldspar	20%
Ball Clay	5
Kaolin	55
Flint	20
	100%

Refractory fiberboard is used for the hot face and element housing; a part of the board should be test fired a cone above your anticipated working temperature to see if it can really handle high temperatures without warping. Each panel assembly consists of an 8×10-inch fiberboard section with a 1×9-inch section at the top and four 2×9-inch sections spaced every 2 inches; 2×8-inch sections overlap the 9-inch-long sections to form the element slots. The sections are anchored in place with resistance wire threaded through a porcelain tile to form a long staple, pushed through the fiberboard, passed through another tile and the ends twisted together. Ceramic fiber cement in combination with the anchoring pins works well. When the four element panels are complete, pin them together with resistance wire staples 2½ inches in length. A square piece of board is then pinned to the bottom. The entire 8×8×8-inch chamber is set on top of 6 inches of fiber blanket, cut with a utility knife and layered on the bottom of the kiln. When working with fiber insulation, use rubber gloves and a respirator.

All of the element wires will exit the kiln chamber to the front where the switch box is located. Therefore, small holes need to be drilled 2 inches apart in the center of the front panel. Two additional holes (for peepholes) should be drilled in one side panel. Correlating holes, large enough for the porcelain conduits to fit through, are also needed in the shell.

If you are unable to find fiberboard rated above 2300°F, use softbrick for the kiln chamber. Element slots are easily cut into eight K-28 (2800°F) insulation brick with a tungsten carbide blade attached to a hacksaw. I used a wooden jig to hold the brick while cutting two slots into each. Holes for the element tails are easily drilled with a nail or screwdriver. To keep the brick from sinking into the bottom insulation, imbed four 6-inch posts to support the center of each chamber wall. The slotted brick can then be stacked in the center of the kiln to form the chamber.

The elements are made from Kanthal wire, available from some ceramics suppliers or from Duralite, Inc., Box 188, School Street, Riverton, Connecticut 06065. Cut four lengths of wire, each 30½ feet long. Make element "tails" by folding over 7½ inches at each end and use locking pliers to twist the doubled wire together. Clamp the inside end of one tail to a 4-foot length of ⅜-inch iron rod; wind the wire around the rod until it meets the opposite tail. (The rod can be secured in a lathe, an electric drill or any device allowing it to turn.) Slide the elements off the rod and stretch the coils only (not including the tails) to 35 inches in length.

Beginning at the bottom, lay the element in the slot (bend corners as you go), passing the tails through the front panel, the porcelain conduits and through the kiln shell. Repeat the process for the remaining elements, packing the space between the panels

Each panel of the test kiln consists of an 8x10-inch refractory fiberboard section with 2x8-inch sections overlapping 2x9-inch strips, all anchored in place with resistance wire and ceramic button tiles.

The four completed fiberboard sections form the chamber when pinned in place with 2½-inch long resistance wire staples. A square piece of fiberboard is similarly pinned to the bottom.

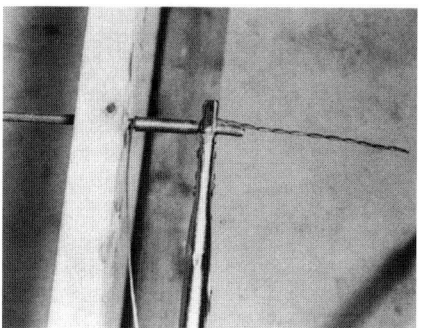
After folding over and twisting 7½ inches at each end of a 30½-foot long Kanthal wire, wind it around a 4-foot length of ⅜-inch diameter rod. Then stretch each coiled element to 35 inches in length.

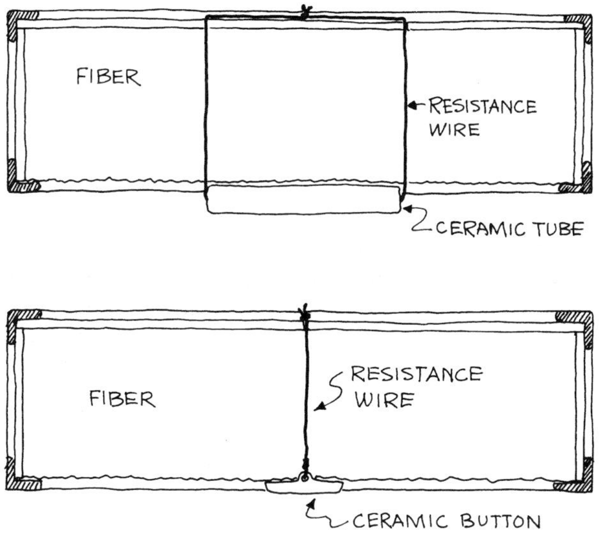

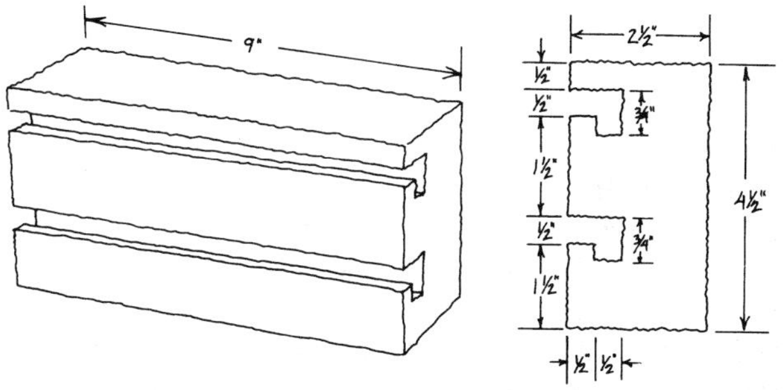

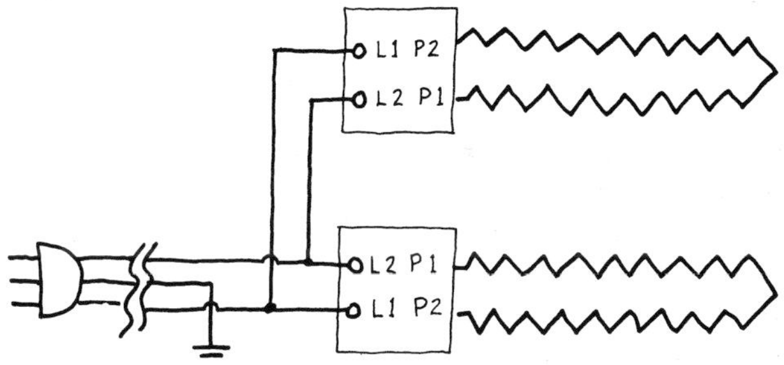

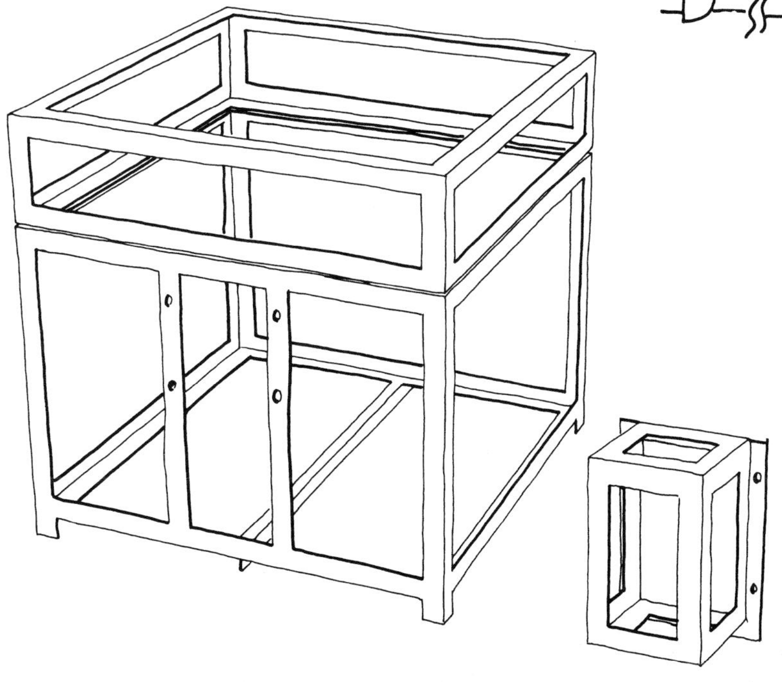

Materials

Angle iron .... 40 feet
Transite or
 galvanized metal ...... 4x8-foot sheet
2700°F refractory
 fiberboard .... 2x3-foot sheet
2300°F fiber blanket ... 50 square feet
Kanthal A-1 B&S
 14 gauge
 resistance wire .... 2 pounds
125-volt, 20-amp
 infinite control switches 2
brass connectors
 or line taps 5
asbestos-covered wire .... 2 feet
12-2 Romex cable
 with ground .... 4 feet
125-volt, 20-amp plug 1

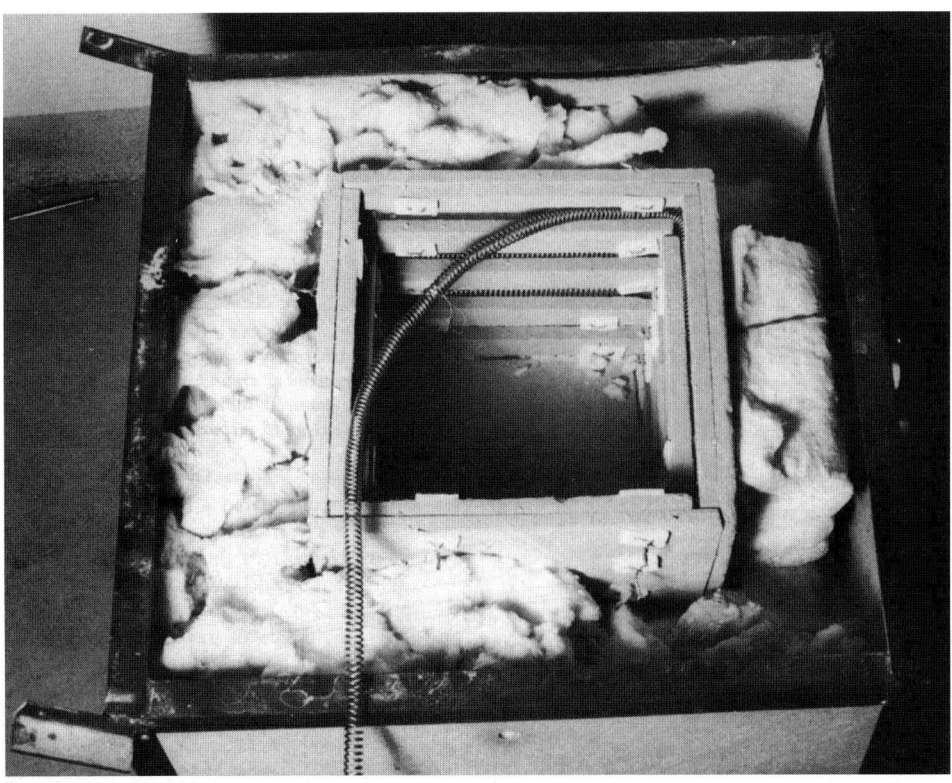

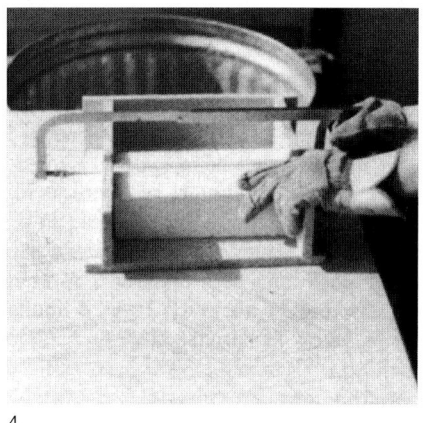

1. Beginning at the bottom, elements are laid in fiberboard slots, bending for corners as you go. Space between the chamber and the shell is packed with refractory fiber blanket or scraps.

2,3. The element tails are passed through porcelain tubes to the exterior with two tails from each pair joined with brass line taps. The remaining tails are connected to lines from the top and bottom switches, and the switch box is attached.

4. Building the kiln of softbrick instead of fiberboard will allow it to be used in frit making. With tungsten carbide hacksaw blade, cut element slots in eight K-28 insulation brick, using a wooden jig guide.

and the shell with cut blanket or bulk fiber (use scraps and old fiber). Remember to position two porcelain tubes in the fiber to assure clear vision through the peepholes.

The last porcelain tubes are used to anchor 6 inches of fiber blanket to the lid. A 30-inch length of resistance wire is treaded through a hole in the lid, down through the fiber, through the porcelain tube and back up through the insulation and shell to the top. The fiber is pulled tight and the wire ends are wound together.

Two infinite-control switches, commonly used on stoves and hot plates, are secured through holes in the front of the switch box. Attach the cord and plug to the switch box with a metal clamp. Using a large wire nut, connect two 8-inch lengths of asbestos-coated wire to each of the two wires extending into the switch box from the cord; one will be black and the other white. The ground is green or bare and should be connected to the metal frame. This will make one black and one white line to connect to each circuit. Connect them to the switches, using black wire on one circuit and a white wire on the other.

Using a brass line tap (available at hardware stores), connect the tail from the bottom element to the tail of the element above it; likewise connect the top two elements. This should leave four tails, one from each element. Connect a line from the bottom switch to the tail of the bottom element and the remaining line to the next element up. Follow the same procedure to connect the top elements to the top switch, then bolt the switch box to the kiln.

Unless you are confident of your electrical knowledge, have a licensed electrician inspect your work and power source. Make sure the outlet can handle a 20-amp load.

Place the kiln on a heat-resistant surface. With the bottom ventilated it can be placed on any surface; I set it on kiln posts lying on their sides. After two hours at Cone 10, the bottom of the kiln is only about 150°F.

Before the kiln is used for testing, it should be properly seasoned. To burn off organic binders, fire slowly with the lid propped open 1 or 2 inches until reaching 1200°F. Then proceed to the maximum cone expected for normal use. After this, the kiln can be fired and cooled as rapidly as desired.

If the kiln is built with a softbrick chamber, you can also make frits. (Fiberboard is less resistant to corrosion from frit vapors, and the longer it is held at a high temperature, the more it shrinks.) Drill a 1-inch-diameter hole through the bottom the kiln. Make a crucible, with a ½-inch-diameter hole in the bottom and a downspout 1 inch long, to just fit into the chamber. I used the following:

Crucible Clay Body
(Cone 8-12)

Talc	18%
Spodumene	10
Kaolin	55
Grog	17
	100%

Position the crucible over the hole in the bottom of the kiln. Place the kiln on a stand with a metal bucket of water 2 feet below. The raw dry ingredients are screened and placed in the crucible. Fire the kiln until the molten frit begins to drip into the water. Maintain temperature until the dripping slows down; do not continue firing until the crucible is empty or the frit will pick up contaminants from the crucible. The frit is then washed, milled and dried.

This test kiln has proved to be a great aid in developing and testing clays, glazes, frits and decorative ideas. Just remember it is designed to fire extremely fast, so don't leave it unattended. ▲

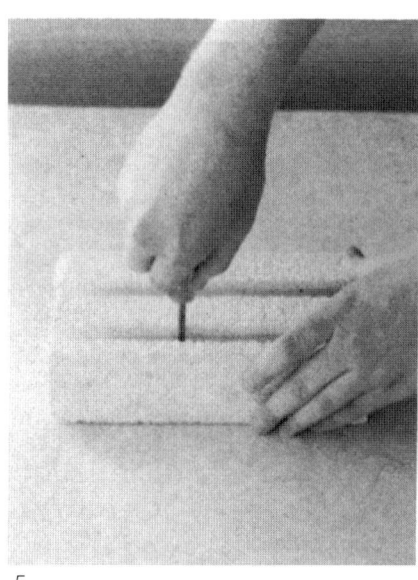
5

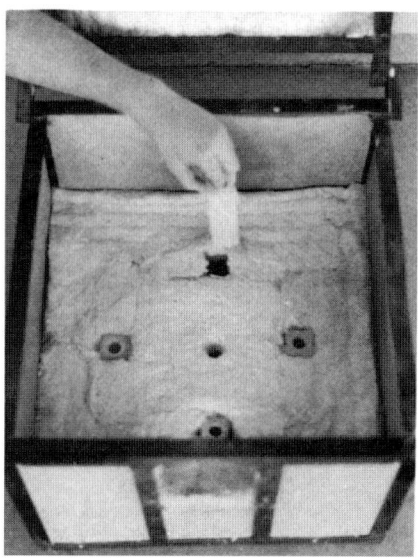
6

7

8

9

5. Holes for the element tails are drilled with a nail or screwdriver.

6,7. Four 6-inch kiln posts are imbedded in the bottom insulation to support the bricks and keep the kiln chamber from sinking. The slotted brick are stacked in the center to form the chamber.

8,9. To make frit in the fast-firing test kiln, throw a refractory crucible, with a ½-inch-diameter bottom hole and a downspout 1 inch long, to just fit the kiln chamber. The downspout should extend into the hole in the floor of the kiln. Raw dry ingredients are placed in the crucible. With the kiln on a stand over a bucket of water, the firing progresses until molten frit begins to drip from the crucible into the water. The frit is then washed, milled and dried.

Building a Modular Kiln

by Bob McWilliams

The modular kiln described in this article was designed with certain priorities: portability, economy, expandability and ease of maintenance. The basic idea was to bolt together a shell from panels of welded angle iron and galvanized expanded metal, then install fiber insulation using a "step-type" layering on the corners so that each side remains a separate panel. The result was a kiln two people can easily dismantle and move, panel by panel. For the urban potter or one who must rent space (never knowing when you might have to relocate), it is a luxury. No more forklifts and flatbeds!

A 24-cubic-foot kiln was designed around three 12×24-inch shelves, and a 16-cubic-foot around two 12×24-inch shelves, but the plans may be adapted to suit your needs. Natural updraft was chosen to avoid the added cost and site limitations of a chimney. Glaze firings to Cone 10 in my 24-cubic-foot kiln vary less than a half cone from top to bottom with excellent reduction.

Before you begin gathering materials, pick a site that is convenient and reasonably level. Be aware of keeping adequate ventilation around the kiln, as well as proper venting from the flues. If the site is inside, I recommend trying to find a used hood or constructing one to fit the top of the kiln; you'll also need a stack at least 12 inches in diameter that will rise above the roof level at least 4 feet. I also suggest installing a fire extinguisher and a smoke alarm.

Construction begins by cutting the angle iron and galvanized expanded metal for the panels; or order these materials precut. Lay out the cut metal parts before welding. Note that the expanded metal parts forming the flues in the roof panel are welded together before the angle iron supports are attached. Also keep in mind where the burner ports go in the sheet metal floor when attaching the angle iron supports. Remember that the angle iron frames on the roof and floor panes flare out (angle in), and the floor of the kiln extends out 4 inches in the front to support the door panel (the shell sits flush with the back).

This article describes how to build and fire a modular kiln designed for the urban potter, or those who rent space, so that each kiln wall is an independent pane. Two people can easily dismantle and move the whole structure, panel by panel.

Place the floor panel on four upright concrete blocks and level it. Assemble the other panels with wire or rope to make sure everything fits before drilling holes and bolting them together. Then unbolt the panels and sand off any rust (or use a solvent to remove oil). Apply a layer of rustproof primer paint on the angle iron and sheet metal, followed by a layer of high-temperature paint.

Once the shell is reassembled, you are ready to install the refractory fiber blankets. (When working around or repairing any ceramic fiber, wear protective clothing-respirator, goggles, long sleeves, gloves, etc.) With heavy-duty aluminum foil, completely wrap the first layer of fiber to be mounted on each panel. This may help retain and reflect heat, but mainly the foil is a barrier against fibers from the outside kiln wall getting airborne and thus into your lungs.

The fiber should be installed in layers, with a "step" effect at each corner. Begin by installing 1-inch-thick Durablanket 2600 in both of the expanded metal flue constructions. Use enough so that you can wrap it under the roof section at least 3 inches. Try to slightly overlap the fiber (this could all be done with the roof panel sitting on a table). Use ¾-inch ceramic buttons (pins) to hold the Durablanket 2600 to the expanded metal: push a piece of Kanthal wire through from the inside; thread it through the hole in the button; push the other end of the wire through and pull the button tight, pushing the point into the fiber; then secure the wire to the expanded metal. The Kanthal wire is imbedded so that it does not oxidize (and thus weaken) in the reduction firings.

Install the first 2-inch layer of 4-pound-density, 2300°F Durablanket in the same fashion-top (use a piece of plywood and boards to keep the fiber in place), back and sides. Any seams can be butted on these inside layers, but try to stagger them. The "hot face" or the 1-inch-thick Durablanket 2600 layer is last and is the most critical. Cut the blanket slightly larger and try to compress the blanket up and into corners; overlap seams at least 3 inches, as the hot face tends to shrink the most and continues to expand and contract during firings.

Remember when securing the fiber with the 2-3-inch-long ceramic buttons, the fewer buttons used without sacrificing holding power is the best. Critical points where more buttons are needed are around the exit flue, along corners, within 2 inches of the front top and along any overlaps.

Peepholes cut through the expanded metal door may incorporate thrown stoneware cylinders or modified softbricks. Approximately 1½-inch-square "windows" are cut through the middles of two softbricks. One face of each brick is then filed down ½ inch, leaving approximately ¼ inch around each window intact to form a raised "frame." The window frame section of each modified brick can then be inserted into one of the holes cut through the expanded metal door. The first layer of insulation (foil-wrapped, 2300°F, 6-pound-density Durablanket) is installed around the softbrick peepholes; the next layer (Durablanket 2600) should go over the brick. These layers should be installed butted firmly against each other. Then add another Durablanket 2600 layer onto the door to fit just within the fiber on the inside perimeter of the sides and top of the shell, i.e., approximately 5 inches from top and sides of the door edge. Overlap the seams on this layer at least 2 inches and secure all with ceramic buttons.

On my 24-cubic-foot kiln I use an interesting door holder. Since the kiln is on cement, I anchored a 3-inch metal pole, vertically, on the left side of the kiln (although it could be on either side). It is anchored from floor to ceiling. A metal "o" ring is attached to the center, top edge of the frame of the door (Fig. 1). Then a horizontal metal structure with angled support is constructed to fit between the vertical 3-inch pole and the center of the "o" ring on the door (Fig. 2). This metal horizontal structure has a movable sleeve that fits around the vertical metal pole, allowing it to swivel 180 degrees (Fig. 3). At the tip where the horizontal metal structure approaches the "o" ring on the door, I welded a large hook to a large threaded screw. This fits through the horizontal structure and has a large wing nut on top (Fig. 2).

The whole idea here is to be able to use the wing nut to screw up the whole door a short distance to be able to swivel the door away from the front of the kiln and out of the way for loading and unloading.

For the floor, determine the placement of the burner ports, then cut holes in the sheet metal. In his book on kilnbuilding, Fred Olsen recommends 9 inches to 12 inches from any corner and a distance between burners of not less than 12 inches nor more than 24 inches. Insulate the sheet metal floor with a 1-inch-thick layer of Durablanket 2600, followed by a layer of softbrick (laid flat), and one more layer of Durablanket 2600.

A manifold for the eight perimeter burners is best made from 1½-inch-square (interior diameter) galvanized tubing, but could also be made from regular pipe. Measure accurately and cut the lengths you need (45° angles at corners), leaving one corner open for attaching the nut that will go to the plumbing controls. Weld the pieces together. Measure where the burners will go, drill these areas, and weld on nuts that the burners can screw into (keep checking to see that everything lines up with the burner ports). The burners should be no closer than 1 inch to the burner port. The manifold can be supported by bricks or wire.

Use conventional gas plumbing parts to connect the two center burners together. This connection should extend out to intersect the other plumbing. They (like the manifold above) will have their own valve and gauge.

For the pilot ring, drill small holes along a ½-inch copper tube approximately ½ inch apart in a straight line. Cap (or crimp) and braze one end so no gas can escape; put a threaded female attachment on the other end. Beginning from the controls side (where the valves and gauges will be), bend the copper tubing around so the holes pass close to each of the ten burners. Wire the tubing in position.

To finish the plumbing, you can buy and assemble already-cut, threaded lengths of pipe (or have a plumber cut and thread them). Use new plumber's tape and use plenty of unions-they come in handy when you want to take things apart. Put the safety shutoff before everything so it will shut off all gas when required. Also put in a shutoff valve somewhere between your gas source and the kiln. Hook the kiln up to your gas source (a typical household line will fire either kiln, provided there are no other major demands on the line, while a minimum size propane tank is 46 gallons). Check each connection by liberally applying soapy water from a squeeze bottle. If it bubbles, tighten it more. Double check. Check all connections on the manifold, middle burners, valves, gauges, etc.

Dampers can be made by wiring some 1-inch Durablanket 2600 to a small piece of expanded metal. For easy adjustments during firing, attach a handle to the expanded metal of each damper.

24-Cubic-Foot Kiln Sample Firing Schedules

BISQUE

Time	Middle Burners	Main Burners	Damper
Preheat 6 hours	½ inch	off	¾ open
Hour 1	1 inch	1 inch	½ open
Hour 2	same	2 inches	same
Hour 3	same	2½ inches	same
Hour 4	1½ inches	3½ inches	same

Gas pressure for each burner is shown in water column inches. Cone 014 should start down at about 4½ hours. Increase gas to middle burners or close damper more to increase heat at the bottom of the kiln.

GLAZE

Time	Middle Burners	Main Burners	Damper
Preheat 1 hour	½ inch	off	¾ open
Hour 1	1 inch	1 inch	½ open
Hour 2	same	2 inches	same
Hour 3	same	2½ inches	same
Hour 4	same	3½ inches	same
Hour 5	same	4½ inches	same
Hour 5½	same	same	¼ open
Hour 6	off	5½ inches	½ open

When both 01 Cones are half over (approximately 1 hour), start glaze reduction. In approximately 1 to 1½ hours, Cone 8 will bend on the bottom first. Wait until Cone 8 on the bottom is halfway over, then achieve 1 inch pressure on middle burners and 7 inches on main burners, and open dampers enough so that you just have a slight trickle of flame. This will even the heat. My average glaze firing takes 8½ to 9½ hours. Remember, middle burners heat up the bottom; increase main burners and open dampers to get heat to move upward (slight flame); just leave the air intake screws on the burners at ¼ inch open.

Before installing the first shelf, choose an exit pattern for the center burners, using bricks laid flat just inside what will be the perimeter of the three 12x24-inch shelves. Level the shelves on these bricks. Next, position twelve 1-inch post on these shelves to support the second set of three shelves. As the center burners are used for preheating, this double shelving acts as a buffer, especially in the bisque firing.

Many aspects of the 24-cubic-foot kiln are duplicated in the 16-cubic-foot kiln; i.e., welding the frame, wrapping the first fiber layer with aluminum foil, ceramic buttons and the progression of the fiber installation. However, the 16-cubic-foot has only one flue. Remember, the size of the flue should equal the combined area of all the burner ports.

Otherwise, the smaller kiln is designed to accommodate up to 4 inches of fiber on the top, walls and door. I recommend at least 3 inches-2 inches of 2300°F fiber and 1 inch of Durablanket 2600. The most efficient insulation would be 2 inches of the 2300°F fiber and 2 inches of Durablanket 2600. The floor should have a layer of Durablanket 2600 under a course of softbrick (high-heat-duty, hard firebrick at points of stress like under kiln posts and where you may lean up against it when loading).

A burner manifold can be fabricated commercially or purchased from California Kiln Company. Explain what gas (propane, natural gas, etc.) you will be using and send a precise copy of your floor plan. Ask for a square manifold out of 1¼-inch pipe. The main manifold has 8 burners and its own valve and gauge. There is only 1 burner in the center, also with its own valve and gauge.

The cost of building a kiln according to these plans will range from $3000 to $3800, depending on size and payments for metal work and/or welding. ▲

Materials for the 24-cubic-foot Kiln

Angle iron: 126 feet of 2×2×⅛-inch angle iron and 22 feet of 1×1×⅛-inch angle iron (for the roof and door).

Brick: 50 K-23 softbrick for the floor.

Burners: 10 burners, with propane or natural gas orifices, rated at 85,000 Btu's each; 8-inch-long burners are available at approximately $15 each from California Kiln Company, 8375 Los Osos Road, Box 1832, Atascadero, California 93422.

Ceramic buttons (pins): Throw approximately 30 porcelain or stoneware buttons to attach the fiber to the expanded metal walls. These should be approximately 2 inches wide at the top and 2-3 inches long. Pierce a small hole through the pointed end of each and fire to Cone 9. Make another 10 buttons about 2 inches wide and ¾ inches long.

Concrete blocks: Four 15×7½-inch blocks to support the kiln.

Fiber: Order 100 square feet of 2-inch-thick by 4-foot-wide 2300°F 4-pound density Durablanket; 150 square feet of 2-inch-thick by 4-foot-wide 2300°F 6-pound density Durablanket; and 200 square feet of 1-inch-thick by 4-foot-wide 2600°F 8-pound density Durablanket 2600. Carborundum Fiberfrax is the most refractory fiber, and is easy to install and order. Note: A great WEB site for info on all kinds of ceramic fiber insulation: www.furnaces-ez.com/furnaces/00251210047966_1.html

Galvanized expanded metal: 105 square feet of 18-gauge (or heavier) expanded metal for five panels and two flue constructions.

Kanthal wire: 50 feet.

Nuts and bolts: ⅜×1-inch bolts to connect the panels.

Paint: Rustproof and high-temperature (at least 375°F).

Plumbing: 155 inches of 1½-inch-square (interior diameter) galvanized tubing for the manifold; 200 inches of ½-inch copper tubing for the pilot ring. Two gas gauges, preferably reading from 0 to 20. One 1½-inch-diameter (interior) safety shutoff valve. Two 1½-inch-diameter (interior) gas valves and one ½-inch-diameter gas valve to operate the perforated pilot ring.

Screw eye bolts and wing nuts: Four sets, with bolts approximately 6 inches long, for use as door fasteners.

Sheet metal: 21 square feet of 16-gauge black iron for the floor.

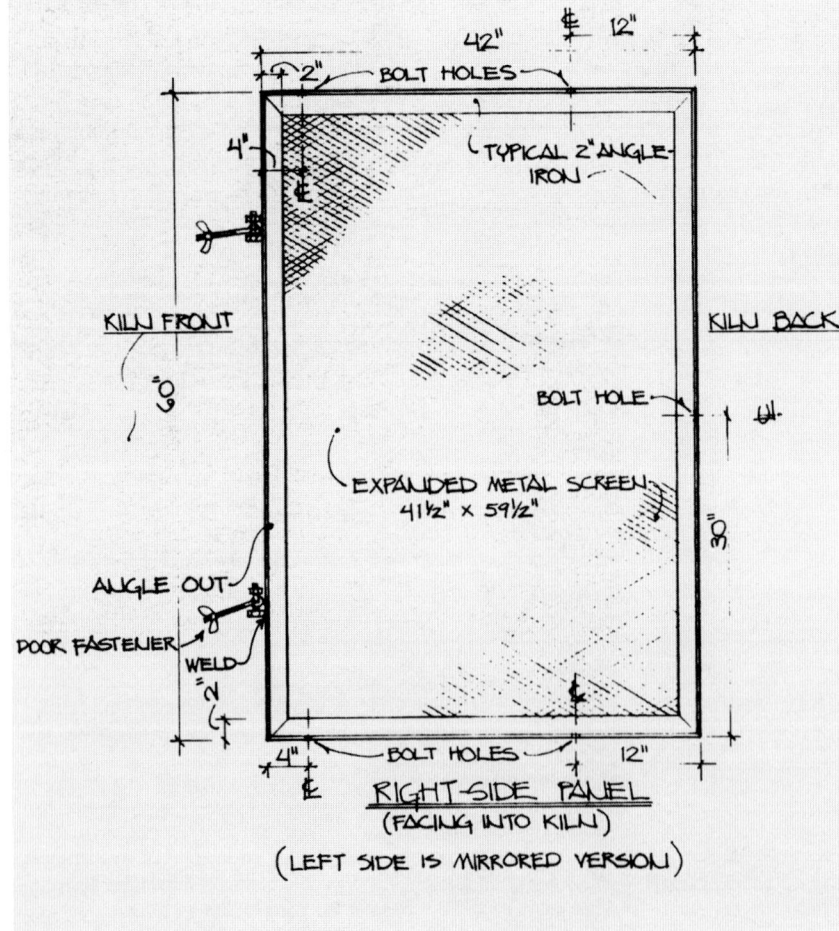

Figure 1

Figure 2

Figure 3

Figure 4

1. Construction of a 16-cubic-foot kiln is begun by positioning upright concrete blocks to support an angle iron floor frame (welded together with angles flaring out). Beneath this framework, the gas fuel manifold is supported by Nichrome wire or bricks so that the burners will be no closer than 1 inch from the ports in the floor panel. A manifold can be welded together from square galvanized tubing or standard pipe (or fabricated commercially) according to the floor plan. Burners, rated at 85,000 Btu's each, are arranged 9 to 12 inches from the corners, and at least 12 inches between other burners.

2. Copper tubing (½-inch diameter) drilled with a dotted line of holes approximately ½ inch apart forms a pilot ring. One end is capped (or crimped), then brazed so that no gas can escape; the other is fitted with a threaded female attachment to connect the ring to the gas line. Then, beginning from the controls side of the kiln (where the valves and gauges will be installed), the copper tubing is bent so that the holes will pass close to the burners.

3. The pilot ring is permanently held in place with Nichrome wire.

STUDIO PRACTICES, TECHNIQUES AND TIPS

4. The expanded metal and angle iron wall panels are bolted in place. Once the shell is assembled, refractory fiber blankets are installed in layers, with a "step" overlap at each corner-for safety, wear protective clothing, goggles and a respirator when working with ceramic fiber. Ceramic buttons and Kanthal wire hold the insulation in place while allowing for firing expansion and contraction. One end of a length of wire is pushed through the fiber from the inside of the kiln; then the other end is threaded through a ceramic button and pushed through the fiber. On the outside of the kiln, the wire ends are pulled tight (thus imbedding the pointed end of the button in fiber), then secured to expanded metal.

5. A damper is simply a rectangle of expanded metal with wire-secured refractory fiber clamped to a handle.

6. Thrown from stoneware, the buttons range from 2 to 3 inches in length.

7. Unglazed, refractory stoneware clay is used to form individual burner bag walls which are thrown cylinders cut in half. They will last through many firings.

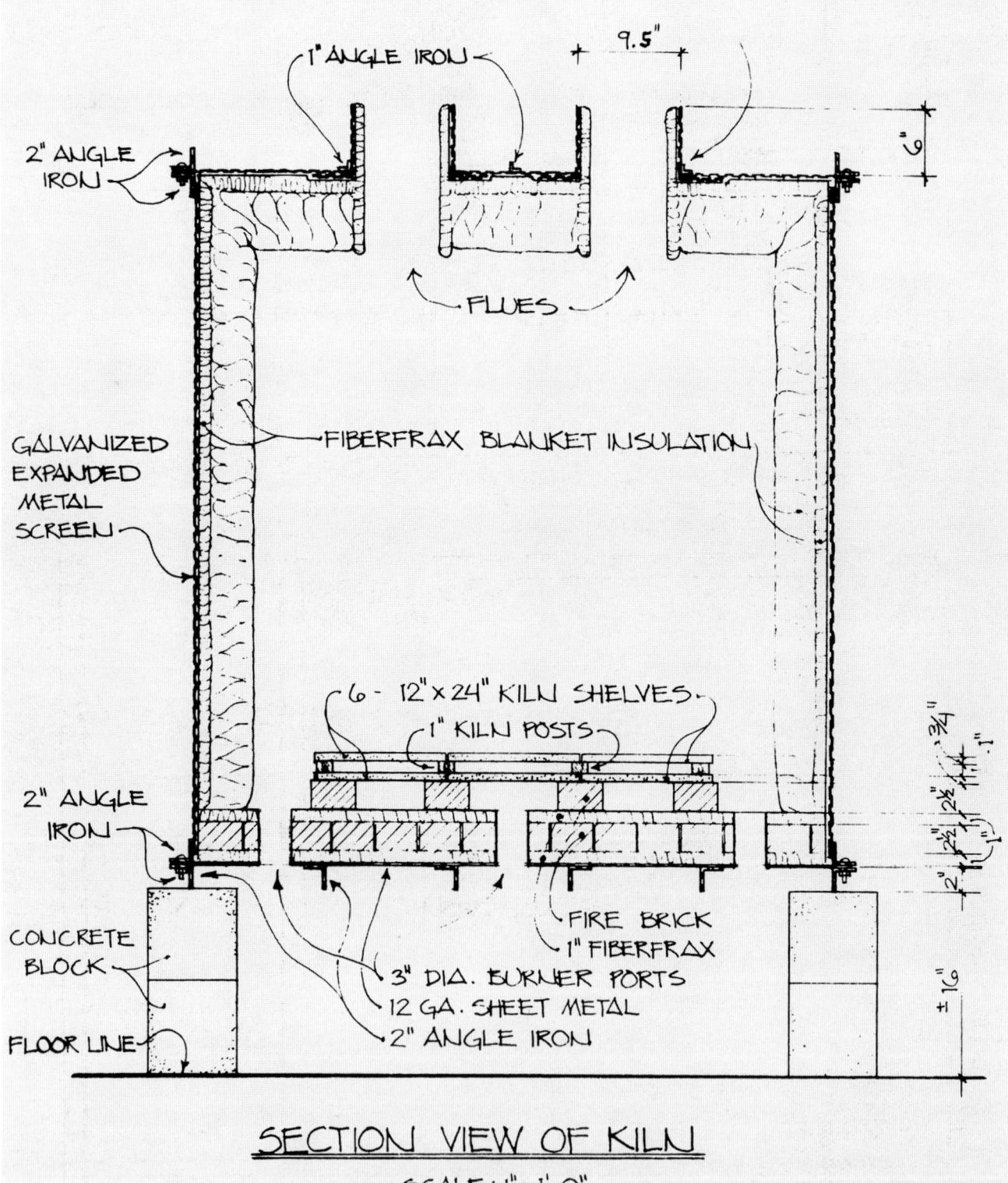

All line drawings accompanying this article show dimensions for the construction of a 24-cubic-foot kiln, while the photos document the building of a 16-cubic-foot kiln in Hawaii. Be sure to check and follow local ordinances when constructing any kiln.

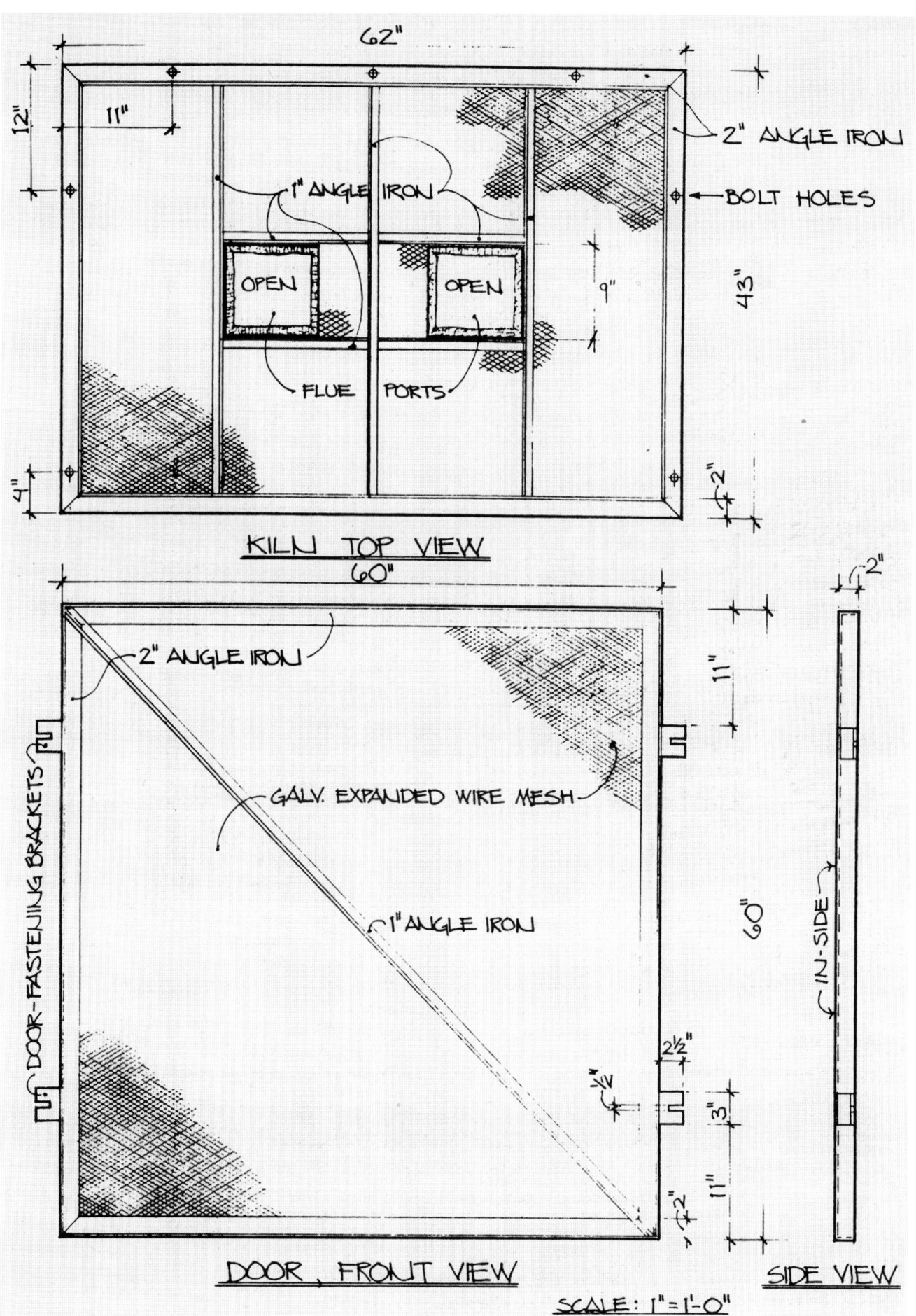

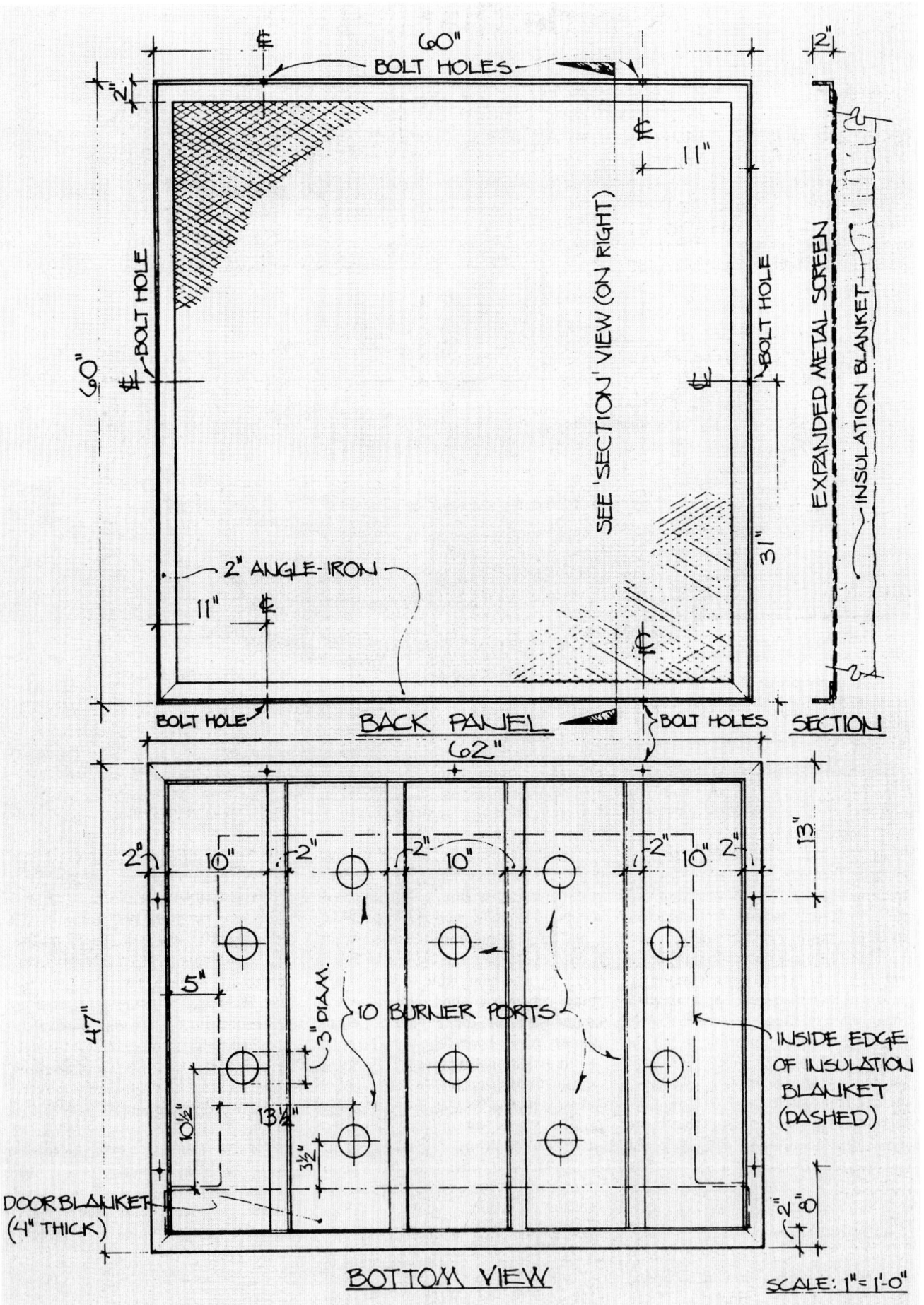

Recycle That Old Kiln

by David G. Wright

I have been salt firing off and on for over 15 years—first as a student at the Philadelphia College of Art, later at the University of Colorado, Peters Valley Crafts Center, University of the Arts, and currently at the Perkins Center for the Arts in Moorestown, New Jersey. My initiation to salt glazing was like many other beginning potters, taking the advice of someone who said, "Don't trash that pot. Put it in the salt kiln. Besides, it couldn't get any worse." Well, it did, and I have since learned that you must make the clay work for the benefits of salt glazing, or as Don Reitz puts it, "The pots must demand it."

I started by using straight salt in a hardbrick kiln and firing about 24 hours to Cone 10. I also experimented with soda and wood firing, and was equally pleased with the results. There is nothing like the rich effects of a wood or salt firing to make you feel closer to the elements of the earth, indeed more directly connected to your pottery.

I eventually dropped my firing temperature to Cone 6 because of the energy crunch and a desire to do my part. I also began using a mixture of half salt, half sodium bicarbonate, and the addition of 3% borax to melt the mixture at Cone 6. This combination resulted in a glossy and fairly respectable salt surface, but with little to none of the orange-peel effect one expects. (More recently, I have eliminated the borax completely.) Nevertheless, the results were acceptable to me because my interest in vapor firing was changing, and I no longer desired the thick, heavy, pebbly look of salt. Rather, I was more concerned with unifying the disparate parts of my pottery and creating a feeling of sensuality on its surface.

At that time, I was using the salt kiln at the University of the Arts, or firing the wood kiln at the Chester Springs Studio (the only place I know that will rent a 40-cubic-foot wood kiln), but I was growing tired of the packing and unpacking, the breakage that occurred, the traveling back and forth, and the extremely long hours involved with the process. Because I work slowly and the pots are small, it took forever to make enough work to fill the kiln. If I had a bad firing, a great deal could be ruined. I especially disliked my dependence on these kilns to finish my work. I needed a change; however, I could not afford to build the type of salt kiln I wanted, so I decided to put salt firing on the back burner for a while and try other things that I had been wanting to do.

Over the years, I had noticed a great number of kilns being discarded, mostly because of broken elements, or softbricks that were chipped. Many of these kilns could have been repaired easily by replacing parts or patching holes. Often the owners were either uninformed or just too lazy. I always felt that too many of these kilns were simply wasted.

As luck would have it, I had the opportunity to conduct a workshop on "Alternative Kilnbuilding" at the Perkins Center for the Arts in Moorestown, New Jersey. So, with the help of a great group of students, I altered an old 12-cubic-foot

The Perkins Center salt kiln, made by removing the elements from an old electric kiln, cutting holes for flues and coating the interior with a wash of equal parts alumina and kaolin.

electric kiln, which was headed for the trash, into a propane-fired, updraft kiln for salt, soda and wood. We fire within a temperature range of Cone 1–8.

This type of kiln is certainly not meant to be a permanent long-time equipment solution, but rather a way of introducing the fundamentals of gas and vapor firing to students, without the usual expense or commitment to construction and space. Eventually, the bricks will disintegrate, but by then the kiln will have served its purpose as a teaching tool.

The particular kiln that we resurrected was circular, just one wall of softbrick, held in place by sheet-metal casing. The floor was connected to the wall and could not be easily separated. We had decided to make an updraft kiln, so we started by cutting a hole in the lid for an exit flue, and another on the lower side of the kiln, just above the floor, for the burner. We

Teapot, 6 inches in height, thrown, altered and assembled stoneware, salt fired.

pulled the electrical components out, and filled the element grooves with a mixture of fireclay, grog and alumina. We also coated the entire interior with a wash of equal parts alumina and kaolin. The shelves we had available to us at the time were made of cordierite. These were washed with the same mixture on top, while the bottoms received a much thinner coating. We eventually replaced these shelves with silicon carbide. To date, I have fired this kiln at least 30 times with very little wear and tear on the sidewalls. The bottom of the kiln, however, has begun to deteriorate and will soon need to be replaced with a hardbrick floor.

The kiln is fired with propane to Cone 5–6 in about five hours. A neutral atmosphere is maintained until Cone 4 starts to bend, at which time both salt and wood (about 2–3 pounds of salt and ten 1×1×12-inch sticks or branches) are introduced. Over the next half hour, the temperature reaches Cone 6 at the bottom, but is usually lower at the top, around Cone 2.

Every firing is unique, as I like to try different approaches and techniques each time. I usually throw any combustible I can find lying around the art center into the kiln. As an inexpensive and experimental teaching tool, this kiln is extremely beneficial and a whole bunch of fun. Of course, we don't achieve the kind of drippy, ash-covered richness that you expect from a Cone 10 firing, but that is not what we're after. The firings are softer and not so severe or labor intensive.

Old kiln bricks are another wonderful resource for small experimental kilns. Many brickyards or tile companies are glad to give away their discards. Building kilns from single bricks is a great learning tool, as you can easily alter the shape of the kiln to discover which design works best. You might build one type of kiln for straight reduction, then rebuild it to be used for sawdust firing.

Many electric kilns, as well as loose soft- and hardbricks are simply tossed away, when they could be put to good use for teaching purposes. The experience of designing, building and firing a temporary kiln is a wonderful group project for all age levels. Before scrapping old kilns and damaged refractories, I hope everyone reading this short article will consider donating them to a local art center to be recycled for just this purpose. ▲

Glazes for Salt, Soda and Wood Firings

Many standard glaze recipes are suitable for salt, soda and wood firings, but because of the differences in temperature within the Perkins Center recycled kiln, I prefer to use glazes that have greater than normal firing ranges.

Amber Gloss Glaze
(Cone 1–6)
Cedar Heights Redart 50%
Gerstley Borate 50
                                           100%

A burnt orange where thin and amber where thick in oxidation; celadon green in reduction. For a purple gloss, add 0.25% cobalt carbonate and 2% manganese dioxide.

Wright's Water Blue Glaze
(Cone 1–6)
Lithium Carbonate 3%
Strontium Carbonate 9
Frit 3110 59
Edgar Plastic Kaolin 12
Flint 17
                                           100%
Add: Bentonite   2%
      Copper Carbonate   5%

A glossy turquoise in oxidation.

Blue-Green Matt Glaze
(Cone 4–8)
Whiting 30%
Cornwall Stone 45
Edgar Plastic Kaolin 20
Gerstley Borate 5
                                           100%
Add: Tin Oxide   4%
      Copper Carbonate   4%

A wonderful glaze for both oxidation and reduction.

Peach Terra Sigillata
Cedar Heights Redart .... 20 grams
Kentucky Ball Clay
   (OM 4) 180
Water 800
                              1000 grams
Add: Calgon   10 grams
For bone-dry ware. Flashes nicely.

"Bagel Bottom Bowl," 8 inches in height, Cone 6 stoneware, by David Wright, Moorestown, New Jersey.